Literatures of the Americas

Series Editor
Norma E. Cantú
Trinity University
San Antonio, TX, USA

This series seeks to bring forth contemporary critical interventions within a hemispheric perspective, with an emphasis on perspectives from Latin America. Books in the series highlight work that explores concerns in literature in different cultural contexts across historical and geographical boundaries and also include work on the specific Latina/o realities in the United States. Designed to explore key questions confronting contemporary issues of literary and cultural import, *Literatures of the Americas* is rooted in traditional approaches to literary criticism but seeks to include cutting-edge scholarship using theories from postcolonial, critical race, and ecofeminist approaches.

More information about this series at
http://www.palgrave.com/gp/series/14819

Helene Carol Weldt-Basson
Editor

Postmodern Parody in Latin American Literature

The Paradox of Ideological Construction and Deconstruction

Editor
Helene Carol Weldt-Basson
University of North Dakota
Grand Forks, ND, USA

Literatures of the Americas
ISBN 978-3-319-90429-0   ISBN 978-3-319-90430-6   (eBook)
https://doi.org/10.1007/978-3-319-90430-6

Library of Congress Control Number: 2018939725

Cover illustration: PM Images Getty Images

Printed on acid-free paper

This Palgrave Macmillan imprint is published by the registered company Springer International
Publishing AG part of Springer Nature
The registered company address is: Gewerbestrasse 11, 6330 Cham, Switzerland

For my children, Rebecca and Marshall—my two best works

ACKNOWLEDGMENTS

I would like to thank the University of North Dakota for awarding me a UND Fine Arts and Humanities Grant, which was instrumental in the completion of this project. In addition, many thanks to the authors of this volume for their invaluable contributions on the topic of parody. Finally, I would like to thank Irene Chikiar Bauer for her permission to use material in Chapter 4 that was previously published in Spanish in *El vertigo de la escritura: jornadas Luisa Valenzuela*.

CONTENTS

NOTES ON CONTRIBUTORS

Jorge Carlos Guerrero is associate professor of Spanish and Latin American Studies, and Director of Latin American Studies at the University of Ottawa. His area of specialization is contemporary Latin American literature, with a particular interest in the Southern Cone and the authors Augusto Roa Bastos and Mario Vargas Llosa. His work includes *Cartografías regionales del Cono Sur* (Iberoamericana Veuvert, 2010); a co-edited volume with Aimée G. Bolaños: *Ficções da História: Reescrituras Latino-americanas* (Universidade Federal do Rio Grande Press, 2014); as well as articles and book chapters on Latin American fiction.

Diane E. Marting is associate professor at the University of Mississippi. She is the author of *The Sexual Woman in Latin American Fiction: Dangerous Desires*, and many articles, translations, and reviews. She is the contributing editor of three volumes: *Clarice Lispector: A Bio–Bibliography; Spanish American Women Writers: A Bio–Bibliographical Source Book of Bio–Bibliographical Essays;* and *Women Writers of Spanish America: An Annotated Bio-Bibliographical Guide.* The second of these books has been translated as *Escritoras de Hispanoamérica.* Marting has been the recipient of two Fulbright awards, an American Council of Learned Societies Fellowship, and several Mississippi Humanities Council Mini-Grants. She is the past president of the Mississippi Foreign Language Association and has recently won their Distinguished Service Award. Currently, she is book review editor of *Letras Femeninas,* the journal of the Asociación Internacional de Cultura y Literatura Hispánicas, and represents Associate Professors on their Executive Board.

Danny Méndez earned his Ph.D. in Contemporary Latin American Literature from the University of Texas at Austin. He is an associate professor of Spanish in the Department of Romance and Classical Studies, and a Core-Faculty member of the Program of Global Studies in Arts and Humanities (GSAH) at Michigan State University. He is author of *Narratives of Migration and Displacement in Dominican Literature* (Routledge, 2012), in which he focuses on contemporary narrative representations of Dominican migrations to the United States and Puerto Rico, analyzing the particular ways in which these narratives challenge conceptions of Latin American literature and Latino Studies.

Patricia M. Montilla received a Ph.D. in Romance Languages and Literatures from the University of Chicago, and joined the faculty of the Department of Spanish at Western Michigan University in 2000. Her research interests are Spanish American narrative and poetry, as well as U.S. Latino literature and culture. She has published articles on the works of Rosario Ferré, Oliverio Girondo, Matías Montes Huidobro, and Judith Ortiz Cofer, among others. She also authored *Parody and the Poetics of Subversion in Oliverio Girondo* (Peter Lang, 2007), and a panoramic study on contemporary Puerto Rican literature of the United States for *A Companion to US Latino Literatures* (Tamesis, 2007). She edited a book titled *Latinos and American Popular Culture* (Praeger, 2013) to which she contributed a chapter on the Latino novel in the twenty-first century.

Fátima R. Nogueira is associate professor of Spanish and Portuguese at the University of Memphis. Her research embraces questions related to the concepts of temporality and becoming in Latin American literary and socio-cultural constructions. She has published the books: *Poéticas del devenir: Lispector y Valenzuela* (Santiago, Chile RIL Editores, 2016); and, in co-authorship with Fernando Burgos Pérez, *Conductividades posmodernas en la obra de Enrique Jaramillo Levi* (Panamá: Editorial de la Universidad Tecnológica de Panamá, 2012) and *Nuevas iluminaciones: la larga trayectoria literaria de Enrique Jaramillo Levi* (Panamá: Editorial de la Universidad Tecnológica de Panamá, 2017). Her articles have appeared in national and international journals such as: *Aérea Revista hispanoamericana de Poesía*, *Alpha*, *Amaltea*, *Afro-Hispanic*

Review, *Arizona Journal of Hispanic Cultural Studies*, *The Coastal Review*, *Confluencia*, *Dissidences*, *INTI*, *Luso-Brazilian Review*, *Revista Chilena de Literatura*, and other academic venues. Currently, she is working on a book devoted to Roberto Bolaño's narrative.

Fernando Burgos Pérez is professor of Spanish at the University of Memphis. He completed his BA at the Universidad de Chile with the degree Profesor de Español and received his Ph.D. in Romance Languages from the University of Florida, where he was awarded a Recognition for Outstanding Contribution. His area of research includes twentieth and twentieth-first-century Latin American narrative. He has delivered more than ninety papers at international and national conferences, and has been invited as a keynote speaker at the Universidad Nacional Mayor de San Marcos, Lima, Perú and at the University of Cincinnati. *La novela moderna hispanoamericana: un ensayo sobre el concepto literario de modernidad* (Madrid, 1985), *Vertientes de la modernidad hispanoamericana* (Caracas, 1995), *Cuentos de Hispanoamérica en el siglo XX* (Madrid, 1997), *Los escritores y la creación en Hispanoamérica* (Madrid, 2004), and *Una temporada en la posmodernidad latinoamericana* (Santiago, Chile, 2017) are among his fourteen published books. He has also published more than eighty articles in European, North American, and Latin American professional journals. He is the recipient of the Alumni Association Distinguished Teaching Award. He has been twice granted the Fellowship for Visiting Scholars to conduct research at the University of Illinois, Urbana-Champaign. He has been the recipient of several research recognitions, including the SPUR award, Superior Performance in University Research, the Alumni Association Award for Distinguished Research and Creative Achievement in the Humanities, the Alumni Association Distinguished Teaching Award, and the Dunavant Professorship award.

Elzbieta Sklodowska is Randolph Family Professor of Spanish at Washington University in Saint Louis. The primary focus of her research is Cuba. She has published widely on topics pertaining to Spanish American literatures and cultures, including the following monographs: *Testimonio hispanoamericano: historia, teoría, poética*; *La parodia en la nueva novela hispanoamericana* (1960–1985); *Todo ojos, todo oídos: control e insubordinación en la novela hispanoamericana* (1895–1935); and *Espectros y espejismos: Haití en el imaginario cubano*. Her latest book, *Invento, luego resisto: El Período Especial en Cuba como experiencia y metáfora* (1990–2015), published by Cuarto Propio (Santiago de Chile) in 2016, explores the ways in which literature, art, and film in post-1991 Cuba reflect upon the dramatic changes after the collapse of the Soviet system. She is currently at work on a project on Cuban women writers and artists.

Patricia Varas is professor of Spanish and Latin American Studies at Willamette University. She is the author of *Las máscaras de Delmira Agustini* (Montevideo, 2003) and *Narrativa y cultura nacional* (Quito, 1993). She has published extensively on Latin American modernity, literature, film, culture, the detective novel, and women's writing.

Helene Carol Weldt-Basson holds a Ph.D. from Columbia University and is a professor of Spanish and Latin American literature at the University of North Dakota. She is the author of three books: *Masquerade and Social Justice in Contemporary Latin American Fiction* (University of New Mexico Press, 2017); *Subversive Silences: Nonverbal Communication and Implicit Narrative Strategies in the Works of Latin American Women Writers* (Farleigh Dickinson University Press, 2009); and *Augusto Roa Bastos's I The Supreme: A Dialogic Perspective* (University of Missouri Press, 1993). Her other publications include two edited collections: *Redefining Latin American Historical Fiction: The Impact of Postcolonialism and Feminism* (Palgrave/Macmillan, 2013) and *Postmodernism's Role in Latin American Literature: The Life and Work of Augusto Roa Bastos* (Palgrave/Macmillan, 2010), as well as *The Prosecutor by Augusto Roa Bastos: Translated with Commentary by Helene Carol Weldt-Basson* (Farleigh Dickinson University Press, 2018). She received the title of Doctora Honoris Causa from the Universidad del Norte in Asunción, Paraguay for her work on Augusto Roa Bastos.

CHAPTER 1

Parody and Ideology

Helene Carol Weldt-Basson

Parody is an ancient literary device that dates back to Aristotle and Aristophanes. Parody has been discussed and delimited in numerous theoretical studies since the 1980s, including in works by such American, British, and French theorists as Joseph Dane (*Parody: Critical Concepts Versus Literary Practices*, 1988); Simon Dentith (*Parody: The New Critical Idiom*, 2000); Gérard Genette (*Palimpsests*, 1982); Linda Hutcheon (*A Theory of Parody*, 1985); and Margaret A. Rose (*Parody: Ancient, Modern, and Post-modern*, 1993). Although there is much written about parody in British and American literature, there is surprisingly little, comparatively speaking, written on the topic regarding Latin American literature, especially on the topic of postmodern parody and its relationship to ideology.

The intersection of parody, ideology, and postmodernism poses two fundamental problems that this volume seeks to explore. First, is postmodern parody a mere deconstruction of previous ideologies, or, in this process of deconstruction, is a new ideology created? If so, how does postmodern parody resolve the conflict between its insistence on epistemological relativism and the enthronement of its own new ideological discourse?

H. C. Weldt-Basson (✉)
University of North Dakota, Grand Forks, ND, USA
e-mail: helene.weldtbasson@und.edu

© The Author(s) 2018
H. C. Weldt-Basson (ed.), *Postmodern Parody in Latin American Literature*, Literatures of the Americas,
https://doi.org/10.1007/978-3-319-90430-6_1

1

Second, is postmodern parody guilty of a political deconstruction totally divorced from the world outside the text, or does postmodern parody in fact possess an ethico-political dimension that engages morally with reality outside itself?

Before discussing the ways in which the essays in this volume explore postmodern parody, a brief discussion of the terms ideology, parody and postmodernism is in order.

IDEOLOGY

Terry Eagleton points out in his book *Ideology: An Introduction* that the word "ideology" has been used to mean very different things. According to Raymond Williams in *Marxism and Literature*, the term "ideology" was coined by the French philosopher Destutt de Tracy as a philosophical concept to refer to the "science" of the study of ideas. From this initial sense, the term evolved to possibly signify one of the following three things:

i.   a system of beliefs characteristic of a particular class or group;
ii. a system of illusory beliefs—false ideas or false consciousness—which can be contrasted with true or scientific knowledge; and
iii. the general process of the production of meanings and ideas (Williams, 55).

Eagleton also acknowledges these varied uses of the term, and critiques the advantages and disadvantages of each. For example, Eagleton points out that meaning (iii) is of little value because it broadens the notion of ideology to include almost everything, thereby severely limiting its utility. Similarly, Eagleton points out that defining ideology as a system of illusory beliefs [definition (ii)], or the idea of false consciousness) implies that ideology is associated exclusively with the notion of the powerful or dominant group. This is not always the case, and such a definition would eliminate the association of ideology with particular groups who are not dominant, such as feminists or Marxists (Eagleton, 6). This leaves us with definition (i), ideology as a system of beliefs characteristic of a particular class or group. Martin Seliger approaches ideology in this manner, calling it "sets of ideas by which men [sic] posit, explain and justify ends and means of organized social action and specifically political action, irrespective of whether such action aims to preserve, amend, uproot, or rebuild a given social order" (cited in Eagleton, 6). However, Eagleton also finds fault with this definition because it eliminates from ideology some of its key elements. Eagleton identifies six important strategies associated with most ideological discourse: the promotion of beliefs congenial to a dominant power; naturalization of beliefs to make them self-evident; universalization of dominant beliefs; denigration of ideas that challenge the dominant power's beliefs; exclusion of rival forms of thought, and obscuring social reality in ways that prove convenient to the dominant power (5). If definition (i) is accepted, strategies key to understanding the notion of ideology would be lost. Consequently, Eagleton argues for the simultaneous acceptance of all three definitions, allowing the contradictions between them to simply coexist, rather than risk losing key elements associated with the concept.

That being said, in this volume ideology will be understood to generally refer to the system of beliefs that characterize a certain group, with the knowledge that when this group is dominant, ideology may involve false consciousness and all the strategies of ideological inculcation delineated by Eagleton in his study.

PARODY

The term "parody," as ideology, has been defined in many different ways, particularly in the twentieth and twenty-first centuries. The three major and most widely cited theorists of parody are Gérard Genette in *Palimpsests* (1982), Linda Hutcheon in *A Theory of Parody* (1985), and Margaret A. Rose in *Parody: Ancient, Modern, and Post-modern* (1993). Genette elaborates an extensive and complex theory of what he terms "transtextuality" defined as "all that sets the text in a relationship, whether obvious or concealed, with other texts" (1). He then defines five types of transtextuality: intertextuality, paratextuality, metatextuality, architextuality and hypertextuality. The larger part of his book is dedicated to the concept of "hypertextuality," which Genette defines as any relationship between a text ("hypertext") and a prior text ("hypotext") upon which it is based in a manner other than commentary. The second text either transforms the previous text by repeating its words, actions, or characters in a new context, or imitates its basic thematic and stylistic characteristics without "necessarily speaking about it or citing it" (Genette, 5). The concept of parody falls under hypertextuality for Genette, and he specifically limits the term "parody" to a playful transformation of a hypotext by its hypertext. He defines all hypertextual relationships in terms of their "mood" and their relation, so that once a text imitates (instead of transforming) another text, it becomes pastiche, caricature, or forgery instead of parody; once one text transforms another in a satirical or serious way, it is no longer parody but either travesty (satirical) or transposition (serious).

In contrast, for Linda Hutcheon, all parody must contain an element of irony. Hutcheon defines parody as "a form of imitation, but imitation characterized by ironic inversion" (Hutcheon, *A Theory of Parody*, 6). Although Hutcheon refers to parody as an imitation (in contrast to Genette, who terms it a transformation), she emphasizes that "the kind of parody upon which I wish to focus is an integrated structural modeling process of revising, replaying, inverting, and 'trans-contextualizing' previous works of art" (11). The concept of "trans-contextualization" is, in effect, similar to Genette's idea of textual "transformation." Thus, the two principal differences between the concepts of parody for these two major critics are that: (a) parodic transformation is only a variety of parody for Hutcheon, whereas it is the very definition of parody for Genette; and (b) parody must be playful in mood for Genette, whereas it must be ironic in nature for Hutcheon.

Finally, Margaret A. Rose offers a detailed evolution of the concept of parody from ancient times to the postmodern era. The section of Rose's work that is relevant for this study is her definition of contemporary parody. According to Rose, the essential difference between ancient and modern parody is that parody in ancient times was seen as both meta-fictional and comic, whereas in modern times parody is not simultaneously seen as both, but simply as either one or the other. Rose states that "late-modern theories of parody from the 1960s and after have tended to emphasise either the powerlessness or the nihilistic character of its comic factors, or its meta-fictional or intertextual aspects, but not both the comic as something positive and the meta-fictional or the intertextual at the same time" (272). For Rose, this combination of the comic and the meta-textual is what defines postmodern parody.

Each critic defines the mood of parody differently—as playful, ironic, or comic. Similarly, each views the function of parody in a distinct manner—as transformation, imitation, or meta-textual commentary. Moreover, each of the critics whose essays appear in this volume has used a different definition of parody. Consequently, rather than offering an over-arching definition of parody, this volume adopts Eagleton's approach to the term "ideology," and accepts the contradictions inherent in the term "parody," allowing each critic to espouse his or her individual view. This approach thus accepts a very broad definition of parody that encompasses all its various interpretations, akin to the general category of "hypertextuality" defined by Genette.[1]

POSTMODERNISM

Many critics, such as Fredric Jameson in *Postmodernism, or the Cultural Logic of Late Capitalism*, and Santiago Colás in *Postmodernity in Latin America: The Argentine Paradigm*, have pointed out the difficulty of providing a fixed definition of the term "postmodernism," because postmodernism is inevitably tied to the particular historical and socio-economical background and time period of the country in which the cultural works have been produced and therefore varies in nature. Jameson specifically ties postmodernism to the period of late-capitalism and views it as lacking depth and a historical consciousness (Colás, 3; Jameson, 47). Ian Gregson, in his book *Postmodern Literature*, indicates that for Jean Baudrillard, another important critic, postmodernism lacks "any sense of the real" which is "lost and replaced by the multiplying of signs and representations" (Gregson, 9), a tendency linked to the influence of technology. Gregson points out that these conceptions of postmodernism (and, more specifically, postmodern literature) have their roots in Saussure's linguistic theory, as well as the deconstructionist theory that subsequently arose from it. According to Gregson, Saussure's theories "call radically into question the common-sense idea that language is simply the means we use to tell each other real things about reality. For Saussure, language is an artificial construct" (Gregson, 3). Although deconstructionists build their theory on the radical break that Saussure posits between language and reality, they take Saussure's theory one step further. While for Saussure it is possible to distinguish the structural features of language, for deconstructionists there is no such possibility (Gregson, 3), and there is nothing outside of language and the text. Although deconstructionism is not synonymous with postmodernism, it is one of the major theories of textual analysis that has sprung from postmodernism.

Despite these concerns regarding fixing a definition of postmodernism, various theorists of postmodernism have attempted to isolate some of its general characteristics, notably Linda Hutcheon and Jean-François

Lyotard. For Hutcheon, postmodernism views all knowledge as a sub-jective, human construct, thus questioning the transparent relationship between history and reality. Hutcheon also emphasizes that postmod-ernism is centered on the concept of difference, underscoring differences of class, race, gender, and sexual orientation. Finally, for Hutcheon, postmodernism inherently rejects elitism and political conservatism in favor of cultural democratization (e.g. popular forms of art), which did not characterize its predecessor, modernism. To these elements, Jean-François Lyotard adds that postmodernism rejects all metanarratives with a pretension to absolute truth.

This nihilistic definition of postmodernism has given rise to the two questions posed at the beginning of this chapter. Does postmodern par-ody (or perhaps literature in general) posit an ideology in its process of deconstruction (and how does it deal with this contradiction)? Can the critique or interpretive process of postmodern parody lead to an ethico-political interpretation that constructs something positive? These questions are examined below in terms of discussions on the relationship between ideology and literature, and postmodernism and ideology.

IDEOLOGY AND LITERATURE

Lennard Davis' *Resisting Novels: Ideology and Fiction* (1987) is one of the few books dedicated to the studying the specific relationship between literature and ideology. In *Resisting Novels*, Davis argues that the novel as a genre is conservative in nature and reinforces passivity in the reader and acceptance of the status quo. According to Davis, a novel "destroys the veil of its own artifice" and appears "as natural as common sense" (25). This parallels the naturalizing and universalizing practices of ideol-ogy as outlined earlier by Eagleton. Davis examines ideology on the level of novelistic form—specifically, the ways in which location, characters, dialogue, and plot are ideological. For example, Davis illustrates how, in the eighteenth-century novel (e.g. *Robinson Crusoe*), locations were intertwined with explanations and defenses for the possession of prop-erty. In other words, Robinson Crusoe's taking possession of an island was a metaphor for European colonialism. For Davis, characters are ide-ological because they reinforce the general ideology of middle-class indi-vidualism in the nineteenth century when novel reading finally spread to the lower classes. Davis also sees novelistic dialogue as "an exten-sion of what Macphersen calls 'possessive individualism' because unlike real conversation, which is social and communal, it is monolithic and non-negotiable, proceeding from the absolute authority of the novelist" (169). Finally, plot is ideological in structure because it refocuses historical change into "less threatening visions of personal and familiar reform" (218).

Davis's ideas are most applicable to the eighteenth and nineteenth centuries, and are largely irrelevant for the twentieth and twenty-first centuries, in which novelistic form has changed greatly; there is frequently no third-person omniscient narrator controlling the novelistic viewpoint and many novels are dialogic in nature. Nonetheless, Davis insists that his schema is relevant for all novels and times, and that only novelistic content (not form) can be radical in its aspirations (226–227):

> It would be foolish for me to deny the fact that novelists have consciously used their novels to make political statements and to ameliorate intolerable social conditions... such novels as these only represent a fraction of published novels ... The political novel is a horse of another color. Those novels that are political are often only in content. That is, it is entirely possible to think as an author that you are making a progressive statement with a novel, and at the same time to have the form of the novel defeat that statement. (224)

Davis's perfunctory dismissal of the ways in which novels can espouse a revolutionary ideology or contribute to social change is refuted by the essays in this volume that show the ways in which postmodern parody contributes to more radical ideology and can be interpreted along ethico-political lines. Indeed, Davis's statement that "novels were rarely if ever conscious of their ideological roles except insofar that novels were overtly for or against something" is refuted by the very nature of parodic novels, which must be acutely aware of their ideological roles in order to perform the transformative function of parody on the previous text that is being parodied.

In his book *The Politics of Interpretation*, Patrick Colm Hogan disagrees with Davis regarding the relationship between ideology and literature. Unlike Davis, Hogan views literature and the novel as potentially subversive in terms of their ideology. Hogan states that literature is one of the three major ideological apparatuses of society, along with religion and education. According to Hogan, through literature "the populace may be presented with either a pacifying fantasy of its own conditions or a mobilizing criticism thereof" (4) and consequently, the act of literary interpretation is "not only possibly a political act, but, in the proper circumstances, necessarily the political act *par excellence*" (4). Hogan critiques deconstructionism and postmodern literary theory because he sees these methods as antithetical to political interpretation, which in his view should be the aim of all literary criticism. Such political critique should be aimed at ethical evaluation, attending to considerations of justice, for which there is no choice but to arbitrarily stipulate its definition. He defines these considerations of justice as a "kingdom of ends" in which each person is treated as an end in himself, and not as a means through which others can benefit themselves (Hogan, 27).

Hogan's work on literature and ideology is important because it posits the question of the relationship between postmodern literary critique and ideological/ethico-political critique. This has preoccupied many contemporary scholars. Linda Hutcheon, a major theoretician of postmodernism, offers a viewpoint completely opposite to Hogan's regarding the relationship between ideology and postmodern literature, at least with regard to postmodern parody. In *The Politics of Postmodernism*, Hutcheon asserts that, since in parody there is a double process of both "installing and ironizing," postmodern parody illustrates how "present representations come from past ones and what ideological consequences derive from both continuity and difference" (89). In other words, postmodern parody problematizes and denaturalizes the politics of representations by foregrounding the contradictions between those of the past and those of the present. It calls to attention "the impossibility of finding any totalizing model to resolve the resulting postmodern contradictions" (Hutcheon, *The Politics of Postmodernism*, 91). Hutcheon notes that, in particular, many contemporary novels "challenge…concealed or unacknowledged politics" through parody and that postmodern parody is a way of connecting the present to the past "without positing the transparency of representation" (Hutcheon, *A Politics of Postmodernism*, 94). In her theoretical discussion of postmodern parody, Hutcheon emphasizes that postmodern parody employs irony and parody in the sense defined by Dominick LaCapra, who claims that irony and parody "play a role both in the critique of ideology and in the anticipation of a polity wherein commitment does not exclude but accompanies an ability to achieve critical distance on one's deepest commitments and desires" (LaCapra, cited in Hutcheon, *A Politics of Postmodernism*, 96). In other words, postmodern parody is not exempt from ideological or political commitment, but finds ways of distancing itself from a total-izing ideological imposition. Hutcheon emphasizes that this politi-cal character of parody is particularly found in Latin American fiction, where it has been employed to critique "the politics of representation and the representation of politics" in postmodern historiographic fiction (Hutcheon, *A Politics of Postmodernism*, 99).

Two important essays, Robert Harvey Brown's "Reconstructing Social Theory after the Postmodernism Critique" and Ian Angus's "Inscription and Horizon: A Civilizing Effect?" discuss the ways in which postmodernism in general can be reformulated to construct a basis for political action. I examine their theories below.

Brown notes in "Reconstructing Social Theory" that, in order to counter the "negative criticality" of postmodernism, one must reformu-late Derrida's declaration that there is nothing outside the text, implying an escape from historical determinism. According to Brown, Derrida's statement:

> may also be construed as an insistence upon the ideological force of a dis-course in general and especially of those discourses that claim to reflect an essential pre-given truth. In this spirit, postmodernists insist that much of the import of a message is contained in what it does not say. The dominant discourse practices of a group or society define not only what is to be said but what cannot be stated and goes without saying. Regimes of truth mar-ginalize certain kinds of knowledge and move others to centre-stage. ... [Thus postmodernism] disables the power of words to go on blindly pro-liferating ideologies and the canonical readings they impose. In this way postmodernism can earn the adjective "critical." It becomes a means of unmasking ideological assumptions. (23)

Brown goes on to point out that although postmodernism is based on epistemological relativism, epistemological relativism differs from judg-mental relativism. In other words, the fact that there are relative truths does not mean that we cannot "discriminate between different forms of knowledge with a view to their relevance or adequacy with regard to a specific goal" (Brown, 24). Alternatively put, "relativism does not entail a society without standards" and the "conjoining of deconstruction and epistemology helps us to recognize when, where, and how the stand-ards are to be established cooperatively" (28). Brown proposes shift-ing Saussure's question of "what stands for what?" to Lenin's question of "who stands for whom?" and from there to the question of "what discursive and cultural practices would support each person standing for themselves and each standing for each other?" (33). Brown's proposition is remarkably similar to Hogan's idea of a "kingdom of ends" by which to judge the moral validity of assertions.

In summary, Brown views ideological critique as inherent to postmodern theory, and, by distinguishing between epistemological relativism and judgmental relativism, opens up the door for postmodernism (and, specifically, postmodern parody) to accomplish an ideological critique from an ethico-political perspective. This line of thought is continued by Ian Angus in his essay "Inscription and Horizon," in which he develops a more elaborate theory of how postmodernism can achieve this type of critique.

Ian Angus is also concerned that postmodernism's cultural relativism runs the danger of rejecting the component of ethico-political evaluation essential to critical theory (79). He thus states that his essay "attempts to redesign the ethico-political evaluative component that can hook cultural studies into a critical theory of society" (79). Angus roots symbolic representations in the issue of the constitution of social relations through what he terms "comparative media theory" (79). He seeks an approach that purports to connect "specific cultural studies and interventions to a reformulated postmodern conception of ideology critique that continues the classic modern notion of a civilizing effect" (87). Essentially, Angus argues that one must study the relationship between a specific object (cultural inscription) and its unthematized background horizon (which is the whole historical and social context). This opens up the possibility of a postmodern concept of critique. In other words, the background horizon (or historical epoch) could be named through the "transversal intersection of a plurality of media" in which each specific cultural production contributes to "the naming of this horizon" which "constitutes its capacity for ideological critique" (87). The plurality of sites of discourse and of translations of one medium by the other cannot be totalized, and this constitutes the postmodern aspect of Angus's theory. Angus concludes that postmodern cultural theory "can retain the civilizing component to the extent that it focuses on the method of passage from a specific production toward the cultural field a whole" (95).

Angus' theory shares the concern and emphasis previously stated by Hogan and Brown, to link postmodernism to ideological, moral, and political critique. The essays in this volume show how such critique is achieved by postmodern parody and how it has manifested itself broadly throughout contemporary Latin American literature.

IDEOLOGY AND PARODY

Similar to discussions on ideology and literature, little theoretical material has been published on the relationship between parody and ideology. Linda Hutcheon mentions the connections between parody and ideology in *A Poetics of Postmodernism*, indicating that parody is a form that points to ideological contexts more obviously than other artistic forms, and is often used by marginalized groups to respond to dominant cultures (35). As previously discussed, she also dedicates a chapter in *The Politics of Postmodernism* to connections between parody, ideology, and politics, but without developing a specific theory regarding their interactions. Her work reinforces the connection between postmodern parody and the social and political world, but only in general terms.

More specifically, Ziva Ben-Porat has published an excellent study on the topic titled "Ideology, Genre, and Serious Parody." In this brief theoretical study, Ben-Porat indicates that every parody contains the coexistence of two codes of representation, or two idiolects (the one of the original text and the one of the parodying text), and that each code of representation in turn contains an ideological factor as one of its components (380). In other words, according to Ben-Porat: "each code of representation is shaped by an ideology which penetrates all aspects of social and cultural interactions" (380). A logical consequence of the coexistence of two ideological factors is that "everything about the original representation is an ideological sign" and any change in that representation may signal an ideological change in the parodying text. However, although every parody contains two ideological factors, many parodies, especially comic ones, share an ideological framework with the texts they parody. Ben-Porat points out that, in order to understand and appreciate the humor involved in carnivalesque parodies, the author of the parody and its readers must share the ideological code of the original text.

Parodies that share the ideological code with what Genette would term their "hypotext" are only one ideological category of parody. A second group of parodies, which Ben-Porat terms "directly satirical," refers to parodies that imitate a "non-modelled reality" (rather than a textual reality). In other words, the hypertext exposes aspects of "reality" that are not actually presented in the parodied text, so that the satire does not deal with a mediated reality. Thus, in Ben-Porat's words: "the biting force of the satire is entirely dependent on the common ideological framework" (380) of the two texts.

The third type of relationship between ideology and parody is when the two texts involved have radically different ideological codes. When these codes exist in a relationship of opposition, what Ben-Porat terms an "indirectly satirical parody" is produced. This type of parody criticizes both the formal features of its model and the represented reality elements.

The fourth type of parody also involves two completely distinct ideological codes and is termed "serious parody" by Ben-Porat. Ben-Porat declares that serious parody exists when there is:

> Equivalence ... in the identical markings of various objects and concepts in different ideological systems. For example, in one system "laborer" is marked as low, or minus for social status ... education, sensitivity, trustworthiness, etc., in a second system "laborer" is marked plus for all of the above ... Only such an equivalence minimizes to the point of total elimination the comic effect of the parodic structure. As a form of imitation, parody may be and often is used for serious purposes; but the serious intention does not in itself oppress the comic potential. (383–384)

Ben-Porat offers Neruda's *Elementary Odes* as a good example of serious parody, and her essay is a useful tool for categorizing how the essays in this volume deal with the ideological implications of the parodies they study.

Michael Issacharoff also briefly discusses parody and ideology in his essay "Parody, Satire, and Ideology, or the Labyrinth of Reference." Issacharoff distinguishes between what he terms ideology *in* the text (the mention of ideological referents, such as political regimes and institutions within the text itself), and ideology *of* the text (the manner in which a text selects and parodies the intertexts it incorporates). Issacharoff acknowledges the ideological thrust of parody stating that "the deliberate distortion of an intertext may be intended to have a social, political and philosophical impact more profound than the immediate purpose of undermining a specific textual target" (216).

It is clear from the previous discussions on parody, ideology, and postmodernism, that parody and postmodernism share a natural affinity. Indeed, Hutcheon signals that parody is a fundamental element of postmodern discourse. Robert Phiddian goes so far as to posit in his essay "Are Parody and Deconstruction Secretly the Same Thing?" that parody and deconstruction are essentially the same, except for a few very modest differences. At the very least, Phiddian proposes that it is most productive to use deconstruction as a method of critical inquiry in conjunction with textual parodies because:

> Deconstruction is routinely used against the texts it studies but you get a very different critical practice if you use it with another sort of textuality, with texts that consent to the movements of deconstruction, foresee them and play with them—if you use deconstruction with parodic texts. My suggestion is that the secret sharer of deconstruction is parody. To use deconstruction with parodies is to commit deconstruction with consenting texts rather than against victim texts because parodies are already thematically and structurally about the play of absence, presence and rhetorical illusion. (679)

Moreover, Phiddian suggests that parody and deconstruction function in the same way, by "operating necessarily from the inside, borrowing all the strategic and economic resources of subversion from the old structure, borrowing them structurally, that is to say, without being able to isolate their atoms and elements, the enterprise of deconstruction always in a certain way falls prey to its own work...and this is precisely what parody does too" (681). Phiddian uses a description of deconstruction in this quotation and shows how it is equally applicable to parody. Phiddian points out that parody contains the seeds of its own ridicule, and is inherently postmodern in nature. Nonetheless, Phiddian does not see parody as divorced from the outside world because:

> For it is true that parody, generically in its forms and linguistically in its textuality, works on fundamental assumptions about the nonreferentiality of language ... but it normally does so cannily, knowing that language does connect with the world, mimesis and intention, however messily. This is where and why parody nearly always turns into satire ... but parody nearly always admits referential impurity. Its first lesson is always to defamiliarize, to show that language forms, distorts and masks the world, that it is an impure medium, and that pure referentiality is a crazy and often dangerous dream. However, there is almost always a supplementary movement in parody (that seldom accompanies deconstruction) which returns the reader to something resembling the world. ... The comic aspects of parody do generate critical perspectives...Political implications may follow from this. (691)

These meditations on parody, and particularly postmodern parody, suggest that, despite its connection to deconstruction and postmodernism, parody does construct ideologies and contain an ethico-political critique. This brings us back to the dilemma of how postmodern parody bridges the gap between its imperative to dethrone absolute discourses, and its own ideological construction. The answer lies in numerous postmodern techniques that the essays in this volume elucidate through their analyses.

Parody and Latin American Literature

Before entering into a discussion of the individual works that comprise this volume and how they attend to the questions of the paradox of postmodern parody and its relationship to ethico-political critique, I would like to offer a brief overview of the work that has previously been done on parody with regard to Latin American literature.

Although there are various books and essays on the topic of parody that examine parody in specific Latin American writers, only seven books on this topic attempt a more comprehensive examination and theorizing of parody: Elzbieta Sklodowksa's *La parodia en la nueva novela hispanoamericana* (Purdue University Press, 1991); Roberto Ferro's *La parodia en la literatura latinoamericana* (Instituto de Literatura Hispanoamericana, 1993); Alejandro Herrero-Olaizola's *Narrativas híbridas: Parodia y posmodernismo en la ficción contemporánea de las Américas* (Verbum, 2000); Juan Carlos Pueo's *Los reflejos en juego (Una teoría de la parodia)* (Tirant Lo Blanch, 2002); Rosa María Díez Cobo's *Nueva Sátira en la ficción postmodernista de las américas* (Biblioteca Javier Coy d'estudis nord-américains, 2006); Charlotte Lange's *Modos de parodia: Guillermo Cabrera Infante, Reinaldo Arenas, Jorge Ibargüengoitia y José Agustín* (Peter Lang, 2008); and Natalia Crespo's *Parodias al canon: Reescrituras en la Literatura Hispánica* (Corregidor, 2012).

Elzbieta Sklodowska offers a comprehensive review of the theoretical literature on parody and a periodization of Latin American parody up until 1985. Although she emphasizes the ironic and critical dimension of parody, she does not dismiss the possibility of a serious or constructive parody. She examines works from the period 1960–1985, ranging from the boom through early postmodernism. Her seminal study, which is the earliest one on Latin American literature, ends with works in 1985. However, Sklodowska continues her theorizing on parody in this volume with her outstanding essay on parody during the special period in Cuba.

Ferro's work on parody is essentially a collection of essays about parody in different Latin American authors. However, it contains a very important essay by Noé Jitrik titled "Rehabilitación de la parodia" which attempts to develop a theory regarding the specificity of Latin American parody. Jitrik states that parody is an imitative act that starts out at one point with the goal of arriving at another. In other words, Jitrik defines parody as "the pure difference in textual identities or as a product of an interaction. In the first case, it is a question of a canonical effect, the 'mocking disfigurement.' In the second sense, the effect would be the modification of the reading but not only of the base text, but of both instances: the change in the reading of text A makes one see text B in a different light" (my translation). It is important to note that although Jitrik shuns foreign definitions, his discussion of parody is not dissimilar from Genette's in *Palimpsests*, where he states that "the most rigorous form of parody, or minimal parody, consists...of taking up a familiar text literally and giving it new meaning" (Genette, 16).

Herrero-Olaizola compares texts written in the 1960s and 1970s (the Latin American "Boom" period) in North and South America. He focuses on the hybrid character of parodic works and on their deconstruction of authoritative discourses. Herrero-Olaizola defines three types of "inter-American" fiction: "fugitive narratives" that deconstruct historical discourse, "residual narratives" that incorporate mass culture and thus redefine the traditional notion of culture, and "apocryphal biographies" that create fictional biographies of fictional writers to reconsider the role of the writer regarding authoritarian discourses and their subversion. Herrero-Olaizola's focus is clearly different than that of this book, not only because his approach is comparative, but also because the period examined is prior to the one considered here. Moreover, he does not consider women or postcolonial writers in his book.

Juan Carlos Pueo's *Los reflejos en juego (Una teoría de la parodia)* [*The Reflections in Play (A Theory of Parody)*] is the most theoretical of the Spanish language books on parody. Although Pueo is from Spain and does not exemplify his theory with Latin American works, his book on parody is the only one written in Spanish that specifically dedicates itself to developing a theory of postmodern parody and is therefore important to include here. Moreover, Pueo's theory of parody has not been discussed by any of the other works on parody. Pueo insists that parody must involve an ironic appropriation of a former text. He essentially agrees with the formulations of parody by Jitrik and Genette, in the sense that one text must take up another with the aim of transforming its meaning in some significant way. However, Pueo limits this "dialogue" between texts to an ironic appropriation, unlike Jitrik's more open-ended concept, and Genette's idea that the word "parody" is restricted to the ludic, while serious parodies become "transpositions" and mocking parodies should be termed "travesties." Pueo coincides with Hutcheon's definition of parody in his emphasis on its "ironic" mode.

Diez-Cobo's *Nueva sátira en la ficción postmodernista* restricts its definition of parody to a satiric reworking of a previous text. Hence, her book is limited in its scope to only satiric works. Like Herrero-Olaizola, Díez-Cobo dilutes her focus on Latin American parody by including works from North American fiction, and thus only discusses two postmodern texts and one Latin American woman writer. Charlotte Lange's *Modos de parodia* concentrates on four male writers from the 1960s. She does not cover the postmodern era in her analysis and only examines parody in boom male writers. Lange does, however, make some effort to theorize the notion of parody and extend it beyond the merely satiric. She indicates that parody can also be aimed at metaphysical reflection, extra-literary meditation, and praise of its pre-text.

Finally, Crespo's book covers a more recent period than the others, focusing on 1975–2000. However, her study is significantly less comprehensive than Sklodowska's, and limits itself to studying two Latin American short stories, two Latin American novels, and one novel from Spain. Although Crespo identifies six types of parody in her typology (historiographical parody, parody of communicative media, total metafictional parody, parody of the detective genre, feminine parody and post-boom parody that criticizes previous aesthetics and aims at literary renovation), she only actually studies this last type of parody in her work.

Postmodern Parodies and Strategies for Self-Critique

There are many strategies employed by postmodern texts to question their own veracity and possible claims to absolute truth. As the essays in this volume illustrate, the following strategies figure prominently among them: dialogism (and contradiction, which may be seen as a subcategory of dialogism), self-reflexivity, linguistic deconstruction, hyperbole, and irony. These characteristics, all associated with postmodernism, are actively employed by postmodern parodies to accomplish a critical analysis of the ideologies they construct while deconstructing the ideologies of the texts they parody. Below, I offer a brief definition of these elements before illustrating how they are exposed in the critical analyses offered in this volume.

"Dialogism" is a term associated with the Russian formalist critic Mikhail Bakhtin. Bakhtin develops an extensive theory of dialogism in his works *Problems of Dostoevsky's Poetics*, and *The Dialogic Imagination*. He analyzes the concept of dialogism on various levels, including the relationship between competing discourses on a topic, as well as the dialogue—or what he terms "double-voicing"—of a single utterance that may contain two voices that intersect within it. With regard to the latter scenario, Bakhtin states:

> Dialogic relationships are possible not only among whole (relatively whole) utterances; a dialogic approach is possible toward any signifying part of an utterance, even toward an individual word, if that word is perceived not as the impersonal word of language but as a sign of someone else's semantic position, as the representative of another person's utterance; that is, if we hear in it someone else's voice. Thus, dialogic relationships can permeate inside the utterance, even inside the individual word, as long as two voices collide within it dialogically. (184)

Similarly, according to Bakhtin, any two discourses on the same topic will intersect dialogically:

> Two discourses equally and directly oriented toward a referential object within the limits of a single context cannot exist side by side without intersecting dialogically, regardless of whether they confirm, mutually supplement or (conversely) contradict one another, or find themselves in some other dialogic relationship (that of question and answer for example) [188–189].

Thus, what Bakhtin terms the "polyphonic" or "dialogic" novel eschews the over-arching viewpoint of a single narrator, and provides multiple perspectives on any given topic. This multiplicity of viewpoints frequently counteracts the enthronement of any single ideological perspective despite the destruction of the ideology of the parodied text and any new ideological construction by the hypertext.

Self-reflexivity refers to the way in which discourses reflect on their own narrative process, or offer an explicit or implicit meta-textual commentary on themselves. Once again, such self-reflexivity is associated with postmodern texts, and is a characteristic often observed in post-modern parody.

Hyperbole is defined as "exaggerated statements or claims that are not meant to be taken literally," while irony is "the expression of one's meaning by using language that normally signifies the opposite typically for humorous or emphatic effect" (*Oxford Online Dictionary*). Linguistic deconstruction, as we have seen through our discussion of deconstruction as a postmodern textual approach, involves the critique of the relationship between language and meaning. Below, I will illustrate how the essays in this volume show how postmodern parodies engage with these strategies.

POSTMODERN PARODIES

The nine essays that comprise this volume illustrate the three fundamental premises outlined in this introduction: first, that although the parodies studied here are postmodern in nature, they fully possess an ethico-political dimension; second, each type of parody can be categorized using Ben-Porat's taxonomy, as engaging with ideological markers of its own text and the previous one it parodies; third, each postmodern parody studied illustrates one or more of the postmodern strategies for self-critique that allows for a questioning of the validity of its own discourse or ideological construction, in an attempt to address the paradox between ideological deconstruction and ideological enthronement.

Chapter 2, "Parody and Intertextuality in the Poetry of Twentieth-Century Spanish American Women Writers" by Patricia M. Montilla, examines parody of patriarchal gender-based metaphors in female poets from the early twentieth century and contrasts them with Cristina Peri Rossi, a more contemporary postmodern poet. Montilla illustrates how poets such as Delmira Agustini, and Alfonsina Storni parody motifs from male poets such as Rubén Darío's swan, or the mystic poet San Juan de la Cruz's representation of the communion with God as an amorous encounter, inverting and subverting the use of these motifs in the original poems in order to bestow agency on the female poetic voice and female image. While Agustini and Storni also mock modernist concepts of artistic creation, Julia de Burgos appropriates the European stereotype of the objectified "*mulata*" in the poetry of Luis Palés Matos and transforms the "*mulata*" into an image of ethnic pride. Rosario Castellanos prefigures Peri Rossi's postmodern appropriation of the objectified images of women in the paintings by male artists in her poem "Mirando a la Gioconda" based on Da Vinci's Mona Lisa. Castellanos breathes life into the Mona Lisa and converts her into a thinking individual rather than a passive object. These efforts culminate in the work of Peri Rossi, whose ironic treatment of the paintings she parodies characterizes her book *Las musas inquietantes* (1999). Montilla shows how Peri Rossi parodies works such as Johannes Vermeer's "The Lacemaker", in which the image of women making lace affirms patriarchal values of females relegated to domestic chores. Peri Rossi subverts this image, boldly having her female poetic voice declare that she does not want to be a lacemaker. Montilla illustrates how women have parodied their male predecessors to subvert patriarchal ideology throughout twentieth-century poetry. Although the earlier parodies lack the degree of self-reflexivity that characterizes more contemporary efforts, Montilla shows how these female poets serve as precursors to postmodern parody in their use of ironic appropriation in these indirectly satirical parodies.

Chapter 3, "Postmodern Parody of *The Enchanted Cottage* in *El beso de la mujer araña*: Molina Leaves the Woods" by Diane E. Marting, explores the ways in which the retelling of John Cromwell's film *The Enchanted Cottage* is converted into parodic discourse in Puig's novel. Marting shows how, although, at first, the incorporation of the movie appears to reinforce patriarchal norms of heteronormative love and female beauty, Molina's ironic retelling of the film actually teaches the character the opposite: to see beyond physical beauty and to accept her own non-conforming body. Marting illustrates how the recontextualization of the movie employs a series of strategies that deteriorate the strict repetition of the story, resulting in a complex, postmodern, retelling, in which the ideology of the original movie is both affirmed and subverted (the ideology is at once shared and satirized by Molina), constituting a true postmodern dialogue. This contradictory dialogue is further enhanced by the novel's numerous footnotes on homosexuality and the social construction of gender. However, it is important to indicate that Puig's footnotes fail to authorize any specific theory of homosexuality or gender affiliation, once again eschewing the enthronement of a specific discourse or ideology in a postmodern fashion.

Chapter 4, "The Re(Naissance) of Texts: Parody and Rewriting in the Work of Luisa Valenzuela" by Fernando Burgos Pérez, examines how Luisa Valenzuela's story "Si esta es la vida, yo soy Caperucita Roja" [If this is life, I am Little Red Riding Hood] is a parody of previous versions of the fairy tale "Little Red Riding Hood," especially the one by Charles Perrault. Burgos illustrates how Valenzuela critiques previous versions of the tale for their tendency to convert "Little Red Riding Hood" into a moralistic fable, fixing the character according to psychoanalytical and other positivistic discourses. According to Burgos, to counteract these static portrayals, Valenzuela creates a version of "Little Red Riding Hood" in accordance with Deleuze and Guattari's concept of "becoming-woman," a fluid, ever-changing process. In other words, Valenzuela allows Little Red Riding Hood to become a figure in constant flux, one who sometimes merges with her mother, grandmother, and even the wolf. She is not a fixed image, but a process, and thus becomes both her own writer and reader. Valenzuela thus views "Little Red Riding Hood" through a feminist lens that deconstructs the patriarchal values espoused in Perrault's version of the story. Nonetheless, Burgos is clear that Valenzuela does not simply replace Perrault's patriarchal ideology with a feminist one but, rather, allows the multiple visions of Red Riding Hood to sound in a postmodern dialogue within her text. Although Burgos acknowledges the political aims of Valenzuela's postmodern Little Red Riding Hood, he emphasizes the story's postmodern characteristics that suggest coexistence rather destruction of previous discourses. Valenzuela's parody is an indirectly satirical one, in which the ideological markers of "Si esta es la vida, Yo soy Caperucita Roja" are clearly in opposition to those of Perrault in the parodied version. Finally, there is a definite reliance on postmodern linguistic deconstruction in the tale, as pointed out by Burgos's discussion of the title of the story collection in which "Si esta es la vida, yo soy Caperucita Roja" appears: *Cuentos de Hades* [*Tales from Hades*], a pun on *cuentos da hadas* (fairy tales) that points to the infernal nature (Hades being Hell) of the previous moralistic versions of Little Red Riding Hood.

Chapter 5, "Of Ideological Continuums and Sentimental Memories: Enriquillo Sánchez's *Musiquito: Anales de un déspota y de un bolerista*" by Danny Méndez, explores this Dominican novel as a parody of the story "Funes el memorioso" by Jorge Luis Borges. The Borgesian character's spectacular memory encompasses a total recall of all events experienced, which serves as a metaphor for History as an all-encompassing discourse or metanarrative. Nonetheless, this total ability to see the past obscures Funes' ability to actually see or comprehend anything at all. Thus, in a postmodern fashion, the novel questions History as an authoritative metanarrative, counterposing it to the bolero, which provides an alternative form of historicizing in the novel. The protagonist, the dictator Funess, attempts to control memory and the past and thus is a parody of his Borgesian namesake, capable of envisioning and thus "controlling" the entire past all at once. Funess, like Funes, is a postmodern contradiction. Just as Funes could see everything and nothing, while Funess's dictatorship embodies the hypermasculinity of the Trujillo dictatorship in the Dominican Republic, the character simultaneously expresses homosexual desires that contradict this doctrine of hypermasculinity. The novel thus deconstructs the ideology behind hypermasculinity, as well as dictatorship and its discourse of modernity and racism, among other ideological postulates. The ethico-political dimension of Sánchez's parody is clear, as is its postmodern adherence to the deconstruction of authoritative modernist and heteronormative discourses. Sánchez parodies both a non-modelled reality (the Trujillo dictatorship), as well as Borges's text, whose ideological markers it shares.

Chapter 6, "Parody as Genealogy and Tradition in *Nazi Literature in the Americas*" by Fátima R. Nogueira, explores Roberto Bolaño's imaginary biographies of various Nazis and Neo-Nazis, frequently portraying them as mediocre artists. Nogueira shows how Bolaño exposes and critiques Nazi ideology through parodic black humor in such tales as "The Mendiluce Clan," "Magicians Mercenaries and Miserable Creatures," and "The Many Masks of Max Mirebalais." Nogueira explores the roots of Bolaño's text in previous works of imaginary biographies that include Borges's *A Universal History of Infamy*, Alfonso Reyes's *Real and Imaginary Portraits* and Marcel Schwob's *Imaginary Lives*. Nogueira analyzes the postmodern technique of ironically using objective, encyclopedic discourse (which runs counter to the postmodern philosophy that all discourse is subjective) to seemingly portray Nazis and neo-Nazis in a "neutral" fashion, while implicitly criticizing these figures and the propagation of fascism in America. A postmodern questioning of the objectivity of any discourse, implicitly including postmodern discourse itself, characterizes Bolaño's work, which is a directly satirical parody of Nazi ideology.

Chapter 7, "Claudia Piñeiro's *Elena Knows*: How Parody in the Crime Novel Explores Disability and Feminism" by Patricia Varas, explores a feminist parody of the crime fiction genre. Varas examines the novel *Elena Knows* as a transgressive appropriation of elements of the detective fiction genre. Varas prefers the term "appropriation" because it implies agency, and the way in which parody questions all aesthetic and paradigmatic norms. Piñeiro employs parody of masculinist detective fiction as a way to inscribe female experience and agency into the genre. Hence, the parody studied by Varas is indirectly satirical, because its ideological markers run counter to those of the parodied genre; it is subversive with regard to patriarchal values. Varas shows how Piñeiro effects an ethico-political critique of the patriarchal institutions that have oppressed women in society through the vicissitudes of her female characters. She also illustrates the manner in which the novel questions many of the conventions of traditional crime fiction, giving an ontological turn to the detective plot, converting it into metaphysical detective fiction, in which the crime is unsolvable, and the detective learns more about him/her self than about the crime. Varas examines how the novel's parodic structure also allegorizes the Argentine military dictatorship and political context through what the author has referred to as "anti-ethical behaviors" that cause oppressive conducts that drive the novel's plot, which also exposes economic inequalities in the country. For example, Elena's search for her daughter Rita's assassin "eerily echoes the search for the disappeared children of the Mothers of Plaza de Mayo."

In addition to the novel's feminism, the novel's protagonist Elena is also disabled, with Parkinson's disease. Varas explores how the novel critiques the discriminatory language used to refer to disabilities. She also analyzes the ways in which the novel, in a postmodern fashion, undermines its own discourse through the character of the protagonist Elena. Although she is the disabled character, she refers to her daughter's boyfriend as "defective," because he has a hunched back. Consequently, through such practices, Elena enters into a contradiction between her own approach to her physicality (in which she is determined to manage her disability and make sense of her life) and the language she uses to refer to others' disabilities. She thus erodes the authority of her own discourse, and the ideology behind it. Postmodern contradictions abound in the parody of the crime fiction genre in *Elena Knows*.

Chapter 8, "No Laughing Matter: Post-Soviet Cuba in the Orbit of Postmodern Parody" by Elzbieta Sklodowska, discusses the ways in which both literary and plastic arts produced during what is known as the "Special Period" in Cuba—the post-Soviet period, immediately after the fall of communism in Germany and the Soviet Union, in the early 1990s—are parodic. Sklodowska's analysis focuses especially on Margarita Mateo Palmer's book *Ella escribía poscrítica* [*She Wrote Post-Criticism*], as well as a variety of examples from Cuban plastic arts, including Ernesto Oroza's collection of material culture collected in

Cuba during this time period and displayed on the internet, and "doctored" images of Havana aimed at perpetuating stereotypes for tourists. Sklodowska's analysis illustrates at least three of Ben-Porat's four categories of ideological relationships in parody through her study of Mateo Palmer's book. There is both comic and indirectly satiric parody of literary intertexts (e.g. Borges, and segments of Cabrera Infante's *Tres Tristes Tigres*, among many others), as well as a directly satiric parody of extra-literary elements of non-modelled reality, such as Palmer's allusion to a non-existent work published by Editorial Pon El Huevo. This, Sklodowska points out, is a parody of a book series (*Pinos Nuevos*) launched in 1994 in Cuba with the goal of promoting young writers. Sklodowska illustrates how Cuban artists engage in political critique through their parodies, including the example of the short-lived installation by Cuban artist Hamlet Lavastida during the 2009 Havana Biennial. Lavastida stenciled a brief quote from Castro's famous speech titled "Intelectuales sin palabras" on the steps of one of Havana's art galleries. This was clearly a parody of Castro's words, and the installation was removed shortly after by the government. Finally, Sklodowska's essay emphasizes the self-ironic, self-reflexive nature of much of Cuban art and literature, that often engages in what is known as the Cuban *choteo*, a Cuban tendency to resort to a self-conscious and irreverent mockery of authority and social norms. Sklodowska shows how Mateo Palmer ironizes and parodies herself in *Ella escribía poscrítica* in numerous instances. For example, Sklodowska tells us that in the 2005 edition of the book, Mateo Palmer includes a text that she first delivered as a speech in a public event held to commemorate her book. It is included as an appendix written by a fictitious professor, Ínclita Mamporro. During the public event, Palmer used the two official medals she had been awarded for her contributions to Cuban culture as earrings, thus mocking her own achievements and enacting a defiant performance against the Cuban cultural establishment. This is an excellent example of self-irony and self-reflexivity that prevents postmodern ideological constructions from deteriorating into discourses of absolute truth. The attribution of her speech to an apocryphal professor is also a self-ironizing act. Through such techniques, Sklodowska shows how Mateo Palmer questions and puts into perspective her own discourse, devaluing its absolute authority.

Chapter 9, "Elective Affinities: The Spectacle of Melodrama and Sensationalism in *Cinco esquinas* by Mario Vargas Llosa" by Jorge Carlos Guerrero, explores a parody of the aesthetics and politics of yellow journalism in Peru in the Peruvian writer's most recent novel. Guerrero illustrates how *Cinco esquinas* is a directly satiric parody of sensationalistic journalistic techniques during the Fujimori regime. Guerrero emphasizes that, despite the novel's happy ending—the end of the Fujimori regime, the triumph of justice—there is a political message that Peru's democracy is imperiled by this form of degradation of public discourse. Guerrero shows how Vargas Llosa also critiques the sensationalism in his own writing through this parody of Peru's yellow journalism, thus engaging in the self-reflexivity so characteristic of postmodernism, and also putting into question the authoritative status of the novelist's own discourse. Vargas Llosa extends this critique by parodying his own previous novel, *La tía Julia y el escribidor.* In this sense, Vargas Llosa also performs an indirectly satiric parody of his previous work. Guerrero illustrates how Vargas Llosa's parody engages directly with the political situation in Peru during the Fujimori era, including a critique of the ideology of the bourgeois class who supported Fujimori and his right-hand man Montesinos, sacrificing national liberty for their own interests and becoming complicit in Peru's oppression.

Chapter 10, "Postmodern Transpositions of the Latin American *novela de la tierra*: *Maldito amor* by Rosario Ferré and *La otra selva* by Boris Salazar," examines the different ways in which Ferré and Salazar parody the Latin American "novel of the land," a variety of regionalist novel that characterized Latin American fiction in the early twentieth century. Ferré's novel *Maldito amor* [*Sweet Diamond Dust*] is fundamentally an indirectly satirical parody of the classic Puerto Rican novel *La llamarada* by Enrique Laguerre because the ideological markers of each novel exist in opposition to one another. In contrast, Salazar's novel, which parodies both José Eustasio Rivera's *La vorágine* and the hard-boiled detective novel, despite attempting to give voice to female protagonists who were silenced in Rivera's novel, actually shares the ideological markers of both *La vorágine* and masculinist detective fiction. My analysis illustrates how each novel deconstructs the ideology behind the parodied text (paternalistic and patriarchal, respectively) and then reconstructs its own ideology in the process (postcolonial and feminist in Ferré, but also patriarchal in Salazar, despite his deconstruction of the same ideology in the previous text). Ferré clearly performs an ethico-political critique of the paternalistic hacienda system that is idealized and viewed nostalgically in *La llamarada*, while Salazar's novel is also a critique of imperialism in the oil industry, because the "bad guys" in the crime fiction plot want to eradicate Rivera's manuscript about the evils of the oil industry (note that this critique was already present, albeit in a different context—that of the rubber industry—in *La vorágine*, the work that Salazar parodies). I argue that Salazar's novel fails as postmodern parody, whereas Ferré's work engages in a postmodern self-critique through its dialogism. The distinct contradictory voices of the narrators in *Maldito amor* illustrate how even the feminist voices cannot be completely validated and accepted, despite Ferré's feminist critique, and the novel's ideological construction is somewhat undermined by the reader's inability to confirm or reject any one of the contradictory versions of the history of the De La Valle family conclusively.

As in any volume of this nature, there are limitations regarding the number of authors who can be included. It is my hope that this book will stimulate further research on the topic of parody and perhaps inspire a sequel that might include some younger generations of writers and illustrate how parody continues to evolve through the twenty-first century. For example, the novels *En busca de Klingsor* [*In Search of Klingsor*] and *El fin de la locura* [*The End of Madness*] by Mexican writer Jorge Volpi (1968–) parody the discourses of philosophy, technology, and science, while the novel *Río Fugitivo* by the Bolivian author Edmundo Paz Soldán (1967–) parodies national symbols such as hymns and the Bolivian hero Eduardo Abaroa (Escobar, 146). Some of the writers included here, such as Claudia Piñeiro (1960–) do belong to this group and initiate the dialogue regarding the continuing prominence of parody among Latin American writers of both the present and the future.

NOTE

1. There is a contradiction between Genette's concept of hypertextuality, which excludes metatextuality and Rose's definition of parody as metatextual. When I use hypertextuality, I am not attempting to exclude Rose's definition, but simply to indicate that a broad view of parody is taken in this volume.

WORKS CITED

Angus, Ian. "Inscription and Horizon: A Postmodern Civilizing Effect?" In *After Postmodernism: Reconstructing Ideology Critique*. Edited by Herbert W. Simons and Michael Billig. London: Sage, 1994. 79–100. Print.

Bakhtin, Mikhail. *Problems of Dostoevsky's Poetics.* Edited and Translated by Caryl Emerson. Minneapolis: University of Minnesota Press, 1984. Print.

Ben-Porat, Ziva. "Ideology, Genre, and Serious Parody." *Proceedings of the Xth Congress of the International Comparative Literature Association.* Edited by James Wilhelm, Douve Fokkema, Edward C. Smith, Claudio Guillén, Peggy Escher, and M.J. Valdés. New York: Garland, 1985. 380–387. Print.

Brown, Richard Harvey. "Reconstructing Social Theory After the Postmodern Critique." In *After Postmodernism: Reconstructing Ideology Critique.* Edited by Herbert W. Simons and Michael Billig. London: Sage, 1994. 12–37. Print.

Colás, Santiago. *Postmodernity in Latin America: The Argentine Paradigm.* Durham: Duke University Press, 1994. Print.

Crespo, Natalia. *Parodias al canon: Reescrituras en la literatura hispánica contemporánea (1975–2000).* Buenos Aires: Editorial Corregidor, 2012. Print.

Dane, Joseph. *Parody: Critical Concepts Versus Literary Practices, Aristophanes to Sterne.* Norman: University of Oklahoma Press, 1988. Print.

Davis, Lennard. *Resisting Novels: Ideology and Fiction.* New York: Methuen, 1987. Print.

Dentith, Simon. *Parody: The New Critical Idiom.* London: Routledge, 2000. Print.

Díez Cobo, Rosa María. *Nueva sátira en la ficción postmodernista de las américas.* Valencia: Biblioteca Javier Coy d'estudis nord-americans, 2006. Print.

Eagleton, Terry. *Ideology: An Introduction.* London: Verso, 2007. Print.

Escobar, Livia. "Desmitificación de los símbolos nacionales en la novela Río fugitivo de Edmundo Paz Soldán." *Estudios Bolivianos* 19 (2013): 145–154.

Ferro, Roberto (ed.). *La parodia en la literatura latinoamericana.* Buenos Aires: Instituto de Literatura Hispanoamericana, 1993. Print.

Genette, Gérard. *Palimpsests.* Translated by Channa Newman and Claude Doubinsky. Lincoln: University of Nebraska Press, 1997. Print.

Gregson, Ian. *Postmodern Literature.* London: Arnold Press, 2004. Print.

Herrero-Olaizola, Alejandro. *Narrativas híbridas: Parodia y posmodernismo en la ficción contemporánea de las Américas.* Madrid: Verbum, 2003. Print.

Hogan, Patrick Colm. *The Politics of Interpretation: Ideology, Professionalism, and the Study of Literature.* Oxford: Oxford University Press, 1990. Print.

Hutcheon, Linda. *A Theory of Parody: The Teachings of Twentieth-Century Art Forms.* London: Methuen, 1985. Print.

———. *A Poetics of Postmodernism.* London: Routledge, 1988. Print.

———. *The Politics of Postmodernism.* London: Routledge, 2002. Print.

Issacharoff, Michael. "Parody, Satire, and Ideology, or the Labyrinth of Reference." *Rivista di Letterature Moderne e Comparate* 42.3 (1989): 211–221. Print.

Jameson, Fredric. *Postmodernism, or the Cultural Logic of Late Capitalism.* Durham: Duke University Press, 1992. Print.

Jitrik, Noé. "Rehabilitación de la parodia." In *La parodia en la literatura lati-noamericana*. Edited by Robert Ferro. Buenos Aires: Instituto de Literatura Hispanoamericana, 1993. 13–32. Print.

Lange, Charlotte. *Modos de parodia: Guillermo Cabrera Infante, Reinaldo Arenas, Jorge Ibargüengoitia y José Agustín*. Oxford: Peter Lang, 2008. Print.

Lyotard, Jean-François. *The Postmodern Condition: A Report on Knowledge*. Translated by Geoff Bennington and Brian Massumi. Minneapolis: University of Minnesota Press, 1984. Print.

Oxford Online Dictionary. https://en.oxforddictionaries.com/. Web.

Phiddian, Robert. "Are Parody and Deconstruction Secretly the Same Thing?" *New Literary History* 28.4 (1997): 673–696. Print.

Pueo, Juan Carlos. *Los reflejos en juego (Una teoría de la parodia)*. Valencia: Tirant Lo Blanch, 2002. Print.

Rose, Margaret. *Parody: Ancient, Modern, and Post-modern*. Cambridge: Cambridge University Press, 1993. Print.

Sklodowska, Elzbieta. *La parodia en la nueva novela hispanoamericana*. Purdue, IN: Purdue University Press, 1991. Print.

Williams, Raymond. *Marxism and Literature*. Oxford: Oxford University Press, 1977. Print.

CHAPTER 2

Parody and Intertextuality in the Poetry of Twentieth-Century Spanish American Women Writers

Patricia M. Montilla

The literary contributions of Spanish American women writers of the twentieth century are vast, particularly in the genre of poetry. For decades, however, these writers were not recognized as poets but instead were labeled in Latin American letters as *poetisas*, a term that is now rejected by poets and scholars alike for differentiating the quality of women's writings from that of men. Women's poetry was "created in patriarchal societies" and was excluded from the canon as well as from anthologies, as Marjorie Agosín affirms in her introduction to *These Are Not Sweet Girls: Poetry by Latin American Women* (22). Notwithstanding, literature became an act of insurgence against the patriarchal order for Spanish American women writers at the turn of the twentieth century. In "*La transformación del discurso crítico en las poetas hispanoamericanas*," Mario Campaña contends that "la literatura adquiere una relevancia particular en la mujer letrada de fin de siglo XIX y principios del XX pues es el único espacio de que

P. M. Montilla (✉)
Department of Spanish, Western Michigan University, Kalamazoo, MI, USA
e-mail: patricia.montilla@wmich.edu

© The Author(s) 2018

H. C. Weldt-Basson (ed.), *Postmodern Parody in Latin American Literature*, Literatures of the Americas,
https://doi.org/10.1007/978-3-319-90430-6_2

dispone para expresarse con libertad. Por eso su rebelión tiene lugar en esos dominios, el de la literatura y el arte" (21–22) [literature acquires a particular relevance in the learned woman of the late nineteenth and early twentieth centuries as it is the only space that she has to express herself freely. That is why her rebellion takes place in those fields: that of literature and art].[1] Poetry provided an ideal subjective space for Spanish American women to express themselves, as well as an effective mode of rebellion. The use of poetry to critique male-dominated literary traditions and social constructs, however, is by no means unique to Spanish America. Sandra Gilbert and Susan Gubar were among the first theorists to examine the topic in *The Madwoman in the Attic: The Woman Writer and the Nineteenth-Century Literary Imagination* (1979). This groundbreaking book is a feminist response to Harold Bloom's *The Anxiety of Influence: A Theory of Poetry*, which was published in 1973 and which is still frequently referenced by scholars studying contemporary poetry regardless of whether they concur or disagree with his approach. Bloom argues that poetic history "is held to be indistinguishable from poetic influence, since strong poets make that history by misreading one another, so as to clear imaginative space for themselves" (5). For Bloom, poetry is passed down from the strong poets or forefathers to their sons, who misread or misinterpret their precursors and in doing so become strong poets themselves; poetic influence is, according to Bloom, "a battle between strong equals, father and son as mighty opposites" (11). In response to Bloom, Gilbert and Gubar argue that "Bloom's male-oriented theory of the 'anxiety of influence' cannot be simply reversed or oriented in order to account for the situation of the woman writer" (48). Unlike the male writer who must battle against his forefather or male predecessor in order to become a strong poet himself, the woman poet must battle "against his reading of *her*" (49). Gilbert and Gubar also note that women writers suffer from an "anxiety of authorship" (51) rather than one of influence because they were traditionally denied the autonomy to create and, in some cultures, were historically excluded from literature. This position of the female writer as described by Gilbert and Gubar is the situation in which many Spanish American women poets of the twentieth century found themselves. In searching for original ways to define and assert themselves as female subjects and poets, these women turned to parody, intertextuality, and textual revisionism as means of challenging the poetics of their male counterparts and the ideologies of patriarchal society, particularly those regarding gender and sex. The present study examines the evolution of parody and intertextuality in the works of five Spanish American women poets of the twentieth century. Specifically, this chapter will discuss how Delmira Agustini, Alfonsina Storni, Julia de Burgos, Rosario Castellanos, and Cristina Peri Rossi employ parody and intertextuality as a form of feminist protest to challenge and subvert literary and social conventions.

There are multiple approaches to the study of parody and intertextuality in the literature and art of the twentieth and twenty-first centuries.[2] For the purpose of this study, Simon Dentith's definition of parody is most useful due to its broad nature and because it is based on "the intertextual stance that writing adopts" (9). According to Dentith, "Parody includes any cultural practice which provides a relatively polemical allusive imitation of another cultural production or practice" (9). This wide definition of parody can easily be applied to the writings of Spanish American women poets who frequently reference or imitate the poetic models of their male precursors and contemporaries. In doing so, however, the roles of the male poetic voice and the silent female interlocutor are transformed or inverted in order to create an assertive position of female subjectivity and authority. Another way in which women poets of Spanish America employ parody and intertextuality is by including and reconfiguring fictional characters, historical figures, and well-known artistic images from other texts. Brian McHale identifies this technique as an "intertextual space" in *Postmodernist Fiction* and explains that:

> An intertextual space is constituted whenever we recognize the relations among two or more texts, or between specific texts and larger categories such as genre, school, period. There are a number of ways of foregrounding this intertextual space and integrating it in the text's structure, but none more effective than the device of "borrowing" a character from another text—"transworld identity," Umberto Eco has called this, the transmigration of characters from one fictional universe to another. (56–57)

This concept of "borrowing" characters provides Spanish American women poets a unique mode with which to challenge the traditional renderings of femininity in male-dominated discourse, to redefine the feminine, and to claim the role of women in literature, art, and society.

Delmira Agustini (1886–1913) of Uruguay and Alfonsina Storni (1892–1938) of Argentina are among the first women writers to emerge in early twentieth-century Spanish America to confront the patriarchal literary canon. Both were well-acquainted with the aesthetic and thematic tenets of *Modernismo*, a literary movement that emerged in Latin America in the late nineteenth and early twentieth centuries and is most often associated with the Nicaraguan poet, Rubén Darío. The *modernistas* were influenced by French Parnassianism and Symbolism; in their works, which are mostly characterized by allusions to Greek mythology and ancient times, as well as images of exotic lands, palaces, swans, peacocks, and princesses, these writers created escapist poetry while advocating the notion of art for art's sake in response to the materialism governing bourgeois society.[3] Jacqueline Girón Alvarado and Cathy L. Jrade have written extensively on the influence of *Modernismo*, and that of Rubén Darío in particular, in Agustini's poetry. In her book on the transformation of the poetic voice in Agustini's poetry, Girón Alvarado affirms that Agustini does not find a lyrical subjectivity in *modernista* writings because the feminine images constitute the aesthetic material; the "other" as opposed to the "yo" or subject of the poem (1). The women represented in *modernista* poetry are either silent, virginal princesses or *femmes fatales*, as in "Sonatina" and "Era un aire suave," two of Rubén Darío's most famous poems from *Prosas Profanas* (1896). Jrade closely examines the representations of woman in Darío's poetry and Agustini's revisioning of them as a means of inserting herself in *modernista* discourse. According to Jrade, Darío and other *modernista* poets frequently utilized "gender-based metaphors to express their literary goals and to assert their natural authorial authority" (23). Jrade observes how throughout *Prosas profanas*, and especially in "Sonatina," poetic language is conceived in the form of a silent and passive woman who must wait for the male writer "to fulfill his role as savior by turning language into *music*" (24). Darío renders this transformation as a sexual union between the male poet and the reticent female "with or through which he is able to create" (24). Agustini inscribes herself in *modernista* discourse by altering this metaphor upon parodying Darío's tropes and giving the silent woman in his poems a voice.

Agustini's poem "El cisne," from *Los cálices vacíos* (1913), shares the same title as one of Darío's well-known poems from *Prosas profanas* in which the swan symbolizes the new poetry and the ideal beauty that the poet strives to achieve. The swan is a recurring leit motif in Darío's writings and, as Sylvia Molloy observes in "*Dos lecturas del cisne: Rubén Darío y Delmira Agustini*," it is archetypically masculine and acquires diverse meanings depending on the poem: "es cultura ("Blasón"),

es la nueva poesía ("El cisne"), es enigma de la creación artística
("Yo persigo una forma..."), es erotismo (los poemas sobre Leda),
es hispanismo (el primer poema de la serie *Los cisnes*)" (64) [it's culture
("Blasón"), it's the new poetry ("El cisne"), it's the enigma of artistic
creation ("Yo persigo una forma..."), it's eroticism (the poems about
Leda), it's Hispanism (the first poem of the series *Los cisnes*)]. In the
first and second stanzas of Agustini's "El cisne," the speaker conjures a
swan on a lake in a park, a portrait that is characteristic of a *modernista*
landscape. Moreover, the image is linked to the act of creating poetry,
as the clear lake is likened to a blank page upon which the poetic voice's
thoughts are printed. But Agustini does not evoke the Greek myth of
Leda, like Darío often does through the symbol of the swan.[4] Instead,
Agustini produces a strikingly suggestive poem in which a feminine
lyrical voice envisions an erotic encounter. Agustini fuses the image of
the swan with that of a male lover through a series of similes that liken
the swan to a prince, its white wings to warm arms, and its beak to burning lips. The poem's oneiric tone also contributes to this fusion. The
swan pervades the speaker's dreams as well as her flesh upon awakening,
causing her to question its existence. The speaker as well as the reader
vacillate between whether the swan is a product of the imagination or
an actual human. In suggesting the latter, Agustini inverts the roles of
the male poetic voice and the silent and passive female. She continues
the *modernista* tradition of representing the creative process as a sexual
act but, in her reinterpretation, the woman is an active participant; she is
no longer waiting for the man to transform her into poetry. Moreover,
the encounter between them is mutually satisfying; the speaker satiates
the swan's thirst by giving him water, which he drinks as though it were
fire. The swan or lover also gratifies the speaker upon burying his beak
on her lap and keeping it still as though he were dead. This highly evoc-
ative image brings to mind the moment after a man reaches climax, suggesting that the poetic voice's yearning is also fulfilled. The poem ends
by further subverting the patriarchal gender constructs depicted in *modernista* writings when the speaker affirms that the swan is frightfully red
while she is dreadfully white. The swan in Darío's poetry is white as a
symbol of all that is sacred and pure. In Agustini's poem, however, the
swan is red, the color traditionally associated with carnal pleasure, and
incites fear. But the feminine poetic voice is equally dreadful due to the
fact that she is associated with the color white, which the *modernistas*
normally associated with chastity and virtue. She expresses her erotic

desire directly and actively participates in a sexual encounter. The poetic voice thus frightens in white because she negates the color's traditional association threatening literary conventions and the patriarchal order.

Agustini, as Jacqueline Girón Alvarado observes, also adopts the techniques of sixteenth-century Spanish mystical poetry as a means of asserting a feminine voice within *Modernismo* and legitimizing her role as a woman-poet within literary tradition (12). Mystical poems such as San Juan de la Cruz's famous "Noche oscura" present the spiritual communion of the soul with God as an amorous encounter between the feminine lyrical voice of the spirit, *el alma*, and a lover. Agustini parodies this tradition in a number of poems in which a female poetic voice addresses a silent male lover. For example, in "Íntima" and "La copa del amor" from *El libro blanco* (1907), the speaker is not only feminine but powerful; it is she who commands her lover to participate in a sexual encounter. The roles of the male poetic voice and the silent female interlocutor are inverted, and the woman's voice assumes a position of authority, but the imagery and positioning used to depict the female subject is still conventional. In "Íntima," the speaker lures her lover to go with her into the night where she will open herself for him as a flower. Similarly, in "La copa de amor," the poetic voice compares herself to a rose that is opening and tells her lover to drink her honey. The speaker uses the imperative mood upon summoning the silent male addressee; however, she passively renders herself, or rather her sex, as a flower and offers herself to her lover. In "El intruso," the female poetic voice describes herself as a lock that is opened by a golden key. The verses bring to mind the unlocking of a chastity belt and the notion of penetration. Lastly, in "Visión," another poem from *Los cálices vacíos* in which the silent male lover is likened to a swan, the speaker surrenders herself while laying down in her bed in a passive if not submissive fashion. Here, Agustini daringly uses the sacred symbol of the Eucharist in describing the lovers' sexual union upon stating that her lover leaned over her like a believer over the communion wafer. The female speaker in these compositions may show little physical agency in the amorous encounters, but her commanding voice nonetheless plays an essential role in creating new poetry while challenging the representations of the silent maidens that inhabit the *modernista* landscapes, and which Alfonsina Storni also questioned in her poetry.

One of the most celebrated woman poets of Spanish America, Alfonsina Storni is best-known for her scathing critique of traditional gender roles and patriarchal society. As Gwen Kirkpatrick observes in *The Dissonant Legacy of Modernismo*, "it is as if the female voice in her poetry speaks from (and against) the vision of the woman embodied in a male discourse" (231). Like Agustini, Storni was also very familiar with *modernista* aesthetics and viewed them as being chauvinistic and passé. In her first collection of poetry, *La inquietud del Rosal* (1916), Storni published two poems about swans: "El cisne enfermo" and "Los cisnes." "El cisne enfermo" parodies Darío's "El cisne," particularly the last stanza of his sonnet in which the new poetry of *Modernismo*, symbolized by the swan, is also likened to the beautiful Helen of Troy, the daughter of Zeus (disguised as a swan) and Leda. In Darío's text, the new poetry is *conceived* by the swan just as Helen was after Zeus and Leda's sexual union. In Storni's poem, however, both the swan and the "nueva Poesía" that it represents are rendered as being exhausted. The poetic voice states that a swan fenced in an old palace is dying and that, instead of gliding upon the blissful current, it has become stagnant and fatigued. The verb "deslizarse" describes the act of one body sliding over another, such as a swan swimming along the water. When used figuratively, however, it means to slip or get away, and thus brings to mind the escapist nature of *modernista* writings. The word "leda" is a poetic adjective meaning happy and content that, ironically, shares the same name as Helen's mother. Instead of gliding smoothly over a body of water (or Leda) as a means of creating new art or evading reality, the swan in Storni's text—who, according to legend, is a swan-poet—has, like *Modernismo* itself, become weary from repetition and worn out.

In the first part of "Los cisnes," Storni subverts the traditional *modernista* image of the male swan by rendering it female. The speaker describes the swans as they swim in the poem's opening stanzas as unstable and coquettish little feminine souls, meekly indolent and tamely feline. Storni strips the symbol of its masculinity and virility by giving the swan traits that in patriarchal society are often negatively associated with the female gender; the swans are fickle, vain, flirtatious, docilely lazy, and indifferent, as well as cat-like and feisty. Storni uses the diminutive "almitas" upon describing their souls as a means of disparaging these male symbols, as she also does in "Hombre pequeñito."[5] Furthermore, she undercuts the beauty that is typically associated with the swan in *Modernismo* by humorously likening its neck to a question mark and, in doing so, mocking the *modernistas'* preoccupation with the mystery of artistic creation. The speaker also affirms that while they are very still, the *cisnes* look like a parenthesis or a dream of the mind that stayed asleep. The use of a singular parenthetical mark rather than a pair of signs is significant because it suggests that the explanatory remark that one would expect between two parentheses is incomplete, indicating that the harmony and perfection sought after by the *modernistas* has not been achieved. The poem desecrates the symbol further upon stating that, when the swans hide their necks under their wings, they become, without a neck, beauty truncated. The ideal beauty represented by Darío's *cisne* is undermined and rendered unattainable by the image of a headless swan.

The depiction of *Modernismo* as a movement that is *démodé* reappears in the second part of "Los cisnes." The first, fourth, fifth, and sixth stanzas underscore the repetitive nature of the symbol in *modernista* writings by beginning with the same assertion that the speaker has seen the swans. The third stanza humorously captures the swans at night, during which their white plumage appears so immaculate that an embarrassed lily camouflages itself in the foliage so as not to tarnish the swan's feathers. As in the first part of the poem, the symbol of the swan is inverted and represented as female rather than male. Here, it is associated with virginity, a virtue that the princesses in *Modernismo* embody as they wait for the male artist to transform them into poetry. Storni ridicules this notion, as well as the self-aggrandizement of the *modernistas*, upon stating that a commonplace lily hides from the white plumage so as not to despoil or deflower the *cisnes*. The poem ends ironically with an exclamation alluding to the many times that the poetic voice has encountered the swans. Storni demonstrates a keen understanding of *Modernismo* and playfully mocks the movement's principles in her revisionism of the swan.

Storni's "Tú me quieres blanca," published in *El dulce daño* (1918), also parodies images of women in Darío's poetry. As Hedy Habra observes in her analysis of the poem, Storni rewrites and subverts the iconography of "El reino interior," directly addressing its erotic imagery and, more specifically, its portrayal of women. Storni creates a female poetic voice that speaks to a silent male interlocutor (the "tú," or "you," in the title). The poem describes the qualities that this male addressee desires in a woman as those represented by the seven white, virgin maidens in Darío's poem. In both texts, whiteness is associated with purity or chastity, virtues that the male interlocutor expects in a woman although he, like the seven diabolical lads in Dario's poem, does not incarnate himself. In contrast, his conduct is chastised by the female poetic voice as being motivated by lust, carnal desire, and overindulgence, and is associated with the colors purple, black, and red. Storni's poem discloses the double standard by which patriarchal society imposes virginity upon women as a virtue that all should actualize while excusing men from having to do the same. The poem ends with a series of commands that the poetic voice gives her addressee in order to undergo a process of purification after which he can only then pretend her pure and chaste, as equals.

The Puerto Rican poet Julia de Burgos (1914–1953) also confronts the issue of gender inequality in literature and society through the use of parody. Although she only published three books in her lifetime, Burgos's poetry marks an important moment in the evolution of Spanish American literature in its revisionism of poetic gender constructs as well as those regarding race.[1] In *Becoming Julia de Burgos: The Making of a Puerto Rican Icon*, Vanessa Pérez Rosario discusses the literary tendencies that were in vogue in Puerto Rico during the time in which Burgos developed as a poet; among these, Pérez Rosario highlights the *Generación del Treinta* or the *treintistas*, who were concerned with promulgating a Puerto Rican nationalist identity in opposition to that of the United States: "The result was a paternalistic literary canon that was written primarily by men, concerned with nation building, and characterized by the metaphor of colonialism as illness" (15). Ironically, these writers' conception of Puerto Rican identity and culture was based upon the island's Spanish heritage and did not "acknowledge the centuries of Spanish colonialism, the struggles for independence from Spain, and the legacy of slavery on the island" (16). A second movement that emerged alongside that of the *treintistas* was comprised of various avant-garde groups or -isms, primarily consisting of poets that turned to Puerto Rico's African roots in their search for creating new forms of expression (17). Both of these trends are visible, albeit transformed, in Burgos's early poetry.

The poems "A Julia de Burgos" and "Pentacromia," both published in Burgos's first book, are among the poet's most famous and frequently analyzed works. Burgos inserts herself in both texts alongside male characters that she borrows from Spanish literature and legends. As Consuelo López Springfield notes in her study on feminism in Burgos's poetry, "During the era in which Burgos published (1937–1946), literary traditions compelled women who aspired to literary careers to accommodate to male constructions of gender" (702). Burgos incorporates long-established notions of gender in her poetry but, in doing so, she criticizes women for accepting the values and roles imposed upon them by patriarchal society while ironically rejecting these norms upon identifying herself with the male gender. In "A Julia de Burgos," the poet addresses the public Julia de Burgos and chastises her for conforming to patriarchal society. Burgos depicts her public persona as a servile and weak housewife while comparing her poetic and "true" self to Don Quixote's horse, Rocinante. The allusion to Miguel de Cervantes Saavedra's *Don Quixote* (1605 and 1615), considered by many as one of the most important novels in modern world history, allows Burgos to demonstrate her knowledge of canonical works while simultaneously helping her carve a place for herself within the literary canon. Rocinante, like Don Quixote himself, symbolizes chivalry and the quest for justice. Represented in Burgos's poem as running wild over the horizon, the horse is also a symbol of movement that contrasts the confinement and lack of mobility traditionally associated with the female gender.

Burgos's ironic appropriation of masculinity as a means of defying patriarchal authority and claiming independence is also highly visible in "Pentacromia," a poem in which she borrows male characters and historical figures from Spanish literature and culture: Don Quixote/Alonso Quijano, Don Juan, and los Siete de Ecija, a legendary group of bandits from nineteenth-century southern Spain. Throughout the poem, Burgos expresses her desire to escape from the gender constructs that restrict her artistic and personal freedom by declaring her wish to be a man in each of the poem's six stanzas. Don Quixote, Don Juan, and los Siete de Ecija exemplify free will and rebellion against societal norms. Burgos discloses the double standard that exists between the male and female genders upon appropriating these characters and expressing her own yearning to rebel against the principles governing literature and society. The men in the poem challenge authority, exert power, and demonstrate agency. As Vanessa Pérez Rosario also observes, the popular figure of Don Juan is virile and sexual, while the women in Burgos's text live cloistered in a convent "and are denied their sexuality" (41). The poem's last stanza closes with a disturbing image of self-infliction as the speaker expresses her wish to be a man like Don Juan, kidnap and seduce two nuns, and rape Julia de Burgos. The desire to violate Julia de Burgos can be interpreted as a reflection of the poet's wish to negate her outward, conventional self as expressed in "A Julia de Burgos." According to López Springfield, "self-violation signifies a victory over female passivity. Unrestrained by social conventions, the rebellious self purges 'Julia de Burgos' of pretension and false piety" (707). Burgos parodies and subverts rigid, male-constructed notions of gender by assuming a masculine identity, which allows her to subdue her more publicly complacent female self and to give authority to her literary voice. She empowers and gives voice to the Puerto Rican *mulata* in a similar fashion upon parodying and challenging representations of blackness and femininity in the poetry of her male contemporary, Luis Palés Matos (1898–1959).

Best-known for his Afro-Antillean poetry, also referred to as *poesía negra* or *negrista*, Palés Matos was among the avant-garde artists in Puerto Rico whose works opposed the nationalist literature of the *treintistas*. As Matías Pérez-Miñambres affirms, Palés Matos was one of the first artists to introduce the European avant-garde movements, as well as blackness (or *lo negro*), to Puerto Rican letters with the publication of *Tuntún de pasa y grifería: Poemas afroantillanos* (1937). Although Palés intended to exalt Puerto Rico's rich African heritage, his poetry fails to represent its social and historical context and is replete with Eurocentric stereotypes (Pérez-Miñambres, 73–83). Among the negative representations of *lo negro* in Palés's book is the portrayal of the *mulata*. She is eroticized in "Majestad negra," and appears moving her hips and buttocks seductively to the beat of conga drums in a dance that is associated with the harvest of sugar cane. The poem highlights the *mulata*'s body parts, and the dance is described as a sexual act culminating in orgasm. Similarly, in "Mulata-Antilla," Palés uses the *mulata* as a metaphor to glorify the Antilles. She is depicted as sensual and exotic, and is objectified through a series of comparisons that liken her body to the sea. The poetic voice compares sexual intercourse with her to swimming in the Caribbean. As in "Majestad negra," the *mulata* is rendered sweet as sugar and dark like molasses. She is also reduced to her body parts, which are likened to the land curves of an inlet or cove and to tropical fruit. Palés Matos emphasizes the *mulata*'s sexuality and fertility. However, Burgos reconfigures this representation of the *mulata* in Palés' *negrista* poetry in "Ay, ay, ay de la grifa negra."

Rather than provide a sexually charged description of her body, Burgos gives the *mulata* a voice in "Ay, Ay, Ay de la grifa negra." In the first stanza, she describes herself from the neck up as grifa" (kinky-haired) and as having big lips and a flat nose—physical traits that are negatively associated with blackness in Puerto Rico. In the second stanza, she depicts herself as a black statue. However, it is a statue that she herself creates. In employing words that are commonly used pejoratively in Puerto Rico to denote blackness such as "grifa," "cafrería," and "chata," she transforms them into terms of self-affirmation and ethnic pride. Like an artist, she is sculpting her own image and identity, which she traces to the experience of slavery on the island. The speaker alludes to the historical and social factors to which Puerto Rico owes its rich African ancestry: slavery. Moreover, she denounces the slave master's actions while identifying with her enslaved grandfather. The poem, therefore, transforms the poetic image of the sexualized *mulata* characteristic of Afro-Antillean poetry into one of an assertive woman who embraces her history and heritage.

Like Agustini, Storni, and Burgos, the Mexican poet Rosario Castellanos (1925–1974) also critiques traditional representations of women in poetry as merely aesthetic material. In "Poesía no eres tú," first published in *En la tierra de en medio* (1969) and later included in the anthology of the same name, *Poesía no eres tú: Obra poética 1948–1971* (1972), Castellanos parodies Gustavo Adolfo Bécquer's *Rima XXI*. Gustavo Adolfo Bécquer (1836–1870) was a Spanish Romantic poet best known for his *Rimas* (rhymes) about love. Bécquer's *Rima XXI* consists of a dialogue between a female interlocutor and a male poetic voice. The female speaker asks the male poetic voice what poetry is, to which the male speaker responds that *she* is poetry. In her revision of the poem, Castellanos ironically discloses the male speaker's negation of female subjectivity by telling him that if he existed, then she would have to exist, too. She also denounces the idealization or fictionalization of women, affirming that only when each sex recognizes the other as "other" can true art begin. This notion is reiterated in "Meditación en el umbral," another poem from *Poesía no eres tú* that borrows fictional characters as well as the names of famous female authors to highlight the intertextual relationships that exist among unconventional female protagonists and women writers whose lack of adherence to societal norms results in their demise by suicide, such as with Anna Karenina and Madame Bovary, or in their having to live cloistered in seclusion, like St. Theresa of Ávila, Sor Juana Inés de la Cruz, Jane Austen, and Emily Dickinson, among others. Castellanos affirms at the end of the poem that there should be another mode of being (human and free), or other ways of envisioning women in art and for women to create literature.

Lastly, another way in which twentieth-century Spanish American women writers employ parody and intertextuality is through ekphrasis, a Greek term used to describe the practice of describing or recreating visual art in literature. Both Castellanos and Uruguayan poet Cristina

Peri Rossi (1941–) reinterpret well-known works of art that feature female figures. Castellanos addresses Leonardo da Vinci's famous painting known as the Mona Lisa in "Mirando a la Gioconda," a poem that appears in a section of *Poesía no eres tú* titled *Viaje Redondo*. The female poetic voice identifies herself as a visitor in the Louvre. She interrogates Gioconda in the first verse, asking the Mona Lisa why she is laughing at her. As Margaret Persin observes in her analysis of the poem, the focus of the text is neither the male gaze of da Vinci, nor of the speaker herself but, rather, the gaze of the Gioconda (493). The poetic voice ponders how the Gioconda might view her: a monolingual tourist from a third-world country. Upon inverting the roles of the spectator and the woman smiling enigmatically in the painting, Castellanos gives the Gioconda life. She is the one who gazes upon the many visitors in the Louvre while smiling mockingly. The Mona Lisa is no longer a static, pictorial representation; she is a woman that thinks and that taunts the tourists who believe that they can simply acquire culture by visiting the museum.

Also from *Viaje Redondo*, "La Victoria de Samotracia" is another poem that recreates a work of art from the Louvre: the Winged Victory of Samothrace (c. 220–185 BC), a marble statue, measuring nine feet tall, of the Greek messenger goddess Victory (also called the Nike of Samothrace). However, Castellanos's poem neither describes the female figure's flowing garments, nor the way that these are draped and folded to reveal her breasts, hip, and leg. Instead, the poet focuses on the parts of the body that are missing from the statue; the goddess has no arms and no head. Although Victory/Nike is armless and headless, the speaker ironically suggests that the goddess's posture or positioning make her appear weightless and content. For Margaret Persin, Castellanos's poem focuses on what is missing from the statue from the perspective of the male gaze: "la mujer, sin cabeza, ni brazos, incapaz de pensar ni de obrar" (495) [woman, without a head, or arms, incapable of thinking or acting]. In other words, the male artist or observer objectifies and reduces the female body to simply consist of a torso and legs. Castellanos, however, recovers and returns her head to Victory/Nike in the second and last stanza of the poem, stating that a head is something that has weight and purpose. The poem ends by alluding to the capacity to think and to the attainment of knowledge, attributes that patriarchal society traditionally denies women but that Castellanos gives back to the goddess in the poem.

Like Castellanos, Peri Rossi reproduces famous works of art in *Las musas inquietantes* (1999), a book comprised of fifty poems about canonical paintings, many of which represent images of women. While her female precursors, such as Agustini, Storni, Burgos, and Castellanos, turned to parody as a way of carving out a place for themselves as poets within Spanish American literary tradition, Peri Rossi's use of parody in this late twentieth-century collection is more aligned with postmodernism in its ironic and subversive treatment of the paintings that she recreates in her poems. As Linda Hutcheon asserts in *The Politics of Postmodernism*, "By both using and ironically abusing general conventions and specific forms of representation, postmodern art works to de-naturalize them" (8). Peri Rossi acknowledges her intent to undermine traditional, male-created representations of women in art in her essay titled "Poesía y pintura." She acknowledges that only a few of the paintings in her poems were painted by women, but contends that women are the primary focus of her book, stating that "el lector de este libro advertirá que a través de los diferentes poemas expreso una rebelión contra el papel tradicional, patriarcal de la mujer" (13) [the reader of this book will see that through the different poems I express a rebellion against the traditional, patriarchal role of woman]. Titled after Giorgio di Chirico's *The Disquieting Muses* (1916–1918), Peri Rossi's book dismantles the patriarchal ideologies and images associated with the female gender and of the female body in high art. According to Hutcheon, "Postmodern parodic strategies are often used by feminist artists to point to the history and historical power of those cultural representations, while ironically contextualizing both in such a way as to deconstruct them" (98). Peri Rossi's ideological deconstruction of patriarchal representations of woman and of the female body begins with first ekphrastic composition of the collection, "Claroscuro." The poem is titled after a technique used in oil painting that uses strong tonal contrasts between light and dark to represent three-dimensional forms, and is subtitled after the painting that it recreates: "La encajera" or "The Lace Maker" by Dutch artist Johannes Vermeer. Completed around 1669–1670, the painting is one of many works by Vermeer that show women sewing. According to Parizad Dejbord-Sawan, these paintings had a didactic purpose; they were often placed in Dutch homes to represent domestic virtue (83). "La encajera" features a young woman sitting alone and making lace. She is concentrating on the task and leaning forward. Peri Rossi interprets her posture as a sign of subjugation and the act of sewing itself as the learning of submission and of silence. After providing a brief description of the painting's content, a voice in the first person appears at the end of the poem and emphatically tells her mother that she does not want to make lace, have bobbins, or be a woman. In addressing her mother, the speaker rebels and rejects the domesticity that the painting is meant to instill in young girls as they come of age and grow up to be women. The sharp contrast between the image of the silent and sedentary lace maker and the poetic voice's strong opposition to the domestic virtue the painting represents brings to mind the poem's title: "Claroscuro."

Like Castellanos, Peri Rossi also recreates da Vinci's Mona Lisa in "Gioconda," but from the perspective of the painter. The poetic voice describes Gioconda while she poses for her husband as he paints her portrait. The poem discloses her sorrow, as well as her passivity and lack of agency; she is described as bearing the Florentine sadness of well-bred ladies. Despite enjoying a more privileged status than the lace maker, Gioconda is bound by the rigid notions of gender and propriety that constrain women of high social position and economic class. Peri Rossi's critique of the passive role in art and society to which women have been relegated throughout history is also present in her reproductions of Pisanello's "La princesa de este" (c. 1449) and of the anonymous limestone, fourth century BC Iberian bust known as "La dama de Elche." The nobility of the princess and the Lady of Elche is highlighted as contributing to their stoicism and immobility, but the sense of detachment that these portraits convey is not limited to ancient times or noble lineage. In "Cuarto de hotel," a recreation of Edward Hopper's "Hotel Room" (1931), Peri Rossi focuses on the loneliness of the woman pictured sitting on the bed alone with her head down. Peri Rossi brings to light the social alienation experienced by the women pictured in these portraits and encourages female artists to take action in her revision of "Las musas inquietantes."

Giorgio de Chirico's painting is of two muses wearing classical clothing. One is sitting while the other is standing. They are surrounded by various objects, a Roman statue, and red industrial buildings. What Peri Rossi emphasizes as being disquieting about these muses, however, is not the architectural setting in which they appear alongside diverse and mundane objects but, rather, their mutilated bodies. The muses are incomplete; the standing muse has no arms and the sitting muse is missing a head. Like the very things surrounding them, they, too, are objectified. Peri Rossi rebels against the painting's representation of the dismembered female body by invoking the muses to create art. This invocation can be interpreted as a plea to women artists to empower themselves; to produce art and have authority over how the female body is represented, as Peri Rossi demonstrates upon recreating Gustave Courbet's 1866 painting of a nude woman in "El origen del mundo."

Courbet's "L'Origine du monde" is yet another representation of a woman's headless, armless, and legless body. The painting depicts a female nude lying down with her legs wide open and her genitals and one breast very closely exposed. According to Parizad Dejbord Sawan, the painting is regarded by art historians as pornographic and representative of male sexual desire (88). Like the Winged Victory of Samothrace and de Chirico's muses, the female nude in Courbet's painting is among many works of art in which women are objectified and denied a head (or mind) and limbs (mobility). What sets Courbet's painting apart from other images of severed female bodies and makes it so unnerving and controversial, however, is the voyeuristic perspective from which it presents the nude's torso and sex so intimately. But Peri Rossi, as Dejbord Sawan observes, presents a new interpretation of the painting by reflecting upon its title: "insiste en la importancia de pensar o repensar la imagen en términos de la fuerza creadora y procreadora de la mujer, al usarlo como encabezamiento para su propio poema" (90) [She insists on the importance of thinking or rethinking the image in terms of the creative and procreative force of women, on using it as a preamble for her own poem]. In Peri Rossi's poem, the nude's sex is referred to as the solitary eye of God, perfectly round, complete, impenetrable, incapable of being possessed, untouchable, and incomparable in its ability to procreate. This metaphor recontextualizes Courbet's image so that the female nude is rendered as the observer and creator rather than an object being observed or created. Peri Rossi subverts the voyeuristic stance of the heterosexual male gaze traditionally associated with the painting upon replacing it with that of the female sex, which is rendered as being responsible for generating everything. The poem ends with an empowering vision of woman bringing the world into being. The assertion that she gives life to the world is highly significant because it suggests more than her ability to procreate; it gives her the power and capacity to produce any and all things, including literature and art.

Representing a century of women's poetry in Spanish America, Agustini, Storni, Burgos, Castellanos, and Peri Rossi employ parody and intertextuality in a variety of ways as a means to confront patriarchal literary and artistic history, and to challenge stereotypical and negative images of women. Agustini's appropriation of *modernista* tropes and Spanish mystical poetry allowed her to create a female poetic voice and to express erotic desire and artistic creation. Storni's revisionism of Darío's poetry and her subversion of *Modernismo*'s conception of gender constructs anticipate the movement's foreseeable demise. Burgos and Castellanos's "borrowing" of literary figures allows each poet to disclose and challenge gender inequality among writers and within literary texts. Lastly, Castellanos and Peri Rossi's reinterpretation of famous works of art provide opportunities to rethink the ways in which women and the female body have been traditionally portrayed in painting and sculpture while challenging the gender constructs that these patriarchal representations of woman promulgate. For these groundbreaking poets, parody and intertextuality functioned as effective and powerful vehicles for defining female subjectivity, and for vindicating the role of women in literature, art, and society.

NOTES

1. This translation and all others are mine, unless otherwise noted.
2. See Linda Hutcheon's *A Theory of Parody: The Teachings of Twentieth-Century Art Forms* (1985), Margaret Rose's *Parody: Ancient, Modern, and Post-modern* (1993), and Simon Dentith's *Parody* (2000).
3. For a summary of *Modernismo* and its main characteristics, see Max Henríquez Ureña's *Breve historia del modernismo*. México: Fondo de Cultura Económica, 1954.
4. According to Greek mythology, Leda, the wife of King Tyndareus of Sparta, was seduced by Zeus disguised as a swan. Rubén Darío recreates the myth in *Cantos de vida y esperanza* (1905). Although Agustini does not mention Leda in "El cisne," Jacqueline Girón Alvarado identifies the poetic voice as that of Leda and contends that Agustini presents her from a new perspective as actively participating in the encounter: "el poema quiere despojar al acto violento y doloroso de la violación de Leda de las implicaciones mágico-religiosas que tiene en el discurso machista patriarcal" (198) [the poem wants to strip the violent and painful act of Leda's rape from the magical-religious implications that it has in sexist patriarchal discourse]. Sylvia Molloy, on the other hand, does not see Agustini's text as a revision of the well-known myth of Leda. For Molloy, the swan "es, notablemente, *un* cisne. Se reduce así el campo simbólico, se descultura-liza el emblema dariano, literalmente se lo *desprestigia*" (64) [is, notably, *a* swan. The symbolic field is thus reduced, Darío's emblem is decultur-alized, literally disparaged]. What is clear upon reading the poem is that

Agustini transforms Darío's cisne into something new by rendering it as a male lover and transforming the swan/partner into the female poetic voice's object of desire.

5. Published in *Irremediablemente...* (1920), "Hombre pequeñito" is one of Storni's best-known and most anthologized poems. The diminutive "pequeñito" is reiterated throughout the poem to belittle the male addressee who is not only narrow-minded and incapable of understanding women, but also small in size. See Alfonsina Storni, *Poesías completas*, 151.

6. Julia de Burgos produced three books of poetry: *Poema en veinte surcos* (1938), *Canción de la verdad sencilla* (1939), and *El mar y tú* (published posthumously in 1954). These three books are compiled in *Song of the Simple Truth*, the bilingual edition of the poet's complete works that is referenced throughout this chapter.

WORKS CITED

Agustini, Delmira. *Poesías completas*. Edited by Magdalena García Pinto. Madrid: Ediciones Cátedra, 2000. Print.

———. *Selected Poetry of Delmira Agustini*. Edited and Translated by Alejandro Cáceres. Carbondale: Southern Illinois University Press, 2003. Print.

Bécquer, Gustavo Adolfo. *Rhymes and Legends (Selection): Rimas y Leyendas (Selección): A Dual-Language Book*. Edited and Translated by Stanley Appelbaum. Mineola, NY: Dover Publications, 2006. Print.

Bloom, Harold. *The Anxiety of Influence*. Oxford: Oxford University Press, 1973. Print.

Burgos, Julia de. *Song of the Simple Truth: Obra poética completa*. Compiled and Translated by Jack Agüeros. Willimantic, CT: Curbstone Press, 1997. Print.

Castellanos, Rosario. *Poesía no eres tú: Obra poética: 1949–1971*. México: Fondo de cultura económica, 1972. Print.

Darío, Rubén. *Selected Poems of Rubén Darío*. Translated by Lysander Kemp. Austin: University of Texas Press, 1965. Print.

———. *Prosas profanas*. Edited by Ignacio M. Zuleta. Madrid: Clásicos Castalia, 1987.

Dejbord-Sawan, Parizad. "Prácticas visuales revisionistas en 'Claroscuro,' 'La lección de guitarra' y 'El origen del mundo' de Cristina Peri Rossi." *Chasqui* 36.1 (May 2007): 80–95. Print.

De la Cruz, San Juan. *Poesía*. Edited by Domingo Ynduráin. Madrid: Ediciones Cátedra, 1990. Print.

Dentith, Simon. *Parody*. London and New York: Routledge, 2000. Print.

Gilbert, Sandra M. and Susan Gubar. *The Madwoman in the Attic: The Woman Writer and the Nineteenth-Century Literary Imagination*. New Haven and London: Yale University Press, 1979. Print.

Girón Alvarado, Jacqueline. *Poetic Voice and Feminine Masks in the Poetry of Delmira Agustini.* New York: Peter Lang, 1995. Print.

Habra, Hedy. "Re-escritura y subversión de la iconografía dariana de 'El Reino Interior' en 'Tú me quieres blanca' de Alfonsina Storni." *Alba de América* 24.45–46 (2005): 295–314. Print.

Hutcheon, Linda. *A Theory of Parody: The Teachings of Twentieth-Century Art Forms.* New York: Methuen, 1985. Print.

———. *The Politics of Postmodernism,* 2nd ed. London and New York: Routledge, 2002. Print.

Kirkpatrick, Gwen. *The Dissonant Legacy of Modernismo: Lugones, Herrera y Reissig, and the Voices of Modern Spanish American Poetry.* Berkeley: University of California Press, 1989. Print.

López Springfield, Consuelo. "'I am the Life, the Strength, the Woman': Feminism in Julia de Burgos' Autobiographical Poetry." *Callaloo* 17.3 (1994): 701–714. Puerto Rican Women Writers. Print.

McHale, Brian. *Postmodernist Fiction.* New York and London: Routledge, 1987. Print.

Palés Matos, Luis. *Tuntún de pasa y grifería: Poemas Afroantillanos.* San Juan, Puerto Rico: Edición especial para cultural puertorriqueña, 1988. Print.

———. *Tom-Toms of Kinky Hair and All Things Black.* Translated by Jean Steeves-Franco. San Juan: La Editorial Universidad de Puerto Rico, 2010. Print.

Pérez-Miñambres, Matías. "'Tuntún de pasa y grifería': perpetuación de estereotipos euroetnologocéntricos en el discurso poético afroantillano de Palés Matos." *Chasqui* 22.2 (1993): 73–84. Print.

Pérez Rosario, Vanessa. *Becoming Julia de Burgos: The Making of a Puerto Rican Icon.* Urbana, Chicago, and Springfield: University of Illinois Press, 2014. Print.

Peri Rossi, Cristina. *Las musas inquietantes.* Barcelona: Editorial Lumen, 1999. Print.

———. "Poesía y Pintura." *Revista Canadiense de Estudios Hispánicos* 28.1 (2003): 11–14. Print.

Persin, Margaret. "El principio ekfrástico en tres poemas de Rosario Castellanos." In *Literatura como intertextualidad: IX Simposio Internacional de Literatura.* Edited by Juana Alcira Arancibia, Juan José Camero, Carmen Ortiz, Josefina Plá, and Augusto Roa Bastos. Buenos Aires: Instituto Literario y Cultural Hispánico, 1993. 488–500. Print.

Rose, Margaret. *Parody: Ancient, Modern, and Post-Modern.* Cambridge: Cambridge University Press, 1993. Print.

Storni, Alfonsina. *Selected Poems.* Edited by Marion Freeman and translated by Marion Freeman, Mary Crow, Jim Normington, and Kay Short. Fredonia, NY: White Pine Press, 1987. Print.

———. *Poesías completas.* Buenos Aires: SELA/Editorial Galerna, 1994. Print.

CHAPTER 3

Postmodern Parody of *The Enchanted Cottage* in *El beso de la mujer araña*: Molina Leaves the Woods

Diane E. Marting

In Puig's classic novel, *El beso de la mujer araña* (1976) [*Kiss of the Spider Woman*, 1991], there comes a moment in chapter 5 when Luis Alberto Molina has fallen ill from the poison in her[1] food and wants Valentín Arregui Paz to tell her a movie to distract her from her discomfort. However, Valentín ignores Molina's pleas and continues to study his book of philosophy. Molina tells herself a film that she is sure Valentín would not like, one of her favorites, "una bien romántica" (97) ["totally romantic"][2] (98). Molina tells herself the Hollywood movie *The Enchanted Cottage*, directed by John Cromwell in 1945, renamed for Spanish audiences *Su milagro de amor* [*Their Miracle of Love*].[3] The elements of this movie, when transformed from visual into verbal discourse, are the least studied of those of all the "movie-stories" in the novel,[4] perhaps because the narrative she tells follows most closely the plot of the movie, at least at first. Molina's interior monologue of *The Enchanted Cottage*

D. E. Marting (✉)
University of Mississippi, University, MS, USA
e-mail: dmarting@olemiss.edu

© The Author(s) 2018
H. C. Weldt-Basson (ed.), *Postmodern Parody in Latin American Literature*, Literatures of the Americas,
https://doi.org/10.1007/978-3-319-90430-6_3

49

is a parody of the movie worthy of study because it subverts a heteronormative ideology of love, and shows the insufficiencies and contradictions of this conceptual field. This imitation of the movie is postmodern because, while seeming to uphold traditional gender identities and values, it demonstrates their unsustainability, undesirability, and limitations for goals of social inclusion, equality, and freedom.

Although parody has been variously defined, for this study I have chosen Linda Hutcheon's definition in *A Theory of Parody* (1985), because of the clarity with which the implications of the definition are explored in her book and the wide usage of her terminology since then. As is well-known, Hutcheon asserts that "ironic 'transcontextualization' is what distinguishes parody from pastiche or imitation" in the twentieth century (12).[5] Arguably, the two most important characteristics of parody in Hutcheon's definition are (1) that a work of art is being imitated, and (2) that there is irony in the imitation's relationship to its original. If one considers the movie *The Enchanted Cottage* to be a work of art, and Molina's memory of the movie to be ironic, then Hutcheon's most important conditions are fulfilled. While movies may not always be high art, Hutcheon's proposal is to distinguish imitations of social conditions or physical realities from parodied art objects, and not to consider whether the work imitated was great art or not, especially in the twentieth century when such distinctions blur.[6] The irony in Molina's retelling or "transcontextualization" of Cromwell's movie, resulting in a subtle wearing away of conservative ideologies, is the subject of this essay.

In most of his works, Puig parodied models from high and low art, or hybrids of the two. He parodied popular music and films most of all, and used the parodies for characterization. The Uruguayan poet and critic Roberto Echavarren states that, in *El beso de la mujer araña*, Puig cultivates paraliterary forms as a method of facilitating the reading process for those who are more practiced in listening to the radio and watching movies (Puig CE, 460).

The ways in which Puig's characters interact with movies especially contribute to his portrayal of their personalities and roles, no matter whether they identify directly and simply with the movie, or do so in more complex, fragmentary, or ironic ways. The popular cinematic forms that Molina fetishizes—mostly Hollywood movies—are parodied in such a way as to render the parodies of the movies intricate and significant. Molina does not make fun of these movies and resents it when Valentín jokes or criticizes them. Molina's parodies are closer to fan fiction than to the common idea of parodies as mocking: "Parody, therefore, is a form of imitation, but imitation characterized by ironic inversion, not always at the expense of the parodied text" (Hutcheon, 6). In *El beso* as a whole, Puig uses humor several times when other discourses are imitated, such as in the police surveillance report on Molina outside prison. The police report, rather than a parody of art, is a hilarious satire of police discourse and of the cluelessness of the detectives following Molina, who at first report her jokes seriously as though they were information about terrorist activity. Even this comic treatment, however, is made serious by the fact that the police surveillance narrated in the report brings about Molina's death.

In accordance with Hutcheon's definition of parody as a "repetition with difference," here we examine how Puig establishes contrasts and continuities between *The Enchanted Cottage* and spectators' understanding of the Hollywood movie, and then, regarding the visual/auditory film, a spectator's understanding of the film and of Molina's monologue. Readers of the novel find information in the monologue that leads us to interpretations in contrast with Molina's view. Molina becomes defined by those differences. Specifically, Molina's parody of *The Enchanted Cottage* is about the conventions of romantic love that the character finds attractive. The parody of heteronormative ideology in *The Enchanted Cottage* as narrated by Molina is uniquely hers, rather than one shared with Valentín. That is, the parody of *The Enchanted Cottage* gives readers information about Molina, as well as anticipates plot elements to come, but does not provide much significant data about Valentín. Its inclusion entirely in one chapter and its private nature (it is the only movie not told to Valentín) may also explain why critics have largely ignored this particular movie parody. Given the novel's lack of a narrator who might provide description, this movie-story needs to be understood as a character portrait and as anticipation of the direction the novel will take.

MOLINA'S "TOTALLY ROMANTIC" MOVIE

Marketed on posters with the phrase "Scandal Marked Their Love," *The Enchanted Cottage* deals particularly with the cruel social realities facing veterans returning home from war with physical and psychological traumas. Interestingly, the film also features women not in the armed services who have difficulty integrating into society in a fashion similar to the scarred veterans. These women are also outsiders excluded from normal relations because of their appearance. *The Enchanted Cottage* begins when a blind pianist and injured World War I pilot, Major John Hillgrove (Herbert Marshall), is about to give a concert. The premise is that, due to his blindness, Hillgrove is capable of looking beyond appearances; according to Molina, his eyes "*ven otras cosas, las que realmente cuentan*" (87, italics in the original[7]) [*see other things, the ones that really count*]. The Major's music has been inspired by a local love story, that of Laura Pennington (Dorothy McGuire) and Oliver Bradford (Robert Young). Bradford, disfigured and disabled after his injury at the front, has abandoned the fiancée whom he had planned to marry on the eve of his deployment. Bradford installs himself in the cottage of the title and refuses to interact with the outside world. He will not spend time with his mother Violet Price (Spring Byington), and stepfather Freddy Price (Richard Gaines), because they cannot see beyond his newly injured body. They pity him and insist he needs a nurse, among other offensive behaviors. Two women maintain the cottage that is his new home: the elderly owner, Mrs. Abigail Minnett (Mildred Natwick), the widow of an airman from World War I, and a homely young maidservant, Laura Pennington. The magic of the cottage allows Bradford and Pennington to become physically attractive to one other and to fall in love.

In her brief discussion of this movie parody, Pamela Bacarisse points out some of the mistakes other critics have made when generalizing about the films in *El beso* because they do not take into account *The Enchanted Cottage*. For example, some critics have claimed all the female movie protagonists are beautiful or are victims of tragic circumstances who die, but Laura Pennington is the exception to both statements because she is ugly and becomes happy (*The Necessary Dream*, 109). Furthermore, Bacarisse rightly emphasizes the importance of the frame story of Major Hillgrove.

The pianist is a friend to the younger couple and is one of the first to recognize that it is Oliver and Laura's love-in-isolation that allows them to "see" each other differently, rather than an actual physical transformation from ugly to beautiful. In a last-ditch effort to protect them and their love from the meddling of Oliver's mother and stepfather, Hillgrove tells Violet and Freddy a parable, the parable of the City of Eternal Night, in which residents looked upon their city with the eyes of the heart and did not see the ruins around them. The Major then asks the parents to play along with the lovers' ideas, saying: "You hold their chance for happiness in your hands." But the Prices do not see with their heart instead of their eyes. The film's visual image of the lovers switches back and forth between Bradford's scarred face and his unscarred one, between Laura's "beautiful" face and her homely one. The spectator is held in suspense until Violet remarks "you poor, poor darlings," revealing that she sees only scars and ugliness. As Bacarisse summarizes, "Molina sees himself in this girl: like him, she is not what she appears to be, but the exigent gaze of the sighted is not capable of this discovery" (109; Bacarisse, like most early critics, uses the male pronoun for Molina).

Keith Cohen is also one of the few critics to comment on *The Enchanted Cottage* monologue. He says he does so because "It is in this passage that the sexual practices and institutionally censured attitudes, which remain on the edges of today's dominant culture, take center stage" (21). Molina's story-within-a-story or secondary narrative, for Cohen, is part of a web of entrapment: "The amazing and even perverse thing about this example [*The Enchanted Cottage*] is that, rather than allowing a second-degree story or object to be spoken 'in full;' the ecphrasis serves to veil its darker pictures. It's a peep-show masquerading as a kinetoscope" (Cohen, 21). Cohen agrees with the idea that Molina's movie-stories are crucial for her characterization. In general, however, Cohen's analysis seems to emphasize Molina's incarceration as an indication of crime and guilt, rather than to see Puig's image of state repression and homophobia. This is particularly true when Cohen uses negative words such as "dark pictures" and "peep show" when talking about Molina's monologue. Cohen may be right that Puig does set up part I of the novel to create such suspicions and suspense, but part II shows that both protagonists are actually valiant victims of state authoritarianism, trying to survive. It is important to remember that the footnote in this chapter discounts the common belief that perversion is a cause of homosexuality. The Argentine author controls carefully the information at the readers' disposal to create suspense and to manipulate opinions about the characters, but it is hard to see Molina's love for *The Enchanted Cottage* as part of a peep show.

In *The Enchanted Cottage*, Laura Pennington must work in marginal, low-paying jobs—as maid and dishwasher—due to little formal education and to having grown up in poverty, like Molina the window-dresser. Molina identifies with her also because her body does not conform to societal notions of female beauty and because she is lonely. Laura lives with the self-sacrificing, all-knowing mother-like figure Mrs. Minnett, yet Laura still feels she is completely alone, like Molina who had lived with his mother. And, like the prison cell in which Molina and Valentín find themselves, the cottage exists with its own rules away from the public eye. One can argue that, in the cell, they are not free from prison surveillance, but together with Valentín, Molina feels secluded and separated from the rest of the prison population, though not safe from the warden. In other moments in the novel, the metaphor for the cell is an island; here, it is a cottage deep in the woods.

The small, isolated and decrepit house in the woods becomes a positive home to Laura, as in a fairy tale, because it allows her to escape men's scorn. For a while, Laura works in the village while living at the cottage. At a dance, she attempts to mingle, but the men pointedly ignore her. When she returns home crying, Mrs. Minnett explains to her the isolation of the cottage is something positive that certain types of people need. She includes herself in the group of those who must have solitude:

> Laura, it is not for some of us, for you and for me, to try to live like other people. You think you can sometimes, but there is always the world to remind you. All the things that other people take for granted you have got to make up your mind and your heart they are not for you. You have got to find something else to take their place. Somewhere you can be safe; that is why I wanted you to be here because there is something here for you that there isn't anywhere else. Do you understand?

Laura does comprehend and for the rest of the movie does not try to integrate into society or flirt with the male sex.

Oliver Bradford also understands the need for privacy in order to be happy during his time in the cottage. The success of the relationship between Oliver and Laura in *The Enchanted Cottage* is predicated on willfully ignoring social pressures and normative attitudes about whom one should love and be loved by. The outside world represents danger to a couple that does not conform to a standard of beauty or norm of happiness approved by others; the cottage provides escape from social pressures to conform. At the same time, it allows a couple with nonconforming bodies to achieve a marital bliss normally denied to those with outsider status. The ex-pilot and the maid strike up a romance that is based on inner qualities of refinement, generosity, and understanding.

Paradoxically, in Molina's retelling of *The Enchanted Cottage* to herself, and in the original movie, love still requires a basis in physical beauty. The enchantment, the magic spell of the cottage, causes this requirement to be fulfilled through the lovers' special sight, despite reality. The magic cottage makes lovers *see* each other as beautiful. The danger that comes from the outside world is that other people shatter the illusion of physical beauty that the cottage's spell has provided. Molina describes Laura and Oliver's transformation in this way:

> *Del rostro tan feo de ella, del rostro desfigurado de él, ... la bruma poco a poco se va esfumando, una agradable cara de mujer, la misma cara de la sirvienta pero embellecida, sus burdas cejas transformadas en líneas de lápiz, iluminadas por dentro sus ojos, alargadas en arcos sus pestanas, su cutis una porcelana.* (92, italics in the original)
> [*of her face so ugly, of his face so disfigured, ... mistiness fading little by little, agreeable face of a woman, same as the little maid's face but beautified, the coarse eyebrows transformed into light penciled lines, eyes illuminated from within, eyelashes elongated with curling, skin like porcelain.*] (108)

The actress Dorothy McGuire who plays Laura is changed from her supposedly homely face to a beautiful one and back again. Robert Young's facial scar is removed, replaced, and removed again in similar fashion. In the movie, makeup is used to accomplish changes from beautiful to ugly; depending on the belief of the onlooker character in the movie, the movie images toggle back and forth in the visual representation of the two lovers. Viewers of the movie, viewers such as Molina, observe physical changes to the couple's faces, depending on who is looking at them. In Molina's monologue about the movie, readers discover that Molina hopes to be like Laura in that someone (such as Major Hillgrove or Oliver) will be able to recognize her female *beauty*, and not just her inner qualities. In contrast, Molina's maturation within the novel allows her to see less importance in physical beauty as time goes on—and to assume less about her own non-conforming body.

Once Oliver and Laura's love has been tested by Oliver's mother and stepfather, and still endures, Oliver affirms to Laura: "You will always be beautiful to me." The happy couple inscribes their names alongside other newlyweds in the glass pane of an enchanted window, a glass that had rejected the name of the hypocritical and now ex-fiancée. Their love is inscribed, literally and in the philosophical sense of being recognized by a higher authority or power—the cottage. This magical writing is a stronger bond than their formal, originally sham marriage, which they had held merely to keep Oliver's family at bay. Major Hillgrove and

Mrs. Minnett, Oliver's mother and stepfather, the townspeople, all see Oliver's scars and Laura's homeliness. But the two lovers and the movie spectator see "with the heart" a physical beauty exhibited magically by both lovers.

The pilots of World War I (Mrs. Minnett's dead fiancé and Major Hillgrove) and World War II (Oliver Bradford) are romanticized figures, and the actual conflict in which each fought is rendered less important through the presence of veterans of both wars, rather than a focus on a single war and its particularities. Molina ignores the political side of her movies and would not have minded the mixing of the world wars in *The Enchanted Cottage*. In addition, Molina's apolitical retelling reflects a certain desire for obfuscation of the political situation held by conservatives and elites in Argentina during the time referred to the novel, April to May 1975. State terrorism in Buenos Aires was frequent but diffuse, designed to cause panic and obedience. Many people in the capital and major cities knew someone who was missing, injured, dead, or exiled; yet, the government denied that anyone had been hurt. The government and paramilitary groups said the dead and missing had voluntarily gone into exile, or simply did not want to be in contact with their family. They tried to justify violence against innocent people as a tactic to fight guerrilla movements, but it is likely only pro-government elites believed what the government was saying. Death threats had made Puig leave Argentina as early as 1973, so government statements about the disappeared did not fool him (see Puig CE, 441).

There are three significant revelations in *The Enchanted Cottage* movie-story, in terms of the foreshadowing of later plot elements: the importance of the kiss; Molina's attitudes toward his mother and toward Gabriel, her waiter friend; and the warden's offer of an early release in exchange for information. The motif of the kiss anticipates the kiss of the Spiderwoman later in the novel. Molina talks about: "*labios que se acercan, el primer y húmedo beso*" (Puig CE, 93, italics in the original) [*first and moist kiss*] (108, italics in the original) and "*el beso húmedo de la felicidad*" (Puig CE, 95) [*their wet kiss of happiness*] (112).

Second, in Violet Price, Oliver Bradford's biological mother, and in Mrs. Minnett, the owner of the cottage, we have two mother figures— one negative, the other positive. Bradford's biological mother never understands him; she pities him. Her letter about her upcoming visit to "save" him from his isolation is what precipitates the sudden marriage of Laura and Oliver. This doubling of the mother figure—Price and

Minnett—allows Molina to entertain a more complex view of his own mother, and it makes Molina's comments on his mother more open to question by the reader. Concretely, Violet's failure as a mother to Oliver may have had an effect on Molina's decision to accept Valentín's proposal that he communicate information to his revolutionary colleagues; Molina wants to live more fully and, ultimately, to risk her life, without feeling trapped by the effect her actions may have on her mother's health.[8] The movement in Molina's consciousness from Oliver's mother to Molina's own mother results from a relatively dispassionate contemplation of the women's actions, and of their lives. In contrast, the motherly Mrs. Minnett helps the couple to understand the cottage's magic powers. She is closer to the angelic image of Molina's mother. When Oliver and Laura ask Mrs. Minnett if there has been a physical change in their appearance, she says that there has not been a physical transformation, but she also tells them the secret: that a man and woman who love have a gift of sight that is of their own making. She declares that if her husband returned from the grave now, she would be pretty to him, despite all the years that have passed.

It is a different mental operation when Molina remembers Bradford's transformation back into his unscarred and handsome self, since this movie moment brings Gabriel to mind, Molina's idealized friend (Puig CE, 93; Puig trans. by Colchie, 108). Molina remembers her visits to Gabriel in the restaurant where he works. The memory of Gabriel comes from the association of Bradford with male beauty. Molina fantasizes that Gabriel will come to visit her at the jail, and will wait for her to be released, or perhaps she will be released early because of her cooperation with the warden.

The important information that Molina has an arrangement with the warden for an early release if she cooperates is first revealed in the monologue of *The Enchanted Cottage*: "*¿Cumple la promesa el director de la penitenciaria? ¿Será cierto lo que me promete? ¿indulto? ¿reducción de pena?*" (Puig CE, 91, italics in the original) [*will the warden keep his promise? Is it true what he promised? A pardon? A reduction in my sentence?*] (106).[9] This early revelation of Molina's possible betrayal of Valentín, as with the later explicit one when we read a transcription of Molina's interview with the warden, seems designed to facilitate suspense, by increasing the fear in readers that Molina may be untrustworthy. Readers eventually learn that Molina does not betray Valentín. She is merely trying to have it both ways: to benefit from the warden's offer of a reduced sentence while not revealing any of Valentín's secrets. (She gets her wish with a deadly twist.) But Puig foreshadows the revelation here to enhance the suspense for readers in *The Enchanted Cottage* monologue: what will Molina do?

DESCRIPTION, DIFFERENCE, AND DETERIORATION

One difference between an objective description of the movie and Molina's movie-story in the novel is the Argentine Spanish employed in the monologue by Molina. The editors of the critical edition were able to examine the Spanish subtitles in *Su milagro de amor*, the Spanish version of *The Enchanted Cottage*, and they found that the subtitles do not use *vos* (Puig CE, 97). In other words, even when Molina provides what a reader would expect to be a direct quotation from the film, within quotation marks, the text from the movie has been modified to fit Molina's Argentine Spanish. Furthermore, Francine Masiello reminds us how Molina "transfers" or "translates" the American woods surrounding the cottage to a South American countryside by speaking of *"araucarias"* [*evergreens*] (108), a Latin American plant rather than the pine trees of the United States (cf. Puig CE, 93 and 98 n. 20). In this sense, as imitations with a difference, Masiello compares the movie-stories to the police documents in the novel; these inserted narratives—she argues—dramatize the distance between what is told in them and what they mean. Similarly, Molina's 'translations' into Argentine Spanish and—most importantly—into Molina's world, make her movie-story different from the original movie.

As Molina's narrative progresses, it shows an increasing irony and distance from the movie's tale of heterosexual and romantic bliss, due to the contrasts with Molina's reality. This is part of Puig's written plan for the chapter: to maintain Molina's voice but to show the movie gradually losing its power to distract her from her prison reality. In note 7 of chapter 5, the editors of the critical edition comment on one of Puig's remarks to himself in his manuscript as providing the key to his next revision (Puig CE, 96–97, n. 7). In this metatext, Puig is addressing the way in which he plans to rewrite this movie-story in the next substantive revision: "~~Descripción objetiva pero cursi, no cálido, después degenera. Voces que se pueden disolver otra vez en descripción y pasan a ser la voz de F.~~" (Puig CE, 96–97, n. 7; strikethrough in the original) [~~Objective description but corny, not warm, then it deteriorates. Voices that can dissolve once again into description and then become F's voice.~~] "F" was Puig's abbreviation for Folle, his working name for Molina in early versions of the manuscript. In other words, Puig's intention is to tell the story in Molina's voice and then let Molina's thoughts on other elements of her reality interrupt to make her parody of the movie **deteriorate**.

At first, the planned deterioration of the parody occurs subtly, in moments in which Molina's memory of the movie stumbles. She wonders if the piano is "*¿de pino? ¿de caoba? ¡de sándalo!*" (Puig CE, 87, italics in the original) [*finished in pine? Or mahogany? No, sandalwood!*] (98). It should be mentioned that, to the extent that the novel follows Molina's thoughts and musings exclusively in this movie-story, the dialogic form of the novel becomes less prominent, but dialogue is not entirely erased. The dialogue has moved from one between Molina and Valentín, to one within Molina. Instead of Valentín asking her questions, Molina interrogates her memory of *The Enchanted Cottage*, setting up an inner dialogue.

Another example of deterioration is when Laura tries to help the blind Major Hillgrove in the woods, explaining she was born in the area; but then Molina doubts the word for the region (Puig CE, 88; Puig trans. by Colchie, 100). Molina even wonders if the man who lives in the cottage might be an architect, as if we were in the world of *Cat People*, the first movie-story: "*Y el estudio para el muchacho, ¿arquitecto?*" (88, italics in the original) [*and for the young man's work, a study, an architect perhaps?*] (101). At another moment, Molina wonders about the drawing (*dibujo*) done in the movie (Puig CE, 92; Puig trans. by Colchie, 106–107).[10] Molina wonders about the relationship between love and words, and how Oliver first becomes attracted to Laura. As the narrative continues, these internal debates come more frequently; perhaps the most commonly cited inner debate in criticism is Molina's worry over the distress she has caused her mother, and the contrast between her mother's generous care and Valentín's obstinate refusal to pay attention to Molina while she is sick (Puig CE, 91).

As the "deterioration" of Molina's description of the movie becomes progressively greater, she stops narrating the film and talks about other people: her mother, Valentín, and Gabriel the waiter. Molina associates Oliver Bradford with Valentín. This connection makes sense because both are patriotic in their own way: Oliver has offered his life bravely for his nation, just as Valentín has sacrificed his life for his political ideals. Oliver has been wounded; Valentín has been tortured. The traumatized pilot hides in the upstairs bedroom when his mother, stepfather, and ex-fiancée visit soon after his arrival at the cottage. He refuses to meet with any of them but cannot avoid hearing them outside his door. After they have gone, Laura enters his room in her capacity as a maid, and finds that he has a pistol in his hand. She gently approaches him and takes the pistol, bravely preventing him from a panicked suicide. Molina has just finished ingesting the poisoned plate of food intended for Valentín in the prison cell. Molina cannot prevent Valentín from being poisoned later. Previously, in chapter 4, she knows the food is poisoned, and she has injured herself in place of Valentín. Molina's secret and private action causes her the physical discomfort she experiences during *The Enchanted Cottage* monologue.

When Molina describes Oliver to herself, she slips easily from thoughts of Bradford to thoughts about Valentín, about when Molina finds Valentín staring at her with an accusatory glare because she interrupted his reading (Puig CE, 91; Puig trans. by Colchie, 105). The slippage from Oliver in the movie to Valentín in the cell is achieved through the bridge of immediate emotions—anger, disgust, and fear. Valentín is reading his book of philosophy, willfully ignoring Molina's request for distraction. The deterioration has carried the reader from a story of love to its opposite, a story of resentment and emotional distance. And irony appears in these areas because the difference is not subtle, or a mere adjustment of memory from the original movie. For irony to be at work, elements in Molina's monologue must be the opposite of the movie she is telling. Indeed, there is a marked contrast between the love affair in the cottage and the animus in the prison cell at this point in the plot.

An important researcher in Puig's manuscripts, Julia Romero, mentions that one of Puig's early plans for the novel was to begin with Molina's dying delirium, without saying whose dreams they were. "Stitches" (*puntadas*) of the delirium were to be spread throughout the novel, without identifying the dreamer, in a classic Puig move designed to heighten suspense. Romero comments further that:

> Las "puntadas ocultas" según esta anotación [de Puig], reiteran los motivos: en todos los filmes está presente el planteo gótico de la identidad distorsionada y la doble naturaleza, la creación de una atmósfera de extrañeza que cuestiona la noción de normalidad: la marca, el secreto, la traición enhebran aquellas "puntadas ocultas" que escanden las claves de la intimidad histórica, un relato desplazado, el enfrentamiento con el orden estatal. *Mise en abyme* de la historia, los filmes incluidos narran el vampirismo presente en los sistemas autoritarios. (309)

[The "hidden stitches" of the delirium according to this annotation [by Puig] reiterate the motifs: in all the films there is the Gothic requirement for a distorted identity and a double nature, the creation of an atmosphere of strangeness that questions the notion of normality: the mark, the secret, the betrayal that tangles up those "hidden stitches" that scan the clues to an intimate story, a displaced story, a confrontation with the state order. *Mise en abyme* of the story/history, the included films narrate the vampirism present in authoritarian regimes.]

It is quite possible that the interruptions of the movie-story of *The Enchanted Cottage* by other topics are related to these "stitches" by Molina that Puig initially intended to be sprinkled throughout the novel. Whether or not they are Puig's "*puntadas*," they are ironic moments contrasting with the normalcy reinforced in *The Enchanted Cottage*, a movie in which scars are erased and the miracle of love saves a marriage based on excluding others and hiding away. The reality of the prison is that scars are created there and usual modes of conduct are destroyed. So when Molina switches back to her reality from her memory of the movie, opposites are established, and irony abounds.

Molina's meandering monologue incorporates comments about her mother, Valentín, and Gabriel; ruminations on the causes of love and the relation between words and love; the effect her incarceration has on her mother, the prison warden's offer of clemency, and more. The two mother figures in *The Enchanted Cottage* lead to thoughts about Molina's own mother; Oliver Bradford's anger at his mother and stepfather reminds Molina of Valentín's anger at being interrupted while reading. There are also memories of Gabriel. But, most often, the secondary narrative of the movie-story keeps bringing Molina back to the primary one of the prison. And, in this main narrative, Molina must make a decision about Valentín and what to do about the warden's offer of early release in exchange for information. From a story of romantic love and escape from social pressures, we are taken to one of repression, torture, (lack of) social justice, and betrayal.

To what extent do these jumps from telling herself the movie to thinking about her reality mean that Molina learned lessons from *The Enchanted Cottage*? And, in terms of the norms of heterosexuality, how much do the stereotypes of gender division in the movie resurface in her later thoughts and actions? A great deal. Ricardo Piglia (among others) calls attention to the influence of popular culture on Puig's characters. For Piglia,

Puig "speaks only of 'bovarism,' the sort of reader that Madame Bovary exemplifies, one concerned with how to believe and what models work to make people believe in fiction" (26). Like Madame Bovary, Molina learns her life lessons from the popular culture. She tries to live like the heroine in *The Enchanted Cottage*. The border between life and movie melodrama for Molina is always very tenuous and, as we have seen, in this monologue Molina debates within herself the relationship between the two.

Female Identification and the Gender Binary

The Enchanted Cottage movie-story highlights—at least as much if not more than the other inserted movie narratives—a transitional moment in Molina's circumstances and beliefs. She had identified with Irena in *Cat People* and with Leni in *Destino* [*Her Real Glory*] because of her commonalities with those tragic movie characters; she is an outsider and someone who wants to fall in love and be loved in return. More than identification with a female character, with *The Enchanted Cottage*, Molina aspires to live Laura's life, to be a citizen of the City of Eternal Darkness, and to escape to the isolation of the American woods. Importantly, it is in Molina's interrogation of the happy ending of this movie that we see her articulate for the first time a hope for the possibility of being loved for herself.

At the same time, most criticism asserts that when Molina tells herself *The Enchanted Cottage*, she believes in gender as a given, an inescapable binary, and as a social construction in which she wants to live. Roberto Echavarren, for example, interprets Molina's ideology as rigid, claiming that she devalues her own changes because she subscribes to the essentialism of binary gender norms, desiring to be a total woman (Puig CE, 458; Echavarren uses the male pronoun for Molina). While it is true that Molina sees herself as a (beautiful) woman who wants to be loved as a woman, it does not necessarily follow that Molina must want gender to remain stable and impermeable. It is one of the interesting problems in feminism for women as well as for transsexuals: to what extent is the celebration of women a reification of the gender binary?

What is clear is that the gender division that seems unquestioned in *The Enchanted Cottage* dissolves somewhat in its movie story and later becomes even more fluid in *El beso*, especially after Molina has sex with Valentín because Molina declares the sex between them has erased the divisions between herself and Valentín. Molina thinks she has the mole that is on Valentín's face. That erasure of the limits of self and ego does not make Molina male, any more than identifying with female characters had previously made her female. It is Molina's certainty that she is female that makes her so. But I would argue that, because of her movement between and among social constructions of gender, from being a woman like Laura Pennington to being at one with Valentín, there is an increasing give-and-take in Molina's conception of the genders as *El beso* progresses.

In fact, her female gender identification is portrayed as both crucial and an obstacle to Molina's search for love and happiness. Puig thought that sexual preferences were less important and more flexible than his character Molina does, at least than Molina does in the beginning. In fact, Puig's ideas are quite radical regarding sexuality as a factor in determining identity; perhaps his attitude would be considered gender queer or gender-bending today. In "El error gay,"[11] Puig wrote: "La homosexualidad no existe. Es una proyección de la mente reaccionaria" (cited in Romero, 314) [Homosexuality does not exist. It is a projection of a reactionary mind]. In the same article, Puig adds: "la identidad no puede ser definida a partir de características sexuales, ya que se trata de una actividad justamente banal" (cited in Masiello in Puig CE, 587) [Identity cannot be defined from sexual characteristics, since it is a merely banal activity]. Hence Molina's identification with Laura Pennington, like her identification with the other female protagonists in his movie-stories, may be merely a starting place for Puig's character, as Molina develops in the novel into a more feminist and liberated figure. Molina identifies with Laura but then more fully empathizes with and becomes at one with Valentín.

By emphasizing Oliver's ability to find love with Laura, and thus to change, Molina's internal movie-story is noteworthy for foreshadowing the wherewithal the two prisoners find to come to love one other. The similarity in the struggles of Molina and Valentín lies in their kindred efforts to move toward freedom from repression, and away from social rules about gender, sex, and sexuality, and from authoritarian regimes in the face of impossible obstacles.[12] Importantly, Puig portrays Molina's self-sacrifice at the end to be fully human, neither stereotypically feminine nor masculine; Molina inhabits a place of tension denied to her by society.[13]

From today's perspective of supporting the rights of transsexuals, readers can consider Molina's ability to see herself differently from the sex noted on her birth certificate as evidence of the fragility of social constructions of sexuality, gender, and sexual identity. Even at the early point in the novel where *The Enchanted Cottage* appears, readers discover in this movie-story Oliver/Valentín's capacity to defy social norms and Molina's desire to change herself to find love. Molina's growing sense that the power of love in *The Enchanted Cottage* encourages her to defy society, makes possible for her a more fluid gender and sexual identity. The ending of *El beso* would thus be enriching: a growing, and a maturing that occurs through Molina and Valentín loving one other, as well as through their freedom from heterosexuality and homosexuality as controlling concepts or dominating norms.

Additionally, Puig plants in the conversations between Molina and Valentín the possibility of a synthesis of the positions of the two characters, even on gender issues. Francine Masiello posits that "Puig responde no solamente a impulsos deconstructivos, sino que, al mismo tiempo, propone la posibilidad de una coalición insospechada entre individuos de intereses disimiles" (Puig CE, 576) [Puig responds not only to deconstructive impulses, but also—at the same time—he proposes the possibility of an unsuspected coalition between individuals of dissimilar interests]. Following this line of argument, the characters have salient genders and sexualities, but they can assume other ones for strategic reasons. Here is Masiello again on Puig's textualization of a more flexible Molina:

> Puig busca la producción de una identidad pero no basada en una mentalidad de *ghetto*, sino desde una coalición construida a partir de nuestro sentido común de exclusión. Se trata de un modo en el que el Yo que se halla cuestionado nos permite comprender un Nosotros. (Puig CE, 587, italics in the original)
>
> [Puig is looking for the production of an identity but not one based on a *ghetto* mentality, rather one based on a coalition constructed from our mutual sense of exclusion. It has to do with a modality in which the I that finds itself questioned allows us to understand a We.]

Puig wanted the world to treat sexuality not as a special, intense, or significant element of human experience but as an unremarkable one, so that we could come together, rather than live in our isolated cottages in the deep woods. Thus, when Molina reflects on the happiness in *The Enchanted Cottage*, learning that happiness is conceivable for those with different bodies, she can begin to reach for it in different ways with Valentín than she had with Gabriel.

Other evidence of the undercutting of the gender binary in *The Enchanted Cottage*, in addition to Molina's identification with Laura Pennington, lies in the fact that the movie-story is placed in the chapter with footnote 3, the second footnote dealing with the causes of homosexuality. (The other previous footnote concerns the Nazi brochure about the movie *Destino.*) This footnote in chapter 5 discusses D.J. West's refutation of the three most common non-physical causes of homosexuality in common opinion (Puig CE, n. 86; Puig trans. by Colchie, n. 97). The three causes listed and then debunked in this footnote are perversion, seduction, and segregation. While all three themes are relevant to the novel, the third is particularly highlighted in *The Enchanted Cottage.* The heterosexual couple's love in the movie flourishes precisely because they are able to separate themselves from society and its pressures long enough to ignore its dictates. On the other hand, the footnote reinforces that segregation from the other sex, such as that which has been forcibly imposed on Molina and Valentín, "está más vinculada con la fuerza e imperiosidad de la necesidad de una descarga sexual que con la libre elección de su objeto amoroso" (Puig CE, 86) [has more to do with the imperative demands for sexual discharge than with any willful choice of sexual partner] (n. 100). West is saying that segregation alone cannot create the affective bonds found between Molina and Valentín by the end of the novel.

Regarding Argentine law, consensual homosexual activity has been legal in Argentina since the end of the nineteenth century. But it was not until democratization in 1983 that Argentina saw the kind of legal changes that have made the country one of the most advanced in Latin America (and in the world) in terms of same-sex marriage (known as "egalitarian" marriage) and sexual rights.[14] According to Balderston and Masiello, Puig was familiar with the gay liberation movement in Argentina when he was about to write *El beso*:

A small group of activists founded the journal *Nuestro Mundo* in 1970 and the Frente de Liberación Homosexual in 1971; ... According to José Sebreli, Osvaldo Bazán, and Flavio Rapisardi and Alejandro Modarelli, who have written histories of this period, Puig attended meetings of these groups, although he was not a spokesperson for them... . (6)

Echavarren believes that one of Puig's intentions in *El beso* was exactly to reflect and to write on seventies-era protests for gay liberation (Puig CE, 461). The Argentine dictatorship also noticed the protest against government repression that the novel represents; *El beso* was banned in Argentina from the time of its first publication in Spain in 1976 until 1983.

IMITATION, IRONY, AND IDEOLOGY

The imitation in Molina's retelling of *The Enchanted Cottage* unravels in several directions that are particularly ironic, as we have seen: interruptions from Molina's current reality and disturbances of her memories cause Molina to change the movie monologue from a straight description of the movie to a parody, an "ironic transcontextualization." Molina mixes Oliver Bradford with Gabriel and contrasts him with Valentín; she remembers mothers less saintly than her own. All these ways in which the narrative unfolds make ironic Molina's desire to be Laura Pennington, particularly because the emotional logic bringing forth these elements reminds readers of the many differences between Molina's current imprisonment and her fantasy of love in the forest.

Yet the reader and Molina learn in the movie-story of *The Enchanted Cottage* that a lover can accept a non-conforming body, and that Molina need not be a traditional woman or a beautiful woman to be happy in love. Mrs. Minnett and Major Hillgrove encourage everyone to "accept this blessing" of loving and being loved, without worrying about the opinions of others. If they love each other, what does it matter if others pity them? In contrast, the women from the other movie-stories remain suspect in their respective contexts, though ultimately Molina makes them sympathetic in their tragedies. Irena the cat-woman, Leni the Nazi sympathizer, and Mrs. Rand the zombie and her nurse—each had a problem without a solution. These other film women do not live happily ever after with the men of their dreams. Only Laura Pennington does that. If Molina takes to heart Laura's message of resistance to outside pressures, then neither the surveillance of the penitentiary nor society's admonitions of who can or should be loved will have the same hold on her. She can value herself more, risk more, hope for more. For the length of time she tells herself this parody, Molina manages to hold some of the contradictions of her life in suspense, as everyone must do in order to feel good about themselves.

Valentín does not yet mirror Oliver Bradford's transformation into someone who can "see other things, ones that really count," and Molina becomes angry about it. Her monologue of *The Enchanted Cottage* ends with an affirmation of love between Oliver and Laura, followed by her resentment against Valentín: "*este hijo de puta y su puta mierda de revolución*" (Puig CE, 95, italics in the original) [*this son of a bitch and his pissass of a revolution*] (112). After Molina's monologue, in the brief dialogue with Valentín that ends the chapter, Molina watches Valentín accept the poisoned food and does not object. Telling the story of *The Enchanted Cottage* ultimately has tipped Molina toward punishing Valentín for his mean-spirited and selfish manner. Remembering *The Enchanted Cottage* was provoked by, and further provokes, dissonance within Molina's consciousness of being "in the movie" vs. being in the cell. She has been recruited to spy on Valentín, and she must now decide what actions to take. Constrained and confined, under duress, Molina is unsure how to act to achieve her utopia; her first thought is to let Valentín experience what she has just endured and eat the poisoned food.

The eruptions into spoken dialogue with Valentín during and after Molina's internal movie monologue about *The Enchanted Cottage* are surprisingly abrupt. The lack of transitions between the parody and the conversation with Valentín are brusque segues that mitigate the impact of the ideology of a movie that relies on magic and isolation to prop up heteronormative love. Puig's decision to have the objective telling of the movie "deteriorate" by mixing other elements into Molina's thoughts regarding the movie mark Molina as a character in motion, moving in the gap between her imaginary and her reality. And the reader, through access to Puig's footnote, learns the opposite of at least one of the messages in Laura's story: isolation—like essentialism and lack of feminist ideals—is not compulsory for people who love those whom society disdains.

The Enchanted Cottage presents Molina with binaries: male-female, alone-together, beautiful-ugly, loved-lonely, Argentina-United States. But after telling herself the story, she tries to not be defined by either side of the dualities and, instead, to transcend limits placed on her, as Laura and Oliver do. Later, in her sexual relations with Valentín, Molina is able to dissolve more fully the gender categories to which she had previously adhered by becoming one in her mind with Valentín. But during this movie-story, she mostly enters and exits, mentally, consciously, the cottage and the cell, finding herself leaving one only to find herself in the other. But this back and forth movement can rob the binary of its coercive power because one becomes aware that neither alternative is everywhere, nor is either part of the binary all powerful. Molina is still attracted to the idea that in isolation she can be happy, but she now recognizes that hiding away from those who wish her harm may not be an option. This recognition is a first step toward "leaving the woods," or asserting herself in society as someone worthy of others' respect and of freedom from persecution.

From page 1, Molina is a sympathetic character that suffers abuse at the hands of society, prison officials, and even Valentín at first, who gains the reader's trust through the pleasure of her storytelling and whose actions create suspense. Nevertheless, Valentín and the novel as a whole show the character to be mistaken in her early inflexibility about gender identification, her ideal of male dominance in the heterosexual couple, and her wholehearted acceptance of heteronormative love. Even though these themes predominate in *The Enchanted Cottage*, in her retelling of this movie-story Molina reveals a new awareness that being a woman is not enough. Molina discovers a key to happiness in the blindness of a love that disobeys society. The apparent contradiction of learning from a traditional movie how to be free from gender tradition disappears in Molina's rendition of a parody of the movie that emphasizes inner qualities, privacy, and resistance. For all the corniness of this solution through magic, Molina gains strength and clarity from this Hollywood cliché. To Molina's credit, she realizes that *The Enchanted Cottage* champions removing stigma and ostracism from people whose distance from the norm have been seen negatively by mainstream society. Molina's retelling of this movie-story ironically and paradoxically allows her to keep an image of love as a force capable of magically making others' criticisms lose their sting. This is the postmodern way—to undercut while affirming.

Puig's critique of homosexuality in "El error gay" and his portrayal of Molina as conservative in her opinions of female-male relations may seem harsh in light of reading Molina as a victim. Even harsher is the portrayal of Molina as identifying with a Nazi sympathizer in *Destino*. But the author also has Molina figure out how one might discard the political and the social construction of gender that had bound her to subservience as a woman: she can feel worthy of love, and be brave and loyal. Valentín's belief in her in later chapters solidifies Molina's newfound self-confidence and strength hinted at here. Molina does die like the women from her tragic movie stories, but she gains the willpower to stand up for herself against Valentín first, and later against the police. Although she believes she will likely die, she tries for a better life and the possibility of happiness, due to *The Enchanted Cottage*, among other factors.

Valentín is more easily associated with a desire for positive social change because he is an activist. But reader engagement with Molina's evolution represents a kind of milestone. Readers see her find a path leading to self-respect and dignity, first in her comprehension of *The Enchanted Cottage* and, later, as reinforced by Valentín. Today, when transsexuals and LGBTQIA (lesbian, gay, bisexual, transgender, queer, questioning, intersex, and allies) individuals have won a degree of greater acceptance by mainstream society, Molina's change of heart about politics, gender, love, and life has become all the more meaningful.

Notes

1. There is a debate about the vocabulary for describing Molina. Is Molina a homosexual, gay, queer, transsexual? In my classes a decade ago, my students to a person felt that Molina was a homosexual; for my students today, Molina is transsexual. (It is interesting to note that, during this decade, my students' support for Molina, and for the novel's construction of love and deconstruction of heteronormative relationships, has also greatly increased.)
   Here, I respect Molina's preference by using the female pronoun for the character. While the debate over which pronoun and which nomenclature to use is outside the purview of this article, I feel it is important to recognize the problem existed from the beginning of criticism of the novel. In the introduction to the manuscripts in the critical edition, for example, José Amícola discusses the problem of what language to use, because it is precisely the effort of the novel to question stereotypes and to advocate for human rights (Puig CE, XXIII; hereafter references to the critical edition are indicated in the text as "Puig CE" with page numbers).
2. All translations from the novel are from the Vintage translation by Thomas Colchie.
3. All translations not from the novel are mine, unless otherwise indicated.
4. As of July 2017, Wikipedia in English does not even list *The Enchanted Cottage* in its discussion of the novel.
5. Under Hutcheon's definitions, for the imitation of the movie to be pastiche there would need to be visual text, actual movie clips, inserted into Puig's novel. Literal quotations from the original movie could be considered pastiche, only if spoken aloud in English. But even if Puig used some actual Spanish subtitles for some of Molina's interior monologue (Puig does use quotation marks to distinguish Molina's memory of speech in the movie from Molina's other paraphrased memories of the movie), that pastiche would not diminish the importance of parody for the movie-story's overall ironic messages.
6. Keith Cohen calls this movie-story an ecphrasis (or, more commonly, ekphrasis), again considering *The Enchanted Cottage* a visual work of art,

one that has been described and/or commented on verbally in literature. I have chosen to use the word "parody" rather than "ekphrasis" for Molina's movie-story to emphasize the twentieth-century use of imitation for ideological purposes, hence Hutcheon's definition and discussion.

7. The italic typeface indicates flow of consciousness and is not an indicator of parody or emphasis. For instance, Valentín's morphine-induced dream also is stylized as italicized phrases separated by commas, although the narrative is told in a more normal Spanish, less poetic, and easier to understand, even if more unexpected and surprising in content. Another example of the form of breathless phrases, told in italicized insertions, occurs in chapter 10 when Valentín is sick and Molina is telling the movie-story about the Caribbean slave trade (based on *I Walked with a Zombie*).

8. Several of the zombie movies that are the source for Molina's zombie tale also have terrible mother figures.

9. Most first-time readers of the novel may not understand this brief insertion, since the change of topic is sudden and unexplained. Many of my students do not realize that Molina has agreed to be an informant until the report on Molina's interview with the prison warden in part II. But, in fact, the existence of the deal is revealed in chapter 5, several chapters before the end of part I. As mentioned earlier, Puig is extremely meticulous in his construction of the novel and his manipulation of the reader's understanding.

10. Another mistake of Molina's memory is that the "drawing" belonged to Bradford when, in fact, in the movie it is a woodcut made by Pennington. This mistake has often been repeated by critics—even by careful ones such as Echavarren (1986, 81).

11. Published originally in *El Porteño*, IX (September 1995).

12. A frequent idea in the criticism of *El beso* is that the novel and the movie "endorse forthrightly the Marcusian hypothesis that sexual liberation and political liberation are in fact the same process" (Foster, 126).

13. Not everyone agrees with this idea. After recognizing the greater complexity of the novel, David William Foster's chapter on the film adaptation directed by Héctor Babenco (1985) stresses that the adaptation "leaves it unclear whether there is any absolute motivation of selflessness in Arregui's and Molina's behaviors" (127) despite the appearance of "ideological exchange between the cell mates" (126). Foster argues the film relies on Molina's presence as a "hovering angel in times of Arregui's distress" (134) in order "to appeal to most spectator's investment in the maternal imperative" (134). The movie adaptation and William Hurt's "acting protocols" cater to stereotypes, Foster argues, rather than showing an increasing freedom from them.

14. The wide acceptance of forward-looking LBGTQIA legal protections in Argentina is seen by scholars to be a reaction to the loss of rights for everyone under the totalitarian dictatorships of the late 1970s and early 1980s (see e.g., Carlos Figari).

Works Cited

Bacarisse, Pamela. "'The Kiss of Death': *El beso de la mujer araña* (1976)." In *The Necessary Dream: A Study of the Novels of Manuel Puig*. Totowa, NJ: Barnes & Noble Books, 1988. 86–125. Print.

———. "The Female Image." In *Impossible Choices: Implications of the Cultural References in the Novels of Manuel Puig*. Calgary, Canada: University of Calgary Press, 1993. 37–50. Print.

Balderston, Daniel and Francine Masiello (Eds.). "Materials." In *Approaches to Teaching Puig's* Kiss of the Spider Woman. New York: Modern Language Association, 2007. Print.

Cohen, Keith. "Unweaving Puig's 'Spider Woman': Ecphrasis and Narration." *Narrative* 2.1 (1994): 17–28. Print.

Echavarren, Roberto. "*El beso de la mujer araña* y las metáforas del sujeto." In *Manuel Puig: Montaje y alteridad del sujeto*. Edited by Roberto Echavarren and Enrique Giordano. Santiago, Chile and New York: Monografías del Maitén, 1986. 77–87. Print.

———. "Género y géneros." *El beso de la mujer araña*. Edición crítica, José Amícola, Jorge Panesi, coordinadores. Colección Archivos. ALLCA XX, 2002 (abbreviated as Puig CE in these References and in this chapter): 456–471. Print.

Figari, Carlos. "Queer Argie." *American Quarterly* 66.3 (2014): 621–631. Print.

Gómez-Lara, Rubén L. *Intertextualidad generativa en* El beso de la mujer araña. Miami, FL: Universal, 1996. Print.

Hutcheon, Linda. *A Theory of Parody: The Teachings of Twentieth-Century Art Forms*. New York and London: Methuen, 1985. Print.

Masiello, Francine. "Fuera de lugar: silencios y desidentidades en *El beso de la mujer araña*." Puig CE: 574–588. Print.

Piglia, Ricardo. "Overture: The Puig Effect." Translated by Susan Benner. In *Approaches to Teaching Puig's* Kiss of the Spider Woman. 18–27 (see Balderston and Masiello). Print.

Puig, Manuel. *Kiss of the Spider Woman*. Translated by Thomas Colchie. Reprint of 1979 Edition, Published by Knopf. Vintage, Random House, 1991. Print.

———. *El beso de la mujer araña*. Edición crítica, José Amícola, Jorge Panesi, coordinadores. Colección Archivos. ALLCA XX, 2002. Print.

Romero, Julia. "Del delito a la escritura al error gay." *Revista Iberoamericana* 65.187 (1999): 305–325. Print.

CHAPTER 4

The Re(Naissance) of Texts: Parody and Rewriting in the Work of Luisa Valenzuela

Fernando Burgos Pérez

The most seductive power of a truly parodic work resides in its proposed audacity, substantiated by a subversive act toward sustained modes of cultural production whose prolonged persistence might come to constitute in itself a seal of impermeability toward change. For that reason, the irreverent nature of parody begins through a moveable and, to some degree, uncomfortable reading on the part of the author, which later will be transformed into a critical and differential vision with respect to the perceived inalterability of those modes that have become programmatic formulas of the cultural establishment. The reading by the author to which I refer is an ontological attempt whose ample registers range from a sign as intuitive as the understanding of love, to such metaphysical pursuits as the comprehension of existence and the question of being in the universe. Everything is readable as cognitive discernment and sensorial perception: a book, a body, the elements of nature, the movement of the

F. Burgos Pérez (✉)
University of Memphis, Memphis, TN, USA
e-mail: fburgos@memphis.edu

© The Author(s) 2018
H. C. Weldt-Basson (ed.), *Postmodern Parody in Latin American Literature*, Literatures of the Americas,
https://doi.org/10.1007/978-3-319-90430-6_4

stars, the play of children, the awakening of puberty, the look of falling in love, the aroma of nature, the fleeting nature of the word. Writing creatively involves the aim of the Borgesian reader of the Universal Library to the extent that the impossible encounter with a partial or total confluence of books prepares the reader to grasp what is not print, so that the reading finally becomes a convocation of signs, a penetration of what is imaginary within what is real. From this type of reading, the marvel of art emerges:

> Leer, leer, leer es la consigna. Mucho más allá del material impreso. Lenta, penosamente, vamos aprendiendo a leer la vida, leer las oscuras intenciones, leer la contradicción y la paradoja instalada en muchos de nuestros actos, leer con el cuerpo, con todas las vísceras. Y entonces escribimos. Y pasamos a ser leídos en la letra impresa, e interpretados y desmenuzados . . . . Toda escritura es un intento de lectura, un buscar el tono y la respiración adecuados para cada acontecer, imaginario o no. (*Peligrosas palabras*, 79 and 187–188)
>
> Reading, reading, reading is the chant. Much beyond the printed material. Slowly, laboriously, we are learning to read life, to read obscure intentions, to read the contradiction and the paradox installed within many of our actions, to read with the body, with all our entrails. And then we write. And we come to be read in the written word, and interpreted and thoroughly analyzed . . . All writing is an attempt at reading, at seeking the appropriate tone and breath for each occurrence, imaginary or not.

The preceding assertions should already forewarn us that it is not at all illuminating to point out that a work of art is a parody of another, or of a complete literary genre, or of a certain theme, historical figure—and thus, consequently, of the innumerable representations, historical circumstances, and socio-cultural artifacts that bear parodic viability. Such assertions are deceptive when they counterpose a work of art to an artistic entity or other type of entity, as if it were a question of totalities in which what was parodied would have specific properties, limited temporally and spatially, and the work that is parodying would emerge as its antithesis in view of its satiric, carnivalesque, comical, or deeply deconstructive levels with regard to what it is parodying.

In the realm of art, neither the most classic nor the most extreme postmodern representations of parody function in such a symmetrical way or in such a definite order of correlation as that previously described since, in that event, one would be understanding parody as only a rhetorical mechanism, a formal medium, which Hutcheon rejects: "Parody is not just to be considered as a formal entity, a structure of assimilation or appropriation of other texts" (49). That parody transcends the erroneous attribute of a purely formal condition is explicable because, since its origins, parody entails a reading of what it is going to parody that involves the total educational background of an artist, his ontological aspirations, his vision of the world, and his ideological framework in the creative articulation of that vision.

For these reasons, one can assert that a parodic text is the aesthetic representation of a political statement provided that the text's purpose involves planes that go far beyond the ideological. Since the new configuration includes the work that one wishes to abandon, the parodied work, upon being converted into a parody, cannot, in reality, be completely abandoned. This is because literary parody does not necessarily seek to dissolve contents, or plots, or characters but, rather, to transform them in order to become an acclaiming political body of difference. In that space, the power of artistic writing and the creative spirit of invention meet, simultaneously joining the diverse foundational moments of the polis in an intimate vision, as well as the most constitutive peculiarities of the planes that induce cultural change. The parody of the picaresque, bucolic, and chivalrous novels which Cervantes wrote at the beginning of the seventeenth century constituted a significant aspect of the foundation of the first modern novel in Western literature. When reading *Don Quixote* four centuries after its publication, not only do we encounter one of the finest dialectical resolutions of the universal literature of all-time with respect to the continuous search for the imaginable and the boundaries of what we suppose is reality, but also we read again, evidently in another manner, the picaresque, bucolic, and chivalrous novels.

In other words, inadvertently, parody also functions as a register of cultural memory that includes the components that have made its renovation possible. Thus, through parody, one can observe, understand, and reflect upon the socio-political components of artistic modes and epochal reception; that is, all that which gradually has permitted—and, many times, lamentably blocked—the socio-cultural development of humanity. In this regard, parody is simultaneously an act of temporal residence and one of continuous displacement. Parody cannot totally dismantle what it parodies, but neither can it continue to inhabit what is being parodied. In literature, parodying becomes a primordial creative force in terms of its representational dialectic potential, sustaining a new construction that inaugurates the parodic, as well as the evocation and comprehension of a constituent past, culture, and civilization—especially when, from the present of postmodernity, the parodic focus goes back to works temporally distanced, as is the case of the work of Valenzuela that I discuss here. With respect to the idea of the new perceptions of the past that parody permits, Hutcheon indicates: "Parody is, then, an important way for modern artists to come to terms with the past—through ironic recoding or, in my awkward descriptive neologism, 'trans-contextualizing'" (10).

Parody is daring, but would not be able to exist without an intimate knowledge of what is being parodied and without a political stratum. Deep down, this last assertion requires that parody maintain a relationship with the cessation of the act of writing in the sense described by Blanchot:

> The end of the act of writing does not lie in the book or in the work. As we write the work, we are drawn by the absence of the work . . . . The book (the civilization of the book) declares: there is a memory that transmits things, there is a system of relations that arranges things; time becomes entangled in the book, where the void still belongs to a structure . . . . The absence of the book makes an appeal to writing that does not commit itself, that does not settle out, is not satisfied with disavowing itself, nor with going back over its tracks to erase them. (148–149)

That civilization of the book to which Blanchot refers, and consequently the polis that its political body proclaims, results in a creative paradox in Luisa Valenzuela's work since, by understanding itself as a continuous form of cessation of writing, Valenzuela's work has to remake itself and reconfigure itself each time. It is a dialectic that emerges from a lack of conformism that cannot allow itself the luxury of being satisfied. Following this direction, in Valenzuela's work, parody supposes a critical revelation of the manner in which cultural discourses are dictated through the games of social power and ideological dogmas of each era. Thus, one of the planes of rewriting that Valenzuela makes from traditional fairy tales—Charles Perrault (seventeenth century), the Brothers Grimm and Hans Christian Andersen (nineteenth century)—will expose the political dimension embedded in the cultural products of these works. In doing so, she protects herself from replacing this political dimension with the logic of discourse. Distancing itself from impositions,

Valenzuela's rewriting thus accepts characterizing itself as the outbreak of a continuous reading susceptible of parodying itself and with the resulting implication of not having arrived at anything definitive.

This aesthetic design results in one of the great charms of the parodic writing of "Cuentos de Hades" [Tales from Hades] by Valenzuela, which resides both in a practice of axiomatic dissolution and in the absence of a finished work. The first practice indicates that, for this Argentine writer, the use of parody does not function as an act subject to the political correction in fashion, or as a work that carries new ethical tenets, or as the creation of texts of socio-cultural salvation. In this manner, the texts from "Cuentos de Hades" become profoundly critical and subversive. The second point is related to the slippery nature of the parodic, which undermines the idea of a finished work that has emerged from the deterioration of the previous one and, consequently, the revision of the work being parodied. The sensation, rather, is that texts keep moving away from themselves as well as from socio-cultural canons and, upon doing so, they start achieving their relevance in displacement itself. Otherwise, they would be lifeless, devoid of any interest. This sense of the movement of works of art allows for the virtual disappearance not only of the parodied texts, which inevitably will be converted into something different, but also of the new text that emerges upon being conceived as a language that is already changing direction, as Blanchot states. Since its stage is no man's land, the end of the act of writing can only reside in the act of continuing to write. This is a practically spontaneous impulse of parody and comprehensible considering the fact that the essence of parody resides in its state of fluidity. This last aspect is thus pointing to another challenge of parody, succinctly sketched in the previous paragraph, which consists of the risk that, as a political body critical of a number of discourses and socio-cultural positions, the parody could end up convening other visions that eventually would also lose their validity. This is the trap that Cervantes consciously avoided by conferring on Don Quixote and Sancho a philosophical sense of humanity and an absolute mode of freedom in the realization of their projects, thus distancing himself from social practices and transcending any convention. He also privileged the amalgam between imagination and free will to such a degree that both protagonists were wrong and neither of the two was wrong. Cervantes's intention never was to represent characters subject to being corrected but, rather, to follow the adventure of their interconnected destinies and to appreciate the continuous dialectic that emerged from that relationship. That Don Quixote had seen a princess in a simple village woman and that Sancho had seen the contrary was neither a question of deceit or truth, nor of fantasy or reality, but, rather, the admission of heterogeneous perspectives and of a contingent configuration of existence. In other words, one does not wish to install absolute truths through parody; neither does one wish to replace the potential dogmatic profile of what is parodied with other ideological frameworks current in that present.

Thus, parody is not instituted as an aesthetic pronouncement. It does not operate as a manifest of artistic principles; neither does it wish to destroy a particular work. What is demolished are socio-historical dogmas, by critically examining the various dominant cultural codes in a given epoch, or their extended persistence in time through a new reading. There are no impositions of any kind, since the reading undertaken by an enduring parody owes everything to a creative liberty that responds to disperse sensations in a "history of instants that flee like the fugitive paths that are seen from the window of a train" (Lispector, 78).

In her book *Simetrías* [*Symmetries*], Luisa Valenzuela includes a section of six short stories titled "Cuentos de Hades" [Tales from Hades] which, in principle, refer to the written tradition of fairy tales initiated by Charles Perrault with the publication in 1697 of *Fairy Tales from Past Times with Morals,* continued in 1812 with *Children's and Household Tales* by the Brothers Grimm, and later with the stories by Hans Christian Andersen published principally in the third and fourth decades of the nineteenth century. Stories such as "Little Red Riding Hood," "Sleeping Beauty," "Blue Beard," "Cinderella," "Snow White," "The Princess and the Pea," and "The Frog Prince" are activated through the mark of a postmodern writing, as well as by the sensibility of a writer who is very distant from the entertainment of literary salons of the seventeenth century in France and who, three hundred years later, would achieve a parodic and caustic reading of these texts, sometimes mixing them with, or making allusions to, other fairy tales in the principal text. The fact that Valenzuela has chosen stories that survived for a long time, not only as a source of reading but as part of the collective conscious of the Western world, shows from the start that the rewriting of any of those stories or a mixture of them is not only based on the re-inscription of the text, but also on the signs of cultural survival that transcend the written work and whose original aspect in this case is found in the rich and millenary oral tradition of folkloric tales.

For this reason, the parody in Valenzuela's work allows the texts to be reborn from a distant past because of the ascribed memory in them, although this memory will be revisited with such a colossal sarcasm that all the elements of alienation, mythology, simulation, and falsifications of that memory will converge in a revisionist scrutiny of the cultural parameters institutionalized in the writing. From there arises the play on words *hadas/hades* [fairy tales/Hades]. The second term became synonymous with Hell in the Christian world but, in classic Greek mythology, it was the space of the dead, a type of infra-world. Its convocation in Valenzuela's work is consequently double. First, it constitutes a revisitation of this dwelling or level from which another perspective is generated; second, it is an invective against the ideological domains of those texts in which feminine characters in particular were pre-condemned to a sort of socio-cultural hell. This was due to the prevalence of an ideology that stigmatized through gender discrimination, as well as the represented implacably submissive roles for women who had to survive in a social environment completely hostile to the aspiration of equality and social integration.

In this essay, I concentrate exclusively on the first of the texts included in "Cuentos de Hades": "Si esto es la vida, yo soy Caperucita Roja" [If this is life, I am Little Red Riding Hood] whose most essential parodic source is the original French version (1697) in which Little Red Riding Hood and her grandmother are devoured by the wolf. In the version by the Brothers Grimm in 1812, the hunter who opens the wolf's stomach with scissors to extract the grandmother and her granddaughter is added. The addition of the salvation of the grandmother and granddaughter in the story by the Brothers Grimm is not of interest in Valenzuela's parody which mentions that "la presencia del leñador es pura interpretación moderna" (*Cuentos completos y uno más*, 64) [the presence of the woodsman is a purely modern interpretation (*Symmetries*, 108)].[1] Valenzuela refers to this aspect, moreover, in an essay where one can appreciate her reading of the classic versions motivated by the intrusion of a masculine figure: "La figura del leñador me resultó difícil de ubicar en este esquema...Busqué entonces la primera versión escrita del cuento, la de Perrault publicada en 1697, y comprobé para mi sorpresa que allí no hay leñador alguno, Caperucita simplemente muere junto con su abuela bajo las fauces del lobo" [The figure of the woodsman seemed to me difficult to fit into this scheme...I then searched for the first version written of the story, that of Perrault published in 1697, and I verified to my surprise that there is no woodsman there at all, Little Red Riding Hood simply dies along with her grandmother in the jaws of the wolf] (*Peligrosas palabras*, 213).

By eliminating the hunter and his protective action, the narrative universe of Perrault's text is circumscribed to three generations of women without external elements of protection (hunter/woodsman): the grandmother, the mother, and the daughter. Although, in theory, each one of them would suppose, in turn, a tacit double functioning (that is, the first as grandmother and mother, the second as mother and daughter, and the third as daughter and granddaughter) the clear narrative course of Perrault's text on the dangerous games of adolescence activates only this last relationship. He shows the harmful amusement of the young girl in the elements of the forest while the deceitful and calculating wolf has managed to extract the necessary information from the gullible girl, emphasizing the interest in Perrault's moral commentary and the revelation of the true role of the wolf, as the man who pursues young girls at home and outside:

> Children, especially attractive, well-bred young ladies, should never talk to strangers, for if they should do so, they may well provide dinner for a wolf. I say "wolf," but there are various kinds of wolves. There are also those who are charming, quiet, polite, unassuming, complacent, and sweet, who pursue young women at home and in the streets. And unfortunately, it is these gentle wolves who are the most dangerous ones of all. (Perrault, *Little Red Riding Hood*)

On the one hand, the sexual background of Perrault's version was evident in the dynamics of the text itself, as well as externally, based on the fact that these stories were not only written by adults, but also addressed to adults. On the other hand, the justification for the didactic and illustrative tone of the text lay in the ideology of the elite literary salons and what the morality of the era could tolerate on an explicit level. Hence there was the necessity to add the moral. The focus was the rationalization of sexual awakening, which obviously was an impossible purpose, since the sexual connotations of the language of the story and the contexts of deceitful seduction made it difficult to fail to perceive the nonsense of any ethical prevention: eating a young girl as a sexual activity; the wolf's invitation to Little Red Riding Hood to go to bed with him; the young girl's undressing before lying down with the wolf; the girl's shock, more ludic than ingenuous, regarding everything that is big about the figure of the wolf disguised as the grandmother. Perrault and other classic versions simplified the participation of the mother and the grandmother. The former, who remains protected at home, sends her daughter on the journey through the woods with a cake and a jar of butter for the grandmother, who has been ill. No other alternative is offered to the latter than that of passively remaining at home waiting for her granddaughter. The center is the young girl who faces the risks of her trip without anyone's help. The only other character in Perrault's story is the wolf: the beast in his dual human transformation of concealment and violence. At this point, it is necessary to specify two observations by Valenzuela regarding her own reading of the story. The first resides in the manner in which she perceived the inseparability of the three women and the significance of the forest: "El viaje de Caperucita es un tránsito, una verdadera travesía que va de la condición de púber a la de la abuela. El bosque es en realidad el tiempo a lo largo del cual se van cosechando experiencias (para meterlas en la canastita). Tres instancias de una misma persona en simultaneidad: Caperucita, su madre y la abuela" (*Palabras peligrosas*, 212–213) [Little Red Riding Hood's trip is a transit, a true journey that goes from the condition of puberty to that of the grandmother. The forest is in reality the passage of time whose experiences are being harvested (in order to put them in the basket). Three instances of the same person in simultaneity: Little Red Riding Hood, her mother, and the grandmother]. The second observation has to do with the manner in which, from Perrault on, the oral sources of these stories were becoming deformed and, in that process, writers such as Perrault forced ideological impositions into their adaptations: "Estuve tentada de investigar a fondo y analizar cómo se distorsionaron los primitivos cuentos orales cuando cayeron en manos de este magno representante del patriarcado, Charles Perrault" (*Palabras peligrosas*, 214) [I was tempted to investigate fully and analyze how the primitive oral tales were distorted when they fell into the hands of this great representative of the patriarchy, Charles Perrault].

The environment that the oral sources of the story transmitted could not be more stripped down: no villages or cities; no labyrinths or tunnels. In addition, the number of main characters could not be more minimal: the young adolescent and the wolf, while the mother and the grandmother would, instead, function as equidistant points in Little Red Riding Hood's trip: her beginning with the mother and the purpose of her visit; her arrival at the grandmother's house, preceded by that of the wolf with the goal of consummating his trick. And, nonetheless, in the apparent simplicity of the elements of the story lay a network of signifiers that gave rise to the interest in putting it in writing, and from there it continued through numerous versions, the production of multiple exegeses and the conversion of Little Red Riding Hood into a cultural icon through time. This icon was reproducible not only in the different story versions over more than three hundred years, but also in other literary genres—such as poetry for example. In addition, the icon was reproducible in comic strips, the movies, music, public advertisements, the internet—that is, in various artistic manifestations and in all the communication media that modernization and postmodernization made possible.

The written text that Valenzuela parodies is Perrault's. However, as far as the hermeneutic level of the story is concerned, in terms that allow its rebirth through parody, Valenzuela explores elements of the story connected to the signifying stratum of its orality and, from there, offers her own reading, enriched by an exploration of different socio-cultural and philosophical aspects that the text suggests. She is disturbed by "lo que Perrault se encargó de distorsionar" (*Peligrosas palabras*, 214) [what Perrault was responsible for distorting] which is why, upon rewriting "Little Red Riding Hood," the Argentine writer does it with preferences suggested by Foucault in his reading of the book by Deleuze and Guattari titled *Anti-Oedipus. Capitalism and Schizophrenia*. The discourse created by Valenzuela in this way becomes adept at the "multiple, difference over uniformity, flows over unities, mobile arrangements over systems. Believe that what is productive is not sedentary but nomadic" (*Anti-Oedipus. Capitalism and Schizophrenia*, XIII). From this point forth, Valenzuela captures the generational interaction in the characters of the grandmother, the mother and the daughter, thus permitting a philosophical approach through the concept of becoming discussed by Deleuze and Guattari.

Valenzuela thus takes up again the representational ubiquity and multiplicity of Little Red Riding Hood, making the young adolescent into a nomadic reader and writer since she will have to travel along the wide-ranging space of her *errata*—that is to say, of all the writings and readings that converted her into a passive entity, into an institution for study and of morals, into a case of psychological textuality to be dissected, into an adolescent prevented from controlling her own existence. At this point, the parody exposes one of its privileged faculties, which is the expansion of its signifiers with which the story of Little Red Riding Hood will be, in Valenzuela's hands, that of becoming-woman and her historical circumstances. However, one should not understand by this that I am referring to a phase of transition in which Little Red Riding Hood passes from adolescent to woman. In this regard, Deleuze and Guattari specify that: "It is not the girl who becomes a woman; it is becoming-woman that produces the universal girl" (*A Thousand Plateaus*, 277), since the French thinkers associate the concept of becoming with a molecular dimension whose emission of particles approximates disorderly growing without regard for hierarchical structuring, through its differentiation and rhizomatic capacity. Valenzuela portrays the universal adolescent dynamically and controversially as the result of her becoming-woman. Thus, she stops serving as a text for psychoanalytic study guided by the parameters established by Freud, Jung, Otto Rank, or Erich Fromm. Fromm, in particular, saw the red hood that the grandmother had given as a gift to Little Red Riding Hood as a symbol of menstruation, and therefore his focus was on the sexual, translatable through symbols. In reality, the idea of becoming for Deleuze and Guattari has nothing to do with symbolic or metaphorical constructions but, rather, with the intensity of desire. It is not an identification but, instead, an experience through which, in the case of Valenzuela's story, what matters is the manner in which she extracts Little Red Riding Hood from her psychoanalytic corporeity by making her a reader and writer. This is completely connected to the idea of becoming-woman, since the experience of writing is initiated in that type of becoming, independently of whoever writes, whether man or woman: "It must be said that all becomings begin with and pass through becoming-woman. It is the key to all other becomings" (*A Thousand Plateaus*, 277).

As parodic writing of a fairy tale that had been imbued with moral apprehensions and institutional safeguards from its first written version at the end of the seventeenth century, Valenzuela's text "Si esto es la vida, yo soy Caperucita Roja" reterritorializes the supposed sexuality of the narrativity, vindicating the function of Eros as a power of the word, writing, and the imaginative. It rescues the symbols of Eros, which are figurative and inert regarding meanings, convoking them like signifiers. By parodying with audacity, Valenzuela converts the sexual awakening and signaling of the erotic into both a concupiscent reality and a sensual experience. Bluntly, without sinuous narrative routes, Valenzuela's short story is built on a creative writing cleansed of ethical registers in which the parameters of mediation of the admissible and the inappropriate disappear, and, for the same reason, Valenzuela's story ends in complex textures of references and proliferating meanings. As parodic rewriting of the classic version's inscription in the textual base, "Si esto es la vida, yo soy Caperucita Roja" disturbs the story (the making literary of what is told) and disdains History (the fixation of its supposed temporal passage).

In the first case, by maintaining the minimalism of the classic narrative elements, "Si esto es la vida, yo soy Caperucita Roja" opts for the creation of an environment of sensuality in the forest and in its protagonists in its parodic construction. It frees the protagonists from their theatrical and bookish staging, granting them the humanism of a changing skin through which they search, grow, lose hope, become bitter and exalted, and principally are transformed beyond the dermis, toward an innerness that not even they themselves can recognize. This occurrence is a favorite one of a parody that eschews proclamations and restraints of any kind. In the second case, with the imaginative fervor of a writing rid of its academic, literary, and moral bonds in the irreverent breaking of decorum, conventions, and cultural and psychological formulas, the portraits of Little Red Riding Hood and the wolf not only parody the narrativity of the story, but also its relationship with History. That is, the positivist concept of progress is parodied since, although both protagonists are different in the passage of the centuries that separate the classic and postmodern versions, their discrepancy separates itself from judgments of good and bad, thus underscoring once more the *difference* of their conduct and development instead of their critical *optimization*. Valenzuela rejects the construction of a Little Red Riding Hood who has "progressed" and "evolved." The new dimension of Little Red Riding Hood resides in manifesting itself as an experience without social or scientific mediations. It signals, rather, directions that have not been experienced and that can lead to another changing state, or to nowhere. In other words, dangers also lurk in the power of writing and of being a writer that Valenzuela has given to Little Red Riding Hood: "La escritura nos tironea, nos empuja al frente; surge con la fuerza de un maremoto. Entonces, tratamos cuando podamos, de encarar el abismo. Pienso que escribir es un salto al vacío sin saber a ciencia cierta si abajo nos esperan las rocas o el agua" (*Peligrosas palabras*, 184) [Writing pulls us, pushes us to the front; it emerges with the force of a tidal wave. Then, we try, when we can, to confront the abyss. I think that writing is a leap into the vacuum without knowing for sure if below the water or the rocks are waiting for us].

With its parodic versatility, Valenzuela's text eliminates the conversion of characters into prototypes, humanizing them and making them thus contradictory, uncertain, and unpredictable. They can now synthesize the turbulence of their subconscious, expressing a dark flow of passions, fears, fervor for change, irritations, sadness, joys, and desire: "Hay frutas tentadoras por estas latitudes. Muchas al alcance de la mano. Hay hombres como frutas: los hay dulces, sabrosos, jugosos, urticantes. Es cuestión de irlos probando de a poquito" (*Cuentos completos y uno más*, 64) [There are tempting fruits in these latitudes. Many are within reach of her hand. There are men who are like fruit: they are sweet, tasty, juicy, and irritating. It's a question of tasting them one by one (*Symmetries*, 108)]. A multivocal sign is highlighted through the volubility generated by a parodic narrativity that opts for reimagining and transforming the characters without the need to give them a purpose. These mutations are expressed without bonds to the point that the dimensions of the wolf, whatever they might be, from the appetite of his sexualities and mechanisms of control to his impotencies and retractions, can converge in Little Red Riding Hood, the grandmother, and the wolf himself, making them a sole figure, as if the rhizomatic proliferation of the psyche were of an imponderable magnitude, defiant of systematizations.

Hence, Valenzuela utilizes parody not only to give a voice to Little Red Riding Hood, but also, and mainly, to allow Little Red Riding Hood to become a writer. I associate this type of becoming with what, from a philosophical position, is understood as becoming-writing. Fátima R. Nogueira—following the ideas of Deleuze and Guattari—approaches this concept with clarity:

> El devenir-escritura es la máxima potencialidad de la representación artística sin condicionamientos que hayan sido mediados por su medio de producción o por su productor. No es una categoría ni menos una clasificación, sino *el happening* de la creación entendida como una incesante y caótica actividad generadora. . . . Es por lo mismo la potencialización de lo que se escribe y de lo que se lee. . . La esencia del devenir escritura es su estado de incompletitud. El devenir escritura es en suma una función exponencial cuyo ritmo de crecimiento es desconocido. (*Poéticas del devenir: Lispector y Valenzuela*, 175)

> Becoming-writing is the maximum potential of an artistic representation
> without restrictions that have been mediated by its medium of production
> or its producer. It is not a category and by no means a classification, but
> *the happening* of the creation understood as an incessant and chaotic gen-
> erating activity . . . . It is consequently the potentiality of what is writ-
> ten and of what is read . . . . The essence of becoming writing is its state
> of incompleteness. Becoming writing is, in short, an exponential function
> whose rhythm of growth is unknown.

This approach implies that, when Valenzuela restores the becoming-
writing to her character, she has allowed not only the becoming-writer
of Little Red Riding Hood, but also her capacity as a reader. The protagonist herself of the story is the one who can perceive in the prolonged
trajectory of her existence that the conformation of her literary figure is
also an extended sum of ideological constructions ratified by the political concerns of each one of the epochs in which it was her turn to live.
Those versions left no other alternative to her ingenuous and passive
portrait than that of adapting to the stereotyping of the character satu-
rated by the simplistic view of symbols. The becoming writer-reader of
Little Red Riding Hood that occurs in Valenzuela's parody incites this
character to take charge of her distorted representations and, therefore,
of her mistaken readings. However, as a reader of her *errata*, she cannot proceed to correcting them as if she had galley proofs in front of
her because her cultural inscription is already fixed. Consequently, reading her *errata* helps her to understand her re-conformation. From this
point forward, the woman writer is going to be equipped in Valenzuela's
text with a reflexivity that will allow her to examine the attributions with
which she had been saddled, capriciously and artificially, and from this
point achieve her transformation. On the other hand, as a writer and
reader, the adolescent Little Red Riding Hood, woman, mother, and
grandmother, is inundated with more doubts than certainties, with more
dilemmas than convictions. The Argentine writer is, therefore, using the
concept of parody to reflect on the cultural codes of the role of women.
Her purpose is to disrupt them as much as possible, so that her character
Little Red Riding Hood not only rids herself of the recommendations
of her mother,[2] which indicate to the daughter that she should not get
distracted in her journey through the forest and that she should arrive
intact to the protection of her grandmother: "De lo otro la previne, también. Siempre estoy previniendo y no me escucha...Cuidado nena con

el lobo feroz (es la madre que habla)" (*Cuentos completos y uno más*, 61–62) [I warned her about the other thing too. I'm always warning her and she doesn't listen...Watch out for the big, bad wolf, dear (it's the mother speaking)] (*Symmetries*, 103–104). In addition, Valenzuela makes Little Red Riding Hood master of her trip, exploring the forest, challenging the supposed dangers, and even desiring a voluptuous encounter with the wolf: "A veces cuando duermo sola en medio del bosque siento que anda muy cerca, casi encima, y me transmite escozores nada desagradables. A veces con tal de no sentirlo duermo con el primer hombre que se me cruza, cualquier desconocido que parezca sabroso. Y entonces al lobo lo siento más que nunca" (*Cuentos completos y uno más*, 66) [Sometimes, when I'm sleeping alone in the middle of the wood, I feel him very close, almost on top of me, and I experience a not wholly unpleasant tingling sensation. Sometimes, so as not to feel him there, I sleep with the first man I meet, any tasty-looking stranger will do. And then I'm more aware of the wolf than ever] (*Symmetries*, 110).

In the process of parodic reimagining, Valenzuela's text refuses to decipher or decode. The wolf comes to live within Little Red Riding Hood and the latter finds herself inside the wolf: "Y cuando por fin llego a la puerta de su prolija cabaña hecha de troncos, me detengo un rato ante el umbral para retomar aliento. No quiero que me vea así con la lengua colgante, roja como supo ser mi caperuza, no quiero que me vea con los colmillos al aire y la baba chorreándome de las fauces" (*Cuentos completos y uno más*, 69) [And when I at last reach the door of her neat log cabin, I stop for a while on the threshold to catch my breath. I don't want her to see me with my tongue hanging out, red as my cape once was, I don't want her to see me with my teeth bared, and my mouth drooling] (*Symmetries*, 114–115). It is a reimagining of sexuality as an integral experience. Without forbidden zones, the search for pleasure as the creative joining of voices, writings, and desires retakes its place. The reunion of bodies and experiences in Valenzuela's stories is, moreover, a fight against the segmentation imposed by social constructions. In place of the generational segments (grandmother, mother, daughter, granddaughter), Little Red Riding Hood absorbs all of them in a body that has no marked roles. Valenzuela replaces threatening wolves and ingenuous adolescents, as well as the omnipotent presence of the devouring man-wolf and the image of a diminished and inexperienced young girl who is devoured, with the formation of networks united by the expression of desire. She replaces the traditional Little Red Riding Hood with a protagonist who, because of walking so much through the forest, already has her hood worn away and who laughs at the idea of ferocious wolves since "Las caperucitas de hoy tienen lobos benignos, incapaces. Ineptos" (*Cuentos completos y uno más*, 69) [Red riding hoods nowadays have kindly, incompetent wolves. Inept.] (*Symmetries*, 114). Valenzuela's story distances itself from linear and binary representations. The parody transforms "Little Red Riding Hood" by distancing itself from the notion of a discourse proposed as knowledge-power that would precisely resemble what Foucault counterposes to an art of initiation. The initiation in this parodic re-version by Valenzuela is sexual and writerly. It cannot be any other way, since the sexual has been separated from the organized system of knowledge as power.

As a writer and zone of desire, Little Red Riding Hood is unclassifiable in Valenzuela's story, as is the wolf and the integration of both. Through parody, the story dares to leave the terms of pathology on the shelves of positivism, dismissing the rationalization of what it is simply not possible to rationalize. Such classifications as those of perversions or dominations, among many others that have been attributed to a dynamic narrative of the story that flows beyond those codifications, are disdained in the text reimagined by the Argentine writer. This is the source of the games of the imagination and the constant transferences of the characters, and the superposition of fairy tales in Valenzuela's text, such as that of the story "Snow White": "El hecho es que al retomar el camino encontré entre las hojas uno de esos clásicos espejos. Me agaché, lo alcé y no pude menos que dirigirle la ya clásica pregunta: espejito, espejito, ¿quién es la más bonita? Tu madre, boluda! Te equivocaste de historia-me contestó el espejo" (*Cuentos completos y uno más*, 66) [The fact is that when I returned to the path, I found one of those classic mirrors amongst the leaves. I crouched down, I picked it up and what could I do but ask it the classic question: Mirror, mirror, on the wall, who is the loveliest of them all? Your mother, arsehole! You're in the wrong story, the mirror replied] (*Symmetries*, 111). With intrepidness, Little Red Riding Hood writes, therefore reconstructing her literary story again in order to make clear that her new body, stemming from a dialectical joining of woman and writing, is going to be a disappointment as much for moralizing and encyclopedic practices, as for those who wish to see the construction of a defined woman. Little Red Riding Hood does not write in the text of the Argentine writer "to confess" or to explain herself. She writes in order to be: in order to be heard, in order to be the writer of a writing that integrates its oral aspect, above all, in order to be reimagined. She writes (following the line of thought of Deleuze and Guattari) to become woman: "When Virginia Woolf was questioned about a specifically women's writing, she was appalled at the idea of writing 'as a woman.' Rather, writing should produce a becoming-woman as atoms of womanhood capable of crossing and impregnating an entire social field, and of contaminating men, of sweeping them up in that becoming" (*A Thousand Plateaus*, 276).

Through parody, Valenzuela has allowed Little Red Writing Hood to leave the immense cultural machinery that has positioned her since the seventeenth century as a case study of psychological, moral, and ideological material. Her parodic constitution allows her to fight against her story and against History, and makes her intolerant of codifications and decoding processes. She wants, on the contrary, to imagine herself and to be imagined in her becoming-woman. Her sexual awakening as a curious, imaginative, and passionate adolescent runs counter to Perrault's prudery, counter to the social and academic protectionism of the French writer and his limited cultural understanding. Leaving the end of the century in which she is literarily born, Little Red Riding Hood almost simultaneously enters into the sanctions of the Enlightenment, where she was the object of pedagogical attention and exemplification. In the last decades of the eighteenth century, she could have been rescued by the imaginative romantic spirit of Novalis and incorporated into the zone of new explorations that he prepared for the fairy tale, but she was not. After the Enlightenment, she falls into the hands of nineteenth-century empiricism where, besides figuring as an educative figure, she is principally converted into a body of evidence destined to prove theories and, consequently, suggest therapies.

In other words, for Valenzuela, parody—besides being a reflexive channel—is a powerful and inventive artistic medium of cultural exegesis. The Argentine writer's story shows us the manner in which Little Red Riding Hood has arrived at being a point of observation, scrutiny, and clinical vigilance. She has been an adolescent, mother, wolf, grandmother, and a forest that symbolizes positivistic thought. Little Red Riding Hood thus constituted the birth of a case that, together with all the consequences that it produced, would not be appealed to as an imaginative creation but, rather, as a perverse rarity. Even in the nineteenth century, which at least offered non-hegemonic alternatives with regard to art, Little Red Riding Hood could have been transformed into the mixture of subconscious and logical games of Lewis Carroll, or portrayed by the early modernity of writers such as Thoreau, Poe, or Darío, but this opportunity was not given to her either.

It is time to break down the signifiers in light of the new being who has been reconstituted in a parodic manner: Little Red Riding Hood was not swallowed by a wolf, neither was the wolf opened by the blade of an object in the hands of a hunter. Little Red Riding Hood was devoured by the jaws of a number of cultural impositions, and the wolf was dissected by the scalpel of sciences in formation where knowledge was domination and power. With rare exceptions—for example, that of Daudet, tenuously, in the nineteenth century—the readings and resulting versions of Little Red Riding Hood are framed in what Foucault terms *scientia sexualis*. She is portrayed through that imperious necessity of creating absolute discourses that are therefore despotic regarding something that, even today, we call "sexual knowledge." It is as though the disciplines of various sciences had arrived at true determinations of psychic human events, and there were nothing more to do than to attribute the articulation of their categories to the protagonists and to apply the discourse in fashion to the text, with the same subversive gestures of science later transformed into dogmas.

Reimagined through her parodic dimension, Little Red Riding Hood stops being imbued with culturally acceptable public discourses, and ambushed by what one supposes she should be. The Argentine writer is very conscious that the problem is not that little has been said about the sexuality of Little Red Riding Hood. In fact, she knows that too much has been said about it. The problem becomes the behaviorist treatment of sexuality, especially when the notion of sexuality is understood in a limited manner by the overused and biased term "sex," and what one expects to find is a correlation of texts and characters with a theory validated by its postulation of truth. The significant connection that the author of *El gato eficaz* finds for the games of sexuality in her tale is the power to express oneself verbally and in written form. The inventive use of parody in Valenzuela's hands frees Little Red Riding Hood, allowing her to be, by writing and writing herself.

Little Red Riding Hood has been, and will continue being, a construction in time. She belongs in the Foucauldian sense to a history of sexuality—an ideological projection of what sexuality represents in the contingency of its different cultural nodules. In this notion of reading, the various signifiers of the text begin to come together, and the sexual dimension emerges with many other dimensions that the story offers—such as the problematizing of writing, the dominion of speech, fundamental expressions of freedom, the meaning of silence, and the voluptuousness of living. It is the zone, consequently, in which one begins to experience a sense of the transcendence of Valenzuela's characters joined by the kingdom of the real and the symbolic (both terms in the Lacanian sense). Once this recognition occurs, one begins, in the same way, to feel, at each step, a sense of participation in the story with regard to the construction of a human being and the resonance of the desires of reading. Hiding the relevance of sexuality in "Little Red Riding Hood" seems to coincide more with Puritan doctrines of the strictly reproductive attributes of sex and the survival of human development than with the aesthetic portal of the text and, especially, with its oral sources. Moreover, as I previously discussed, sexuality is not an issue in this story of classification of knowledge but, rather, sexuality is tied to an erotic awakening and its relationship with imagination and creativity. In this way, and upon further reflection, the split with a dogmatic position occurs through the story's restitution of erotic planes and, thus, of the entire collective unconscious that produced it. The prior close-minded views of Little Red Riding Hood would not take us far from suggesting that, apart from a supposed spiritual or religious transcendence, the human trajectory would have nothing to do with the development of an experience of games and volitions, of erratic realizations, of dreams, of adventures and accidents but, rather, with the recognition of a disposable materiality, stripped of any hedonistic fulfillment.

Little Red Riding Hood was invented in the transmitted orality of a long past and in the present of each one of those pasts that succeeded in being an invention of her futures, therefore plural, in order to disassemble that meaning of security and even of permanence that the "I" tends to seek. The extraction of her changing figure from that past assures us the existence of a character inscribed in History (a History that is many histories) and of the fact that the configuration of any resulting "I" is not unidimensional, and that it can be multiplied in the replacement of cultures and in the construction of numerous social discourses.

In the ontological realm (its temporal proclivity), in the cultural perspective (its critical condition), and in the psychological dimension (its sexual-erotic-imaginative becoming), Valenzuela's text encounters a dialogic point of realization. Voice, word, reflection, critique, and interpretation as integrated elements of her writing constitute the source of access to the process of reimagination in Valenzuela.

The necessity to parody installs the urgency of imagining future texts to be written as though they already belonged to the library of the present, alerting us to our socio-cultural limitations. The birth of the most sophisticated cultural whole that we can conceive neither guarantees infallibility nor legitimates the definitive establishment of "truths" thus constituted. In this sense, all cultural construction is a vulnerable fortress, an architecture that at some point in its historical occurrence is going to be demolished. Parody in this case anticipates the relativity of knowledge accumulated by social institutions at the same time that it prepares its survival as a legacy disposed to its recreation. On the other hand, the act of reimagining texts already written in a parodic manner supposes a movement toward the future of the past—that is, toward the doors that that text left open and which in that past remained unexplored or, rather, toward the cracks that were closed because of socio-cultural, ideological, or other reasons, or the prejudices that marked its realization, or the questions dissolved in the time of history. Hence, we should not understand that parody acts only as a transgression of works. First, because as Hutcheon indicates: "Parody is the custodian of the artistic legacy, defining not only where art is, but where it has come from" (75). Second, because the discourse that parody is reading with another perspective is directly related to the political and socio-cultural codes that form part of the set of that work. Parody does not emerge from the threat or destruction of a work but, rather, from the manner in which it addresses the ideological conformation of the parodied work.

The parodic re-elaboration of works from a given artistic tradition supposes that they are texts from our legacy and human belonging, independent of the fact that they diverge from the aesthetic vision—and from its ideological and philosophical base—that permeates its realization. Returning to these texts through parody is not different from the desire to see the production of our cultural present reread and remade by that future that awaits at the turn of the corner—that is, by the multiplicity of readings that transform and re-inscribe writing. In this sense, the future to which I refer is not a chronological time but the malleable opening of the text that writes and reads at the same time. On the other hand, the readings omitted from a text in its contemporaneous era can reappear after an extended period of time. In this case, thinking that we are reading a text from a more "prepared," "understanding," "sophis-ticated," and "correct" future coincides with the pretentiousness of the human condition, since all future will be another past and the return of the text is an installation in that present of the text anticipated as a future. This is why we return to the text even to strike blows at it and radically transform it. The "good," "enjoyable" texts—those without contradictions, that lack universal projection, except within their cele-brated, albeit insignificant present—will be able to be read again through the enunciating faculty of their testimonial stratum, but not as creative challenges that impact the psychology of our desires, or the metaphysics of our hopes.

Parody induces recoveries. In the Argentine speech of Little Red Riding Hood, in her use of the "*vos*" form, her conversion into the wolf, in her oral reunion with the grandmother—the wolf, the mother, and she herself—in her hobnobbing with wolves of all lineages, in her occa-sional blasphemy, in the effusive illustration of her lust, in her baptism of the wolf...oh, finally, a name...her tango-dancing Pirincho, a magnif-icently energetic and motivational portrait is revealed of how a woman assumes her erotic potential—whether it is that of the wolf, that of the man-wolf, or that of writing itself. Little Red Riding Hood does not transform into an adult. This would eventually lead to her fossilization. She becomes, rather, the universal young girl of the woman: the writer of her writing and the reader of her story. In this instance of the parodic portrait of Little Red Riding Hood, Valenzuela's art distances itself from moral blocks and corrections imposed by cultural codes. It does not por-tray the character as better or worse than the wolf, perhaps as tormented as he is, as indifferent as the mother, as fearless as the grandmother, as ingenuous and astute as Little Red Riding Hood, so herself, so wom-anly, so human. In Valenzuela's work, the parody ends up being an act of reimagination guided by the humanistic impulse that does not attempt to rectify anything and even less so, to impose new patterns of moral-ity, conduct, or definitions of how a character should be. Hutcheon has said, regarding the fact that parodic art or any other type of renovating art that impels change does not demonstrate that art evolves toward a scale of improvement and of absence of contradictions: "The forms of art change, but do they really evolve or get better in any way? Again, my definition of parody as imitation with critical difference prevents any endorsement of the ameliorative implications of the formalists' theory, while it obviously allows agreement with the general idea of parody as the inscription of continuity and change" (36).

In reality, Valenzuela does not want her character to be anything specific, which explains her parodic construction within this transformational idea of parody. The parody of the obedient or disobedient pubescent girl also justifies having untied her, pressing her to tackle the journey through the forest in her different being. Her parodic conversion has freed her from mothers, grandmothers, wolves, and even herself. It has made her become herself, a woman, a woman who speaks, reads and writes, and invites the reactivation of the writing of her reimagination again and again.

The wolf of the fairy tales in their numerous versions is always one, the "lone wolf," the solitary wolf, the wolf that unequivocally translates some determined symbols. Valenzuela's rewriting rejects that fake bookish representation in which the role of the character must fit a certain preconceived idea of the reading or of its ethical framework. Instead, it wants that wolf to belong to his natural displacement in the pack. For Valenzuela, this dimension of the pack pluralizes the signifiers with respect to what Little Red Riding Hood wants as a woman and writer of her story. In other words, having noticed in the stereotyped portrait of the wolf an establishment of the reading originated in specific literary inscriptions, Valenzuela resolves to take up in her text again the plurality of the representation of the character in the literary tradition—the fable, for example—opting also for a parodic representation of the wolf. The creature is a wolf of multiple facets that is donjuanesque and easy to seduce, shameless and shy, ingenuous and false, benign and ferocious, tamable and savage, candid and cunning, without being presented in the binary mode as was exemplified here. Rather, Valenzuela finds the integration of these characteristics, their human disparity and malleability, their disconcerting protean faces, their conversion into diverse men and into Little Red Riding Hood.

The parodic characterization of the wolf and of Little Red Riding Hood in Valenzuela's story supplies clues of transformation disseminated throughout the text, prefigured in those significant synesthesia by Little Red Riding Hood: "Noto entonces que el bosque poco a poco va cambiando de piel" (*Cuentos completos y uno más*, 67) [I notice that the wood gradually changes its skin] (*Symmetries*, 112). From the moment in which Little Red Riding Hood acquires a voice, everything is put in motion. Not just any movement but a playful one. In the next step, corresponding to that acquisition that Little Red Riding Hood will make of writing, nothing is impossible for her, even being the wolf, or experiencing the holistic sensation of being Little Red Riding Hood, mother, grandmother, and wolf at the same time.[3] The complex parodic nature with which the Argentine writer confronts the re-incorporation of Little Red Riding Hood into a narrative world created by dialogue between classic and postmodern versions resists a univocal signaling of the symbolic.

NOTES

1. Note that all translations of "Si esta es la vida, yo soy Caperucita Roja" come from *Symmetries* by Luisa Valenzuela, translated by Margaret Jull Costa. London: Serpent's Tail, 1998. All other translations, unless otherwise noted, are mine.

2. In Perrault's version, there are no recommendations from the mother about the dangers of the forest or the presence of the wolf. In the version by the Brothers Grimm, the recommendation to "behave" and that of not straying from the path are made explicit, although they do not point toward the wolf but, rather, the possibility that Little Red Riding Hood might fall and break the bottle of wine and her grandmother would lose the objective of the errand.

3. Nogueira observes that this fusion is a form of becoming wolf in Little Red Riding Hood, which in her conception would integrate the four characters and would create, in addition, an indivisible temporality: "El proceso de devenir-lobo de la niña no solo postula una disolución de identidades individuales donde se aglutinan Caperucita, la madre, la abuela y el lobo, sino que también subentiende una temporalidad no cronológica que puede extenderse en un presente indefinido que es el tiempo que constituye el microcosmos del bosque, así como desdoblarse en la narración en pasado y futuro constantemente" (*Poéticas del devenir: Lispector y Valenzuela*, 62) [The process of becoming-wolf of the little girl not only postulates a dissolution of individual identities where Little Red Riding Hood, the mother, the grandmother and the wolf are brought together, but also a non-chronological temporality that can extend itself into an indefinite present, which is the time that constitutes the microcosm of the forest, as well as splitting into a narration constantly in the past and future] (my translation). On the other hand, Nogueira also includes the question of sexuality and the processes of language in Little Red Riding Hood's becoming-wolf.

WORKS CITED

Blanchot, Maurice. *The Gaze of Orpheus and Other Literary Essays*. Edited by P. Adams Sitney and Translated by Lydia Davis. New York: Station Hill Press, 1981. Print.

Daudet, Alphonse. *Le Roman du Chaperon-Rouge. Scénes et Fantasies*. Paris: Michel Lévy Frères, Libraires Éditeurs, 1862. Print.

Deleuze, Gilles and Félix Guattari. *Anti-Oedipus. Capitalism and Schizophrenia*. Preface by Michel Foucault. Translated from the French by Robert Hurley, Mark Seem, and Helen R. Lane. Minneapolis: University of Minnesota Press, 1983. Print.

———. *A Thousand Plateaus. Capitalism and Schizophrenia*. Translation and Foreword by Brian Masumi. Minneapolis: University of Minnesota Press, 1987. Print.

Foucault, Michel. *The History of Sexuality. An Introduction*. Vol. I. New York: Random House, 1990. Print.

———. *The Use of Pleasure. The History of Sexuality*. Vol. II. New York: Random House, 1990. Print.

———. *The Care of the Self. The History of Sexuality*. Vol. III. New York: Random House, 1990. Print.

Grimm, Jacob and Wilhelm Grimm. "Little Red Cap. Rotkäppchen." In *Little Red Riding Hood. A Casebook*. Edited by Alan Dundes. Madison: Wisconsin University Press, 1989. 7–12. Print.

Hutcheon, Linda. *A Theory of Parody. The Teachings of Twentieth-Century Art Forms*. New York and London: Routledge, 1991. Print.

Lispector, Clarice. *Agua viva*. 3rd ed. Madrid: Siruela, 2012. Print.

Nogueira, Fátima. *Poéticas del devenir: Lispector y Valenzuela*. Santiago, Chile: RIL Editores, 2016. Print.

Perrault, Charles. *Contes*. Texts Established by Gilbert Rouger. Paris: Editions Garnier Frères, 1967. Print.

———. *Little Red Riding Hood*. http://www.pitt.edu/SQUIBBLEdash/perrault02.html. December 19, 2016. Web.

Valenzuela, Luisa. *Symmetries*. Translated by Margaret Jull Costa. London: Serpent's Tail, 1998. Print.

———. *Cuentos completos y uno más*. México: Alfaguara, 1999. Print.

———. *Peligrosas palabras*. Buenos Aires: Temas Grupo Editorial, 2001. Print.

CHAPTER 5

Of Ideological Continuums and Sentimental Memories: Enriquillo Sánchez's *Musiquito: Anales de un déspota y de un bolerista*

Danny Méndez

Enriquillo Sánchez' first novel, *Musiquito: Anales de un déspota y de un bolerista* [*Musiquito: Annals of a Despot and a Bolero Writer*] marked an important moment when it was published in 1993 in the Dominican Republic. Incorporating recognizable traces of the dictator novels by Gabriel García Márquez, Augusto Roa Bastos, and Mario Vargas Llosa, Sánchez's novel dared to directly criticize the ongoing political repression lived in the Dominican Republic during the 1980s and 1990s through his presentation of the comically absurd fictional dictator, Porfirio Funess. Funess' name directly refers to Jorge Luis Borges' short story "Funes el memorioso" and to the eccentric figure of the Mexican dictator Porfirio Díaz, who was in power from 1876 to 1911. The incorporation of this precise literary text along with the reference to a key historical figure in the political sphere of Latin America are central to the

D. Méndez (✉)
Department of Romance and Classical Studies, Michigan State University, East Lansing, MI, USA
e-mail: mendezda@msu.edu

© The Author(s) 2018
H. C. Weldt-Basson (ed.), *Postmodern Parody in Latin American Literature*, Literatures of the Americas,
https://doi.org/10.1007/978-3-319-90430-6_5

97

characterization of Porfirio Funess, and they subtly illustrate a key idea: an ideological continuum that is expressed through a postmodern decentering of memory, truth, and history. In this essay, I analyze how Porfirio Funess embodies an ideological continuum in the sense that he illustrates how, in the Dominican Republic, there has been a succession of political regimes whose despotic ideology was very similar. As a composite of the political regimes of Pedro Santana (in power 1844–1848, 1853–1856, and 1858–1861), Ulises Heureaux (in power 1882–1884 and 1887–1889), Rafael L. Trujillo (in power 1930–1961), and Joaquín Balaguer (in power 1960–1962, 1966–1978, and 1986–1996), Funess' absurdity and megalomaniac personality aligns with what has occurred historically in the Dominican Republic.

Much like the narrator of *Musiquito: Anales de un déspota y de un bolerista*, Sánchez was a part of the generation of the 1970s whose members were born and raised under the Balaguer administration. In fact, the publication of *Musiquito* coincided with Balaguer's administration. The effects of living under an ongoing cycle of repressive administrations appear throughout the novel. It is through the filtered memories of the narrator that we get a glimpse of the titular *Musiquito*, his father, and of Funess. More importantly, however, it is through the narrator that we get a glimpse of how many of the societal factors that were present during Funess' regime still exist in the present. The narrator alternates between a retroactive narration of his father's and of Funess' deaths, and of his own precarious living conditions in the Dominican Republic. Therefore, in this chapter, I am also analyzing how the historical conditions that have given rise to absurd and despotic figures in the past are still present, and always ready to reappear in the Dominican Republic.

The ambiguities of power and its association with identity and history are at the center of *Musiquito: Anales de un déspota y de un bolerista*. The title itself conveys this idea with the positioning of the despotic dictator and the *bolerista* alongside the sites where the historical is alternately registered and documented for public consumption: the annals and the boleros. And thus, I suggest, we can sense here an unavoidable postmodern sensitivity that is captured in the opposing characterizations of Porfirio Funess and Jacinto Buenaventura (alias Musiquito). While Funess' characterization is "overtly politicized and inevitably ideological" (Hutcheon, 7), as he embodies the presumably powerful dictator, it is Musiquito who truly manages to capture the sentiments of the population and, in so doing, has access to the public consciousness in a way that Funess does not. Furthermore, what is most obviously postmodern here is the reliance on a number of literary references ranging from Rubén Darío (*El rey burgués*) to Jorge Luis Borges ("Funes el memorioso" and "El milagro secreto") to anchor the novel's incisive critique of the rise and fall of the fictitious Dominican dictator. These specific works comment on the complexities of cultural and political representation, and its unending entanglement with historical discourse and memory. Furthermore, the ability to "freely" express sentiments that one is unable to "voice" or "write" in a repressive political state such as the one erected by Funess is itself parodied in the novel because the *boleros* Musiquito composes are all invested in extolling the spectacular accomplishments of the regime that are, ironically, in the end, epic failures.

In the novel, the notion of governing is in line with a need to control the past and the mechanisms of memory. Confirming the difficulty of full erasure within chronological historical discourses, Funess seeks Musiquito's music because he sees it as existing outside of the annals and historical records and, thus, it is presumably erasable and controllable. Furthermore, Musiquito's ability to provoke feelings of love, despair, and nostalgia is one that Funess needs not only to document the feats of his regime, but to also secure the domain of memories and emotions. The postmodern parody, as Linda Hutcheon has theorized, arises to make evident the contradictory nature of representation. In other words, while we have a long tradition of visual and written representations, there is ultimately a sense of doubt in regard to the effectiveness of these images and the language itself to fully convey the wide range of experiences and identities (Hutcheon, 8). This leads me to conceive the function of the postmodern parody in *Musiquito* in two ways. The first way parodies the eccentric, despotic, and tyrannical masculinity of Funess via literary references, in order to illustrate the waning of his power and, alternatively, the permanence of an underlying political ideology that resurrects figures such as Funess. The second way calls our attention towards the paradox of history as a discourse whose tendency to "repeat itself" is itself ideologically rooted in a notion of History as an all-encompassing national discourse. Here, the bolero and the compositions of Musiquito provide an alternative mode of historicizing that is not by any means directed at "chronicling" one Dominican national experience. Instead, what we see in the bolero is the coming together of (his)story and fiction. In this view, *Musiquito* can be interpreted in the vein of what Hutcheon has called a "historiographic metafiction" in the sense that: "its historical and socio-political grounding sit uneasily alongside its self-reflexivity" (15). While *Musiquito* cannot be fully inserted within either the confines of the dictator novel or those of the genre historical fiction, it does rely on historical references from the Dominican Republic; these are developed and commented on by fictitious characters such as the narrator and Funess himself. The historical discourse is consumed and diffused from the vantage point of the fictitious.

Much like real-life dictators such as Rafael L. Trujillo, in power from 1930 to 1961, Porfirio Funess is obsessed with redefining the past and his identity, as he actively seeks to modify national history. The narrator explains the first layer of Funess' ideological construct in the following way: "Algo le sugería que no podía gobernar si no gobernaba el pretérito" (79) [Something suggested to him that he could not govern if he did not govern the preterit].[1] This is perhaps the most evident parodic literary reference in Sánchez's novel where the subtext of Jorge Luis Borges' short story, "Funes el memorioso" is used to characterize Porfirio Funess' desire to control memory and the past. My use of parody here is tied to the imitative qualities of the concept and the comedic effect of Funess' failures as he tacitly imitates the other Funes. Consequently, the salient figure of Ireneo Funes, Jorge Luis Borges' titular character in "Funes el memorioso," surfaces to illustrate the failing political ideology of the fictitious dictator. If we consider the solitude and tragic ending of Ireneo Funes' character in Borges' story, then the suggestion Sánchez makes in *Musiquito* is quite powerful: the desire to control the past via a control of memory is a project doomed to fail. This is made even more palpable when the narrator describes the underlying quality upon which Funess defined his power: "Su poder se fundaba en saber por sí mismo todo lo que todos sabían todo el tiempo que lo supieran y en saber quién sabía lo que en cada caso él también sabía" (27) [His power was based on knowing for himself everything that everyone knew all the time that they knew and knowing who knew what in each case he also knew]. Ironically, for Borges' Funes, the ability to memorize everything did not lead to a life of fulfillment. Borges' short story, much like Sánchez's novel, is narrated by a homodiegetic character whose encounter with Funes, a solitary man who was able to tell the time without looking at a watch, takes place on two occasions when he meets him while vacationing in Fray Bentos. During the second encounter, the narrator discovers that Ireneo suffered an accident after falling from a horse, leaving him with the ability to memorize everything instantaneously, and to see the world around him in a painfully precise way. Consequently, the themes of solitude, intelligence, memory, and knowledge are central to the story as we see the deterioration of Funes, whose gifted ability isolates him further from society. Trapped in his mind and unable to critically think beyond the facts and numbers he memorizes, Funes tells the narrator: "Más recuerdos tengo yo solo que los que habrán tenido todos los hombres desde que el mundo es mundo...Mis sueños son como la vigilia de ustedes...Mi memoria, señor, es como un vaciadero de basuras" (105) [I have more memories than all men in this world since the world is world...My dreams are like your vigil...My memory, sir, is like a garbage dump]. The imitative gesture is quite apparent here: Porfirio Funess believes himself to be a sort of revised version of Ireneo Funess in the sense that he thinks he knows *everything*, including the memories, of his constituents. But, whereas Porfirio Funess measures his power on the presumption that he controls and knows all the thoughts of the population, Ireneo reveals the futility of memory (and memorization) as tools of control and critical thought, since he is unable to think beyond the facts and memories he acquires.

The novel privileges an unwritten and subjective mode of historicizing, and we are made aware of this immediately, as Funess dismisses the work of historians and biographers as untruthful disciplines. Consciously aware that, in order for him to successfully create a myth around himself he would need a written account, he hires biographers and rhetoricians, but he is also aware that he would need an alternative venue to disperse this myth: "El dictaría, palabra por palabra, los momentos finales de su biografía a la sarta de retóricos a sueldo que le complacían el oído y la imaginación mintiendo por disciplina y hasta por placer cada vez que era necesario e incluso cuando era absolutamente innecesario" (82) [He would dictate, word for word, the final moments of his biography to the string of paid rhetoricians who pleased the ear and the imagination lying for discipline and even for pleasure whenever it was necessary and even when it was absolutely unnecessary]. Musiquito becomes this alternative venue and his boleros are created mostly to "document" Funess' feats. As Manzari asserts: "Here, the bolero, or speech, is privileged over the written histories composed by the appointed historian chosen by Funess" (93). In this formulation, the annals are more associated with an official recording of historical events, and the bolero is seen as an alternative historical and musical discourse that is more popular and dispersed. In many ways, the act of writing, and the documentation of History and its institutional recognition are criticized in this novel because they are deemed as unable to capture the lived experiences of these characters. Alternatively, Funess' rise to power is a meditation between the official documentation of History and the histories that the bolero affectively represents under the themes of love and heartbreak. The boleros that Musiquito composes (at the mandate of Funess) are literally "survival stories" much like those narrated by Scheherazade to save her life, and, if we align them to modernism, they would be the "survival poems" that we would have heard in Rubén Darío's "El rey burgués." Funess' treatment of Musiquito as a sort of imprisoned artist who is now forced to develop his craft towards the advancement and propaganda of the dictatorship is all retold by the narrator. The process of narration for this narrator is invested in the desire to "tell his own story"; however, the spectral weight of the stories of Musiquito (presumably his biological father) and Funess (who could be his father because he also slept with his mother) inevitably crosses him. What is left behind for this narrator, the symbolic product of a succession of dictatorships and ideological continuums, are Funess' useless annals and biographies, and the boleros composed by Musiquito that described the ebbs and flow of Funess' dictatorship.

The need to guarantee a total control of his regime depends, as well, on a retrospective management of the past which, in the novel, is expressed in sexual terms to draw our attention towards the parallels of power dynamics in the crafting of history, and its deep correlation with race, gender, and sexuality. This is best expressed in an early scene of the novel when Funess seeks counsel from the *Academia de la Historia*, that is itself, as all other institutions of knowledge and education in the novel, mocked and viewed as superficial and "outside" of the domain of progress. Funess, who is hoping to rewrite the past of the Dominican Republic and align it directly with a European lineage, soon realizes that he would need to also "erase" the historical consciousness. The solution proposed by one of the professors of the *Academia de la Historia* is that Funess could only *rewrite* history if he could manage a way to rid the island of all remnants or associations with darkness. This act of eliminating darkness from the historical discourse is analogously expressed in sexual terms: "Le explicó que los hechos históricos, una vez consumados, solo existían en la imaginación ética de los hombres, de modo que bastaba soñarlos de otra manera para que desaparecieran de la crónicas mendaces" (79) [He explained that the historical facts, once consummated, only existed in the ethical imagination of men, so that it was enough to dream them in another way so that they disappeared from the mendacious chronicles]. This consummation (and consequent over-writing) of history is in line with the establishment of a heteronormative masculinity whose ability was measured by the idea of "possessions." So, it is not merely the imagination of *any* man that can readily erase histor-ical facts from presumably unreliable chronicles, it is the imagination of an ethical man such as Funess whose virility and power could revise the national historical consciousness.

Sánchez' novel does not merely represent the absurd tyranny and power exerted by Funess, he also integrates gender and sexuality to expose the deeply interconnected nature of these concepts in the Dominican Republic. Notions of masculinity and power are portrayed in a degrading (devaluing) scale, much like the national currency that Funess invents and that loses value as soon as it is printed. The impe-tus for Funess' reign is driven by a desire to document his political and sexual potency, and, conversely, by his inability to identify the one con-stant element that truly defines him: impotence. This notion of impo-tence is made abundantly clear in *Musiquito* in the disturbing scenes where Funess attempts to rape and sexually assault women as an exer-tion of his power, but, in Funess' case, this exertion of power can only be performed with his pinky finger. And thus, the desire to possess and objectify does not fully materialize into the action of domination or con-trol. From a historical vantage point, it is unavoidable to consider how Trujillo's "hyperbolic masculinity" (Horn, 17) factors into the char-acterization Sánchez makes of Funess. For example, the incongruous self-fashioning of Trujillo as a paternal, virile, and unbeatable macho figure in the Dominican Republic was made possible, and popularized, as a reaction to the U.S. occupation of 1916–1924. That first occu-pation was expressed in feminized terms and it was, in the mindset of intellectuals and political figures of the time, a symbolic emasculation by U.S. forces (Calder, xxx; Horn, 17). The eventual withdrawal of the United States and the rise of Trujillo as president and eventual dictator of the Dominican Republic necessitated a restructuring of these senti-ments of political impotence (caused by the U.S. occupation) in order to re-establish a form of national pride and honor that had been pre-sumed lost. The mythical re-fashioning of Trujillo as a guardian of the *patria* and his concerted efforts to erase from the national history those facts (*hechos históricos*) that were deemed to be contrary to his notion of whitened progress were some of the ways that his ideology was put in place. Furthermore, as Maja Horn notes: "The Trujillato's emphasis on virility as a cornerstone of its political discourses in defense of the nation, however, was not merely a quintessential expression of 'Latin' patriarchal masculinity…Trujillo similarly wielded his rhetoric of masculinity to signal the sovereignty of the self and of the Dominican nation-state after its curtailing by U.S. imperial powers" (35). Similarly, we see Funess' adoption of the nickname of the *Poblador* [settler] as an extension of this obsessive desire to wield control over territories whose sovereignty has been in constant jeopardy.

There is also a racist discourse that underlies Funess' political ideology that subtly hints at the sometimes torrid relationship between Haiti and the Dominican Republic. The dictatorship of Trujillo heightened the racial tensions between these two neighboring islands and the quote above (Horn, 35) points towards one of the most violent and horrific acts orchestrated by Trujillo and led by Joaquín Balaguer (who eventually became the president of the Dominican Republic): the 1937 Haitian Massacre. The Haitian massacre was an act of border violence in Trujillo's Dominican nationalist project in the 1930s, which occurred in the midst of an already upsetting history of ethnic and racial cleansing projects. As I have indicated elsewhere, "More than another atrocity, it became, translated into Dominican nationalist terms, a moment of 'liberation,' the central legitimizing act for the regime" (Méndez, 103). In the Trujillo period, a special lexicon was fashioned to explicate and simultaneously visualize the Dominican identity under the system of a so-called "raza dominicana" or, as it was originally envisioned, of "dominicanidad" (formulated in terms of a *Hispanicized* race theory, and not as it is used today). Likewise, here Funess is invested in furthering this racist ideology to signify a Dominican identity but, ironically, this ideology stems from the Trujillo dictatorship, although it is represented in fiction. Trujillo undertook his position as dictator in 1930, and it was one of the longest and most vicious dictatorships in the Dominican Republic. After his assassination in 1961, his remaining supporters shouldered off any adversaries for power until the U.S. occupation of 1965. Trujillo employed violence, censorship, and intimidation to purge all opponents, stopping in this way any group that sought to influence popular cultural expressions from the Dominican people (90). As José Alcántara Almánzar describes: "anti-communism, the cult of Hispanicity, an anti-Haitian racial discourse and Catholicism were some of the most important elements defining Trujillo's ideology and that allowed his effective domination of subordinate classes" (178). Funess' political ideology is evidently nurtured by the specter of Trujillo.

SILENCING THE PAST AND THE VOICE OF FAILURE

"Es mejor. La cultura es tortura permanente" (100) [It is better. Culture is permanent torture]. With these words, the exuberantly grotesque Funess comes to terms with one of his many failed projects. In this case, the failed enterprise was a literacy campaign—as the narrator tells us, the population had not learned to read; instead, they *memorized* the lessons imparted by the campaign managers. The ironic twist here underlies one of the ideological layers sustaining Funess' regime: the population is more adept at memorizing than learning, and thus rendering the idea of books useless. Traditionally, books and literature have been viewed as posing a danger in dictatorships and militant governments due to their potential ability to awaken the minds of citizens. But, in *Musiquito*, the dictator himself orders the campaign to presumably usher in an idea of progress that he initially associates with literacy. However, the citizens themselves refuse this potential tool for rebellion. Funess' response is indicative of the dangers of culture and he only comes to this realization after he confirms that his literacy campaign has failed. It is not only the dangers of culture as a critical sounding board of political discontent, but also the notion of *access* to memory and historical discourses that frighten him.

In essence, the fear of an uncontrollable Dominican past points towards a dichotomy that Funess hopes to eliminate, which is that humans engage in history as both actors and narrators. In this way, the classical dilemma of history as a fundamental uncertainty unravels in *Musiquito*, and this is best illustrated by the narrator's attempt to provide what he perceives as "facts of the matter" in a linear fashion while concurrently, and fragmentally, providing a "story of the process" and personal effects of Funess' reign. The narrator subtly notes this process in one of the first lines of the novel:

> Porfirio Funess gobernó la república durante cuarenta y cuatro años. Fueron cuarenta y cuatro años incesantes-olímpicos, devastadores-, marcados por la huella impar de la bonanza y de la gloria, de la abundancia y de la justicia, de la felicidad y del progreso. Jacinto Aguasvivas, mi padre, fue

bolerista. Estuvieron unidos por una relación avasalladora que duró más de
un tercio de siglo y que concluyó . . . . (9–10)

Porfirio Funess ruled the republic for forty-four years. They were forty-four incessant-Olympic, devastating years-, marked by the odd imprint
of bonanza and glory, of abundance and justice, of happiness and progress.
Jacinto Aguasvivas, my father, was a bolero composer and singer. They
were united by an overwhelming relationship that lasted more than a third
of a century and ended . . . .

Here, it is apparent that the narrator's process of storytelling is
impacted by the stories of Funess and his father, and his own. If, "the
past-pastness- is a position" (15), as Michel-Rolph Trouillot reminds
us, then the narrator of *Musiquito* is forced to provide his account from
multiple chaotic and personal spaces. The narrator, I suggest, is acutely
aware of his position and expresses it this way while trying to describe
his past: "Ni mi madre ni yo sabemos cómo distinguirlos. Ella, derrotada
quizá por la esperanza, vencida por la costumbre simultánea del pretérito
y del porvenir, esos dos países de nadie, mastican su papiamento y sus
estrellas. Yo soy el caos o el cosmos. Erijo al uno en el discurrir minuci-
oso del otro" (10) [Neither my mother nor I know how to distinguish
them. She, defeated perhaps by hope, overcome by the simultaneous cus-
tom of the past and the future, those two countries of no one, chew their
Papiamento and its stars. I am the chaos or the cosmos. I correct the one
in the detailed discourse of the other]. The inevitable shadow of Funess
taints the narrator's personal recollections so much so that neither he nor
his mother can recall a moment in which Funess and Musiquito were not
together. But here the narrator is not only concerned with describing the
relationship between Funess and Musiquito; inadvertently, he also criticizes his mother's complacency with the political ideology surrounding
them. Reminiscent of Trouillot's criticism of positivist historical frameworks, the narrator decides to simultaneously inhabit the chaos and the
order (*el cosmos*), and, in this way, follows Trouillot's rejection of: "the
naïve proposition that we are prisoners of our past and the pernicious
suggestion that history is whatever we make it" (xix). By indicating he
inhabits these two domains, the chronological and the fragmented, the
narrator is symbolically rejecting the one element that allows political figures such as Funess to arise: unchallenged ideas of the past and a
blind faith in the future. Once again, Troillot's interpretation of a positivist historical framework is pertinent here, especially as it relates to:

"The role of the historian . . . to reveal the past, to discover or, at least, approximate truth. Within that viewpoint, power is unproblematic, irrelevant to the construction of the narrative" (5). The narrator's preoccupation with "telling his story" while also putting together the story of his father and his relationship with Funess could be interpreted along the lines of the positivist historian described by Trouillot. However, the narrator in *Musiquito* is not interested in merely reproducing a historical past that is accessible via annals and records; instead, he focuses on the *boleros* composed by his father to illustrate a more complicated process of historical reasoning and recording in which power is not necessarily linked to political authority. In this sense, *Musiquito* does not present an uncritical depiction of power. The portrayal of the relationship between Musiquito and Funess is indicative of power shifts that are described by the narrator as an "overwhelming relationship." Given the fact that there is an asymmetrical power dynamic in this relationship, we must scrutinize what sort of influence or power Musiquito can exert over Funess. I will return to this idea of power and its implicit association with a homoerotic desire that I perceive in the interactions of Funess and Musiquito.

BOLERO AND HISTORY

In *Musiquito*, the bolero—a musical genre born in the Caribbean and an extension of the sentimentality of the modernist movement—surfaces as an alternative mode of historicizing. The fragments of various popular Latin American boleros throughout the novel and the compositions of Jacinto Buenaventura express emotions that go beyond the traditional themes of love and despair, and subtly express sentiments of impotence, sadness, and fury against the political and cultural reality under Funess.

To understand the significance of the bolero as a disrupting force in the historical framework presented in *Musiquito*, it is necessary to briefly define it and situate it here. It is important to indicate that Sánchez's novel is part of a long tradition of Latin American novels that have used the genre of the bolero to express the cultural effects of political repressions.[2] In many ways, the bolero is seen as a way of contesting the linear and chronological depiction of the past in historical discourses. If an event can be categorized and time-stamped in written historical accounts, the bolero allows for a more expansive and subtle voicing of pain (associated in these songs with the theme of love and despair) that can allude to the ongoing effects of political and social upheaval. The guitar-based bolero in Latin

America was initially conceived in Cuba and it dispersed around the world as a consequence of the Wars of Independence (1895–1898) and the subsequent displacements it caused (Pacini Hernández, 5). The boleros were originally spontaneously created and, in this sense, were ingrained in an oral tradition that represented the lived experiences of the popular classes. The bolero was at the peak of worldwide popularity in the 1950s and, in the Dominican Republic, it was a musical genre, unlike the *merengue*, that represented the voices of the rural and lower-class Dominicans. As Deborah Pacini Hernández has indicated, while the *merengue* (specifically the whitened *merengue* from the Cibao region) was utilized during the Trujillo dictatorship (1930–1961) as a musical discourse to promote the regime, the bolero and the *bachata* were genres that exemplified the experiences of Dominicans that were not in the urban sphere of influence of the dictatorship (Pacini Hernández, 44).

The bolero is connected to *modernism* in its content and structure. As Leonora Simonovis rightly asserts, the bolero's ascent coincides with the rise of modernism so much so that the first popular songs were inspired by the poetry of Amado Nervo, Rubén Darío, and Manuel Gutiérrez Nájera among others (Simonovis, 53). For this reason, the boleros epitomize the union of the literary and the historical, and thus create a space for communication that transcends class and genre. Iris Zavala remarks on this communication process when she states that the bolero: "pasa con el modernismo a la burgesía, a los marginados y al pueblo" (50) [goes with modernism to the bourgeoisie, the marginalized and the people]. The bolero diffuses a way of "feeling" history and politics, and I would argue that it provides an affective structure whereby sentiments of love and despair are collectively and subtly expressed. This affective structure I see in the bolero is akin to Raymond Williams' argument regarding other modes of understanding generational differences that are not ingrained solely in literary language. As Williams argues: "Such changes can be defined as changes in structures of feelings. The term is difficult, but 'feeling' is chosen to emphasize a distinction from more formal concepts as 'world-view' or 'ideology'... it is that we are concerned with meanings and values as they are actively lived and felt" (132). Keeping in line with the themes of control and possession that structure *Musiquito*'s main plot, the traditional bolero also relies on a gendered narrative of possession. All of the boleros quoted in *Musiquito*, with the exception of those composed by Musiquito himself to illustrate the virtues of Funess' dictatorship, rely on the theme of domination of men over women, revealing in this way a continuous patriarchal ideology. As Frances Aparicio observes: "The continental, eternal and ubiquitous body of the bolero as socio-musical practice is closely linked to patriarchy and to its male-gendered voices and lyrics" (Aparicio, 128).

Structure and Ideology

The ideological continuum that *Musiquito* proposes is made apparent right from the very first chapter of the novel titled, "De te fabula narratur," which roughly translates into English as "This is your story." This phrase originally appeared in Karl Marx' *Das Capital* and was originally intended to express that the future of Germany was already foretold by England. In other words, Germany figured right from the start in England's plans for industrialization and modernity. In Sánchez's novel, this first chapter provides an unsettling point of departure as we are not fully aware whether the "you" to which the phrase alludes is the narrator, Musiquito's son, or to us the readers. I propose that what we have here is a process of interpellation that dismantles itself via Musiquito and Funess, thus revealing an ideological continuum that has unified fiction and history in the Dominican Republic. I propose here that this ideological continuum is akin to Antonio Benítez Rojo's notion of a repeating island. But here the repetition heavily leans towards Benítez Rojo's pronouncement of "actuar" as one of the characteristics that simultaneously associates and differentiates the Caribbean islands. In his book *The Repeating Island: The Caribbean and the Post-modern Perspective* (1997), Benítez-Rojo uses chaos theory to critically analyze the Caribbean region from a position that does not essentialize it. Although chaos theory points towards a disparate and complex array of elements, Benítez-Rojo adduces that basic repetitions do arise that curtail complex processes. In this sense, Benítez-Rojo recognizes polyrhythm as a mode understanding and illustrating the Caribbean regions without affixing them to rigid historical and political paradigms. In *Musiquito*, the repetition is itself the ideological mechanism that has promoted the resurgence of a despotic figure such as Funess that can survive under different names and guises beyond history. The megalomaniacal and ideological excesses that characterize Funess in the novel parallel those of real-life despotic figures such as Trujillo and Joaquín Balaguer, whose combined reign unfolded in the Dominican Republic for a half century.

The second chapter, titled "Cuarenta mariachis os contemplan" [Forty Mariachis Contemplate You], repurposes a speech given by Napoleon Bonaparte in 1787 in the Battle of the Pyramids to anchor Funess' maneuvering of the historical discourse in the novel. Bonaparte's original phrase was given in front of his troops: "soldiers, from these pyramids, 40 centuries are contemplating us." The chapter title replaces the word "*siglos*" (centuries) with "*mariachis*," and it does so, I believe, to emphasize the idea that chronology and history do not always have to run parallel to one another. That is, history's reliance on chronology makes it blind to other forms of registering the past. In this case, the *mariachis'* music produces a different form of "time-keeping." The rephrasing of Bonaparte's comment is important here because it denotes a careful dismantling of the historical discourse in *Musiquito* that is rooted in a parodical intertext.

Much of the second chapter narrates Funess' daydreaming about bringing progress and modernity to the island. Recurring once again to Borges, the chapter illustrates Funess' daydreaming in such a way that it evokes the main plot of the short story "Las ruinas circulares," [The Circular Ruins] only that, in this case, Funess himself is at the center of the process of dreaming/creating the world around him: "Mientras todos temían (mientras el miedo gobernaba la nación con una eficacia superior a todas sus ejecutorias y a todas sus hazañas de gobernante), Porfirio Funess... Soñaba despierto. Como siempre, soñaba despierto. Era un visionario y lo sabía" (25) [While everyone feared (while fear ruled the nation with an efficiency superior to all his executions and all his exploits as ruler), Porfirio Funess...Daydreamed. As always, he daydreamed. He was a visionary and he knew it]. In this act of creation, Funess sees himself as a god whose power is measured in virility and reproduction, as the narrator indicates: "Era un poblador. Poblaba de urbes los valles y de ruas solitarias las sabanas y de ilusión el miedo y de talleres agobiantes y fragosos la sempiterna menesterosidad de las islas" (25) [He was a settler. He populated the valleys with cities and the savannahs with lonely streets and fear with illusion and the everlasting neediness of the islands with the oppressive and fragrant workshops]. It is impossible not to draw certain immediate comparisons between Funess and Rubén Darío's "El rey burgués," and the protagonists' desire to possess and control all things. In Dario's story, the king's penchant for collecting all "exotic" materials make him unable to truly appreciate the essence of art, and thus, when he meets a poet, he "sees" him solely as a material gain. We are confronted with a similar situation with Funess, who is only interested in building a myth of progress, control, and power around himself. But this myth required a precise mode of documenting itself that would resonate widely and subtly induct the population. Much as occurred during Trujillo's regime and his use of *merengue* to promote his ideology, the *bolero* is presented here as the most effective mode of advertising his feats and securing his place in the collective memory. In contrast to the *merengue*'s more corporeal and dance focus, the *bolero* is more attuned to provoking a mental and reflective experience around the leitmotifs of love and despair, and thus, by guaranteeing the *bolero* as a discourse to promote him and his regime, Funess is symbolically also controlling the mind and emotions of the people around him. When Funess hears Musiquito's boleros, he realizes the impact they had on emotions and thoughts: "Funess no se inmuta. Manejaba la realidad tanto como la irrealidad (había descubierto sus secretos mientras perseguia sus simultaneidades) y decidió en el acto que debia superar los acontecimientos" (28) [Funess does not flinch. He handled reality as much as unreality (he had discovered its secrets while pursuing his simultaneities) and decided in the act that he should overcome events]. However, before Funess tries to overcome the effects of Musiquito's music, he is inspired to reflect on his own identity and his relationship to the musician: "'La insularidad'—decía Funess— 'es deliciosa y omnímoda'. Él era la ínsula. Cuando vio a Musiquito desnudo, cubierta las partes pudendas por una guitarra agurejeada pero invicta, decidió convertirlo a él también en una ínsula, en la otra ínsula, en la ínsula opuesta" (29) ['Insularity,' said Funess, 'is delicious and all-embracing.' He was the insula. When he saw Musiquito naked, covering his private parts by a guitar that was pierced but undefeated, he decided to turn him into an insula, into the other insula, in the opposite island]. This conversion of Musiquito into "the other island" can be viewed as an analogy of Hispaniola with Funess and Musiquito embodying the individual islands that make it up, Haiti and the Dominican Republic. Manzari has indicated that this proclamation of the *insula* as Funess is a way of noting how dictators have sought to define the national identity as something that stems solely from them, but I believe that this proclamation is made to incorporate both Funess and Musiquito as opposing figures that are immersed in a process of abjection. Funess ultimately decrees Musiquito as the official "chronicler" of his regime: "lo nombró Cantor Vitalicio de la Patria. Entonces decretó una Semana Aniversario para conmemorar sus fastos más sonoros y sus hitos más elocuentes desde que había alcanzado el poder" (29) [He named him the Official Singer of the Fatherland. Then he decreed an Anniversary Week to commemorate his most sonorous celebrations and his most eloquent landmarks since he had reached the power]. For Funess, Musiquito was the vessel to expose his messages and victories.

All the chapters in *Musiquito* elaborate, to varying degrees, the absurd power dynamics that have permitted the despotic figuration of political leaders such as Funess and the complicity of constituents that manage to "resist" it subtle ways: I see this especially in Musiquito's reaction to his new situation as the "Official Bolerista" of Funess' regime. Forced to assume the role of an alternative chronicler and pseudo (musical) historian, Musiquito himself reflects on his situation in the following way: "Adivinó en un instante de fulgor helado que le esperaban treinta y cuatro años de abyección y se preparó a resistir, sin armarse de ningún género de heroismo ni de ninguna suerte de discurso ni de ningún tipo de retórica" (29) [He guessed in a frozen moment that thirty-four years of abjection awaited him and he prepared to resist, without arming himself with any kind of heroism or any kind of discourse or any kind of rhetoric]. Abjection surfaces here, and in multiple parts of the novel], not solely as a theme but more so as an existential crisis that arises every time the subject, in this case Musiquito, intends to represent itself. Considered usually within a psychoanalytic framework developed by important scholars such as Julia Kristeva, Georges Bataille, and Jacques Lacan, the notion of abjection is observed as something that disrupts and poses a threat to identity. As stated by Tim Dean, "If desire disturbs identity, arguably the abject does so even more" (872). Consequently, I find Calvin Thomas' framework of abjection useful in his study *Masculinity, Psychoanalysis, Straight Queer Theory: Essays on Abjection in Literature, Mass Culture, and Film*, where he focuses on the abject to understand and challenge a supposed stable and unified idea of a normative masculinity: "Abjection thus involves the general realm of bodily production, expulsion, leakage, and defilement...by constructing arenas of abject powerlessness, lifelessness, and meaninglessness to which its consigns its marginalized others" (xii). So, how is this specter of abjection expressed in the relationship between Musiquito and Funess? How does the literary parody factor into this process? The traces of abjection are presented in Musiquito every time he is forced to compose a new bolero for Funess. The coexistence of fear for his life and shame, because his craft is now at the service of documenting the absurdities of the regime, are further complicated by a sentiment of liberation, because he is being able to create/compose despite his situation.

Musiquito's abjection confronts him to the limits of what he believed was his identity prior to meeting Funess. Something similar occurs to Funess, whose rise to the role of dictator confronts him with other anxieties that are tied to a dread of being forgotten, and thus express his need to control memory and the past (*para gobernar tenía que controlar el pretérito*). But something else arises in this abject relationship with the sentiments Musiquito provokes in Funess, because his *boleros* destabilize his presumed unified identity as a *Poblador* (settler). Towards the end of the novel, we witness this gradual mental breakdown of Funess who, under the spell of Musiquito's *boleros*, comes to a dramatic realization: "hasta que olvidó por completo, sin rastos ni pistas, que una vez en su vida había amado sin confesarlo a dos hombres...Funess sabía olvidar... Había descubierto que los hombres eran poderosos no por lo que recordaban sino por lo que olvidaban" (132) [until he forgot completely, without tracks or clues, that once in his life he had loved without confessing two men...Funess knew how to forget...He had discovered that men were powerful not for what they remembered but for what they forgot]. Thus, the pervasiveness of abjection as a qualifier of Musiquito's and Funess' relationship is not coincidental, as it signals to a sort of Hegelian dialectic whereby each of their social and political realizations stems from their contrasting positions. Along these lines, the layers of Funess' political ideology are also revealed under his obsessive need to manifest an exterior persona that is hypermasculine and virile while seemingly casting to the margins those subjects, such as Musiquito, that he deems as weak and nonproductive to his regime. If both the *bolero* and Musiquito himself represent the abject, and therefore the marginal, in the environment led by Funess, then it could be argued that, dialectically, they have an effect on Funess' sense of self. This is best expressed at the end of the novel when the unexpected eruption of abject desires and emotions invade Funess leading him to renounce the ideological status quo when he surprisingly manifests this wish: "¡Búsquenme un hombre con una verga de loco!" (157) [Find me a man with a crazy cock!]. The voicing of a queer desire contradicts the heteronormative and macho culture that Funess himself had propagated up to this point. However, by virtue of expressing a desire to be possessed by another male, Funess symbolically places himself within the type of traditional *boleros* that treated female bodies as objects (Aparicio, 137), and thus assumes the role of the marginalized.

Funess' symbolic displacement to the margins at the end of the novel does not lead to a complete rupture with the ideological basis that had allowed him to be a dictator in the first place. In fact, the story we read in *Musiquito* is a story told to us by a narrator whose life is still defined by the parameters that were set during Funess' dictatorship and that continued to have an impact in the Dominican Republic. In *Musiquito*, Enriquillo Sánchez provides a powerful criticism of the normalized ideological postulates that have permeated the political, social, and cultural spheres in the Dominican Republic. Although Porfirio Funess is a fictitious representation of a Dominican dictator, through him Sánchez illustrates some of the enduring cultural "norms" that have continued to color the ways Dominican political leaders govern the island.

In *Musiquito*, Enriquillo Sánchez illustrates the permanence of a despotic political ideology in the Dominican Republic. Consequently, the narrative techniques Sánchez incorporates in the novel situate it within a postmodern framework that emphasizes the contradictory ways that Funess, the fictitious blend of real-life Dominican dictators, has been able to wage his control and political clout. In this formulation of contradictions, sexual prowess is made evident by its opposite, impotence, and control of the emotions and historical memory of the population results in the epic failure of campaigns geared towards attaining these objectives. As a result, the function of the postmodern parody in *Musiquito* serves the purpose of mimicking the concept of imminent failure that is attached to the political ideology that inspires Funess, and that is seen as the despotic obsession to control the emotions and the memory of the population. The parody of this failed political ideology in *Musiquito* itself is foregrounded in the literary references to Borges' "Funes el memorioso" to illustrate how it conversely depicts both change and cultural resurgence. As Hutcheon further notes: "The collective weight of parodic practices suggest a redefinition of parody as repetition with a critical distance that allows for ironic signaling and difference at the heart of similarity" (26). So, what is at stake when we consider a novel like *Musiquito* that poses a criticism of ideology in postmodern terms? What is at stake, as I have illustrated in this chapter, is the need to critically reconsider how historical discourses have failed to fully consider how ideological continuums propagate not only in the fictitious despotic regimes of a character such as Funess, but also in the administrations of figures such as Trujillo and Balaguer. With Funess' characterization, Enriquillo Sánchez makes it quite evident that real life supersedes fiction.

NOTES

1. All translations unless otherwise noted are mine.
2. For a substantive analysis of the genre of *the novela bolero*, refer to Vicente Francisco Torres' *La novela bolero latinoamericana* (Mexico: UNAM, 1998).

WORKS CITED

Benítez-Rojo, Antonio. *The Repeating Island: The Caribbean and the Post-modern Perspective*. Translated by James E. Maraniss. Durham: Duke University Press, 1997. Print.

Borges, Jorge Luis. *Narraciones*. Edited by Marcos Ricardo Barnatán. Madrid: Ediciones Cátedra, 2008. Print.

Calder, Bruce J. *The Impact of Intervention: The Dominican Republic During the U.S. Occupation of 1916–1924*. Princeton: Markus Weiner Publishers, 2006. Print.

De Maeseneer, Rita. "Denzil Romero, Enriquillo Sánchez y Zoé Valdés a ritmo de bolero." *Iberoamericana* 5 (1992): 37–53. Print.

Horn, Maja. *Masculinity After Trujillo: The Politics of Gender in Dominican Literature*. Gainesville: University Press of Florida, 2014. Print.

Hutcheon, Linda. *The Politics of Postmodernism*. New York: Routledge, 1989. Print.

Manzari, H.J. "Violence and the Seduction of History in *Musiquito: Anales de un déspota y su bolerista*." *Ciberletras* 14 (2006). http://www.lehman.cuny.edu/ciberletras/v14/manzari.htm. Web.

Méndez, Danny. *Narratives of Migration and Displacement in Dominican Literature*. New York: Routledge, 2012. Print.

Ortega, Julio, Gustavo Pellón, and Martín Gaspar. *Nueva Antología de la literatura de las Américas*. Boston: Vista, 2014. Print.

Pacini Hernández, Deborah. *Bachata. A Social History of a Dominican Popular Music*. Philadelphia: Temple University Press, 1995. Print.

Sánchez, Enriquillo. *Musiquito: Anales de un déspota y de un bolerista*. Santo Domingo: Editora Taller, 1993. Print.

Simonovis, Leonora. "*Musiquito*: La historia de un dictador y su bolerista." *Caribe* 9 (2007): 51–68. Print.

Thomas, Calvin. *Masculinity, Psychoanalysis, Straight Queer Theory: Essays on Abjection in Literature, Mass Culture, and Film*. New York: Palgrave, 2008. Print.

Trouillot, Michel-Rolph. *Silencing the Past: Power and the Production of History*. New York: Beacon Press, 2015. Print.

Williams, Raymond. *Marxism and Literature*. Oxford: Oxford University Press, 1977. Print.

Zavala, Iris. *El bolero. Historia de un amor*. Madrid: Celeste Ediciones, 2000. Print.

CHAPTER 6

Parody as Genealogy and Tradition in *Nazi Literature in the Americas*

Fátima R. Nogueira

La literatura nazi en las Américas [*Nazi Literature in the Americas*] (1996) belongs to the sub-genre of imaginary biographies, and is also close to historiography and satirical pastiche. However, some theoretical observations authorize us to speak of parody in this work, as well as in other texts that have a genealogical relationship with it, as indicated by Bolaño. Gérard Genette, observing the theoretical difficulty in distinguishing efficiently between terms such as parody, pastiche, and travesty, proposes:

> To (re)baptize as parody the distortion of a text by means of a minimum transformation, travesty will designate the stylistic transformation whose function is to debase, caricature will designate the satirical pastiche, and pastiche plain and simple, would refer to an imitation of a style without any satirical intention. (Genette, *Palimpsests*, 25)

F. R. Nogueira (✉)
The University of Memphis, Memphis, TN, USA
e-mail: nogueira@memphis.edu

© The Author(s) 2018
H. C. Weldt-Basson (ed.), *Postmodern Parody in Latin American Literature*, Literatures of the Americas,
https://doi.org/10.1007/978-3-319-90430-6_6

117

In this sense, Bolaño's text surpasses the question of imitation of a style, transforming dictionaries of authors to serve a specific aim. At first, he rethinks literary production and the figure of the author to coincide with his socio-historical surroundings and with the literary institution.[1] Then, upon involving the American historical context as a propitious environment for Nazi ideology, he uses the impersonal language of encyclopedias to reach a critical distancing.

This last aspect is consistent with some of Hutcheon's proposals in *A Theory of Parody* (1986), principally regarding the pre-eminent role of social context and of irony in the parody of art in the twentieth century. In sum, parody is a question of using old forms to create new ones; of making difference emerge through repetition; of inscribing itself within the continuity of literary history and innovating it at the same time (Hutcheon, 34–35).

Inserting his book into universal literature and recurring once more to the dialogue between tradition and artistic renovation, Roberto Bolaño offers us his genealogy:

> This book owes a lot to *The Temple of Iconoclasts* by Rodolfo Wilcock. At the same time, his book, *The Temple of Iconoclasts* owes a debt to *A Universal History of Infamy* by Borges. Borges' *A Universal History of Infamy* too owes a debt to one of his teachers, Alfonso Reyes, who has a book I think called *Real and Imagined Portraits*. Alfonso Reyes' book also owes a debt to Marcel Schwob's *Imaginary Lives*, which is where this all comes from. But at the same time, *Imaginary Lives* owes a major debt to the methodology and form of certain biographies perused by encyclopedic types. (Bolaño, *Bolaño por sí mismo*, 42)

The previous citation confirms what Bolaño had already pointed out in some articles compiled in *Between Parentheses* (2011a).[2]

Although Bolaño insists on connecting *Imaginary Lives* (1896), *Real and Imagined Portraits* (1920), and *A Universal History of Infamy* (1935/1954), Borges does not associate his book with the one by Reyes. However, Borges does admit his debt to Schwob in the prologue to the Spanish edition of *Imaginary Lives*, in which he writes: "Hacia 1935 escribí un libro candoroso que se llamaba *Historia universal de la infamia*. Una de sus muchas fuentes, no señalada aún por la crítica, fue este libro de Schwob" [Around 1935 I wrote a naive book that was called *A Universal History of Infamy*. One of its many sources, as yet unmentioned by literary criticism, was this book by Schwob] (Borges, *Biblioteca personal*: prólogos 112, my translation).[3] Borges's omission of Reyes can probably be justified by the difference between Reyes's work and that of the others. This difference does not invalidate Schwob's influence on Mexican literary production of that era, or the hypothesis that Schwob's work had been one of the sources that inspired Reyes when he wrote his portraits, or the admiration that the Mexican writer provoked not only in Borges, who considered him the best prose writer in the Spanish language (Sorrentino, *Seven Conversations with Borges*, 105), but also in Bolaño, who wishes to identify him as his precursor.

I believe that Reyes's work distinguishes itself from the others due to an emphasis on the application of a series of founding principles of the sub-genre, explained in the author's preface to *Imaginary Lives*. Víctor Gustavo Zonana, in the article "*De viris pessimis*: Biografías imaginarias de Marcel Schwob, Jorge Luis Borges y Juan Rodolfo Wilcock" [*De viris pessimis*: Imaginary Biographies by Marcel Schwob, Jorge Luis Borges and Juan Rodolfo Wilcock] delineates these tenets in a detailed manner. I summarize them here, citing Schwob, when necessary. These are the five founding principles of the sub-genre:

1. The shifting of imaginary biography from historiographical discourse to that of art (Schwob, *Imaginary Lives*, 4);
2. The connection between the individual—founding precept of modernity—and the anomalies and manias belonging to each human being, so that biography, through art, captures for eternity the peculiarities of the individual: "Great men possess only that which is bizarre about them. To describe a man in all his anomalies a book should be a work of art" (Schwob, *Imaginary Lives*, 4);
3. The aesthetic transformation of existence is achieved through an aleatory selection of facts from which existence is fictionally imagined and reconstructed: "As an art, biography is founded upon choice; truth need not be its preoccupation, for out of a chaos of human traits, it can create. Biography should select unique individuals from the realm of human material available" (Schwob, *Imaginary Lives*, 13);
4. Thus, biography is a work of fiction and its fundamental interest is summarized, therefore, in the selection of particular characteristics and in the creation of a realistic character through these characteristics;

5. Manias and anomalies are typical of human beings, and the actions of great men and historical events of the person whose biography is written are not of interest to art. Thus, "the unique existences of men-priests, criminals or nobodies must be recounted with equal care" (Schwob, *Imaginary Lives*, 14).

Departing from the application of the fundamental principles of imaginary biography in the works that he analyzes, Zonana establishes five generic traits of the sub-genre:

1. Encyclopedic will, referring principally to the spatio-temporal environment to which the biographies of each work belong;
2. The desire to synthesize, or the brevity of the tale;
3. Employment of preambles of a general nature;
4. Infamous protagonists; and
5. Black humor (681–686).

We find the principal difference between the imaginary biographies by Reyes and Borges, Wilcock, Bolaño, and Schwob himself, in the second principle and the two final characteristics. That is, Reyes is out of place with the others to a certain degree, although he follows the majority of the founding principles and characteristics of imaginary biographies because he emphasizes singularity and imagination at the service of art. Reyes avoids the sickly, abnormal, or infamous. This behavior results in a parodic procedure that emphasizes the critical analysis of the persistence of an ideology in a specific historical era without necessarily highlighting ignominy, while the other authors I discuss accentuate ignominy, when achieving this same analysis.

Real and Imagined Portraits by Reyes gathers fifteen portraits previously published in Madrid newspapers. They are real people—mostly government officials, kings, literary figures, navigators, conquerors, or religious men—who are described with subtlety and extreme elegance. They are stylistic exercises that seek to aggrandize historical fact, curious details, the ups and downs of chance, and the games of imagination. We could summarize Reyes's strategy in these fictional biographies as something very similar to what he describes in "Chateaubriand in America" where already: "poco nos importa saber hasta dónde alcanzó en sus viajes. Hemos cerrado ya el estudio de la mentira en la América de Chateaubriand; de la mentira biográfica, práctica. Nos falta el estudio de la verdad; la verdad trascendental del viaje, su verdad poética" (Reyes, *Retratos*, 66) [it does not matter to us to know how far he really went in his trips. We have already finished the study of lies in Chateaubriand's America, of the biographical, practical lie. We lack the study of truth, the transcendental truth of the journey, its poetic truth]. What is important, then, is to capture a poetic truth that gives a transcendental sense to existence. In this way, biography is no longer restricted to portraying a particular individual but, rather, the surroundings of an era through the history of a life. These biographies, as Parra Triana suggests: "parten del efecto metonímico de perseguir en un nombre particular los efectos de largo alcance histórico de sus acciones" (Parra Triana, 227) [they depart from the metonymical effect of pursuing through a particular individual the long-range historical effects of one's action].

Reyes's work, instead, seems to have as its objective satirizing certain past events to reflect on the present, as well as analyzing the European and Hispanic cultural imaginaries. By imitating the biographical genre, Reyes opens a space of corruption and textual transformation between his writing and historical writing, connecting parody to the serio-comical and carnivalesque genres, and, even more specifically, to Menippean satire, according to the way in which Bakhtin theorized it:

> Real-life figures from various eras of the historic past and living contemporaries jostle one another in a most familiar way. In the Menippean satire, the unfettered and fantastic plots and situations all serve one goal—to put to the test and to expose ideas and ideologues. [It] is dialogic, full of parodies and travesties, multi-styled, and does not fear elements of bilingualism [and] can expand into a huge picture, offering a realistic reflection of the socially varied and heteroglot world of contemporary life. (Bakhtin, *Rabelais and His World*, 43)

There is a pertinent connection between Bolaño's work and Reyes with regard to historical analysis. Both authors recognize in their work, through certain characters, historical events that reflect long-range effects. In Bolaño, the exploration of certain effects of these events on culture and the American way of being is disseminated through the text. The force of repetition creates a series of internal resonances in his work that make it singular. The excessive use of this procedure exemplifies an era in which culture, or the understanding of an idealized "American being," has reached the climax of its crisis and is headed for its dissolution. The conjunction of those tendencies results in a strategy in which certain historical events mold the chapters of *Nazi Literature*, coming together around the term "Nazi." This offers the opportunity to search for the long-range historical effects of Nazism around the name of Adolf Hitler, whose life crosses directly or indirectly with the lives of the writer-characters in this hybrid book. It is necessary to clarify that Nazism will be one of the themes that Bolaño is going to pursue throughout his literary creation. However, in this book, the resonance created around Hitler's name has the function of formally demonstrating the regenerative power of fascism, which is never completely extirpated. When we eliminate one of its instances, others reappear strengthened.[4] The opening chapter, "The Mendiluce Clan," exemplifies this resonance. In this chapter, Hitler appears as a character, finding himself in Europe with the family matriarch and her children in 1929. This encounter marks the life of the entire Mendiluce family, principally that of Luz, who has a photo with Hitler "enmarcada en un rico trabajo de plata labrada" (Bolaño, *La literatura nazi*, 29) [set in a richly worked silver frame] (Bolaño, *Nazi Literature*, 19).[5] Luz would give two different versions regarding this portrait: the little girl a few months old held by Hitler was successively "una huérfana, una sobrina de Hitler que había muerto a los diecisiete años mientras combatía en Berlín y ella" (Bolaño, *La literatura nazi*, 30) [an orphan, Hitler's niece who had died at 17 while he was fighting in Berlin and it was her] (Bolaño, *Nazi Literature*, 20). In general, when she recognizes reality, Luz digresses: "Hitler la había acunado y que aún en sueños, podía sentir sus brazos fuertes y el aliento cálido por encima de su cabeza, y que probablemente aquel había sido uno de los mejores momentos de su vida" (30) [She had been handled by the Führer. In dreams, she could still feel his strong arms and his warm breath on the top of her head. She said it had probably been one of the happiest moments of her life] (20). In other chapters, Hitler is mentioned, or his name is changed for another whose ideas align with the totalitarian regime or white supremacy. In this manner, to cite a few examples, while the character Pérez-Mason composes the acrostic "VIVA ADOLF HITLER" (65) [LONG LIVE HITLER] (55) in the first letters of each chapter of "Poor Man's Soup," the character González Carrera tries to recover the figure of Mussolini in a poem. To this end, "el poema era una reivindicación de los vilipendiados ejércitos del duce, del burlado valor italiano" (Bolaño, *La literatura nazi*, 72) [(he) vindicated Il Duce, vilified armies and the derided courage of the Italians]

(Bolaño, *Nazi Literature*, 62). Franco, on the other hand, is the figure whom the Mexican Irma Carrasco admires. Sometimes symbols are mentioned like "La suástica negra que Daniela Montecristo llevaba tatuada en la nalga izquierda" (Bolaño, *La literatura nazi*, 72) [the black swastika that [Daniela Montecristo] wore tattooed on her left buttock] (Bolaño, *Nazi Literature*, 62). Other times, the symbol is connected with biographical facts that coincide with those of Hitler. For example, the young Zubieta obtained the iron cross during his combats in World War II, on the side of the Nazi Army, and shared with the *Führer* the habit of preferring to hook up with older women when he was young. Gradually, Bolaño connects the leader of national socialism to the diverse forms of the mediocre and vile failed artist who populates the chapters of his book.

Thomas Mann is the first to observe the figure of the mediocre artist as that of the monster in his famous essay "Bruder Hitler" (1939), published initially in English by the magazine *Esquire*.[6] He reflects on Word War II as the encounter of two wills derived from the resentment of the mediocre individual who attributes the guilt for his frustrations to society. For the German writer, Hitler incarnates this prototype, whose losses are joined to that of the German nation obsessed by the thought of saving its honor, broken in World War I. Mann paints the artist in Hitler thus:

> For must I not, however much it hurts, regard the man as an artist-phenomenon? Mortifyingly enough, it is all there: the difficulty, the laziness, the pathetic formlessness in youth, the round peg in the square hole, the "whatever *do* you want?" The lazy, vegetating existence in the depths of a moral and mental bohemia; the fundamental arrogance which thinks itself too good for any sensible and honorable activity, on the ground of its vague intuition that it is reserved for something else. There is also present the insatiable craving for compensation, the urge to self-glorification, the restless dissatisfaction, the forgetfulness of past achievements, the swift abandonment of the prize once grasped, the emptiness and tedium, the sense of worthlessness so soon as there is nothing to do to take the world's breath away; . . . A brother—a rather unpleasant and mortifying brother. (*Esquire*, 31 and 132)

Mann concludes his essay by evaluating the vanguard arts as well as socio-political transformations, and even the notion of geniality itself, as great distortions of an era. The connection proposed between the reasoning that recognizes Hitler as both an artist and a brother cannot thus be taken seriously because it simultaneously expresses a scorn that casts a somber reflection on art and its contradictions.

Bolaño repeats the same position as Mann, employing irony as a combat weapon against mediocrity, understanding the latter as the source of resentment linked to Nazism. *Nazi Literature* constantly points to the narrator's disdain for the authors whose biographies he provides. This disdain takes different forms. Among them, two modalities connected to parody in *Nazi Literature* are repeated with great frequency: false praise and the separation between mediocre writers that Bolaño portrays and some of the real authors whom Bolaño himself admires, creating a hostility between them. There are numerous examples of this second form: For instance, the fictitious Nazi Pérez Mason is the enemy of Lezama Lima and Virgilio Piñera. Juan Mendiluce Thompson attacks Cortázar, Borges, Bioy Casares, Ernesto Sábato, and Leopoldo Marechal, among others, in the newspaper. Mateo Aguirre hates Alfonso Reyes. Amado Couto does not value Haroldo and Augusto de Campos or Osman Lins. Taking advantage of this last example, one can trace a parallel between the mediocre and infamous artist who, faced with the grandiosity of his own insignificance, does not manage to understand the limitations of his work and feels like the victim of an injustice, and the biography of Adolf Hitler, a common painter who sold his paintings on the Viennese streets through intermediaries. Amado Couto, collaborator in the monstrosities perpetrated by the Brazilian military dictatorship, while thinking about the destiny of literature in his country and how to innovate it, asks himself: "¿Por qué publicaban a Osman Lins y no sus cuentos?" (*La literatura nazi*, 126) [Why did they publish Osman Lins, and not Couto's stories?] (*Nazi Literature*, 116).

This technique of composition in which Hitler successively appears as a character and leader of a group of writers is accompanied by the launching of a random tableau of parallels in biographical sketches, transfigured into diverse symbols of Nazism which are finally connected to the figure of the mediocre artist. This allows for a perturbing dissemination of the figure of the German Nazi leader. Such dissemination is represented in the simulated games of war to whose creation Sibelius dedicates himself in the chapter "Magicians, Mercenaries, and Miserable Creatures," as does Wieder of Bolaño's novel *Distant Star* (1996), a recreation of Ramírez Hoffman, protagonist of the last chapter of *Nazi Literature*. This outline, assembling the similarities between the affirmations of Mann and the imaginary portraits of the mediocre failed and infamous artists, proposes an amplification of the question of the German writer formalized thus: since art brings with it its own contradictions, always reflecting its opposite, which is displaced in the shadow in a specular game—that is, since art in its contradictions and in its internal play always exhibits the possibility of transformation, deformation, or simulacrum, would parody and similar genres not be inherent to artistic manifestation itself? If this were so, then *Nazi Literature* would be a compilation of frustrated writers who, nonetheless, do not abandon literature—"una propuesta seria y criminal" (Bolaño, *La literatura nazi*, 105) [a serious criminal proposal] (Bolaño, *Nazi Literature*, 94)—and, on the contrary, submerge themselves into it. Evidently, the focus on the relationship of the artist to his production amplifies the questions previously proposed on two fronts. On one hand, it makes us return to the theme of a contemporary aesthetic of parody, putting into prominence its auto-referential situation as an artistic exercise consciously overturned on itself, as it reveals its paradox to us. In other words, upon reflecting a fundamentally mimetic aspect of art whose selected option is to mirror itself, parody is transformed into a symptom of a historical process and into a form of its own critical analysis. To put it differently, focused now specifically on the book on which I comment here, one verifies that the self-absorption of art, instead of delving into introspection, externalizes itself in parodic criticism of historical events and of the history of literature with its literary figures. On the other hand, the dissemination of the figure of Hitler and the presence of various symbols of Nazism associated with the games of war, and the very structure of the book itself, "un compendio de maldad absoluta o banal que deviene aventuras de existencias frustradas, fragmentos de quien a través de la escritura se extravía de sí mismo" (González, 142) [A compendium of absolute or banal evil that becomes adventures of frustrated existences, fragments of he who loses himself through writing], brings us to the configuration of the artist as an infamous subject who utilizes his writing as a reflection of what he is or that which he desires to be.

Let us return to the ambiguity that the order of the genealogy of *Nazi Literature* establishes. On first reading, it seems to insist upon the association between Reyes and Borges, as well as to suggest a greater proximity between Wilcock's *The Temple of Iconoclasts* (1972) and *Nazi Literature*. Thus, the similarities between *A Universal History of Infamy* and the book by Bolaño would be filtered through Wilcock's book.

We have already seen that Bolaño seeks to connect his writing to that of Alfonso Reyes by shifting Reyes' work toward that of Borges. Wilcock acts the same way toward Borges. For this reason, in the previously cited interview, moments before offering us the genealogy of *Nazi Literature*, Bolaño, when referring to the Argentine Vanguard affirms: "for me, what's important is Borges" (Bolaño, *Bolaño por sí mismo*, 42). For Bolaño, all roads lead to Borges. Upon ideally constructing a center through a genealogy revelatory of the inspirations of his work, Bolaño privileges the writing of a very peculiar type of parody, promoted by the encounter of diverse approaches on this aleatory point of imaginary biography. As we have seen, the imaginary biography is based on art, on the imagination, on the irregular and unusual, imitating a specific genre. This type of biography—which as soon as it imitates cannot help but parody— argues, transgresses, transforms, and deforms the perception of historical events because it situates itself precisely on this borderline where the limits between reality and fiction disappear. Another hidden history is gradually inscribing itself there, implicit, unfinished, unknown. However, upon revealing its ignominies through a parodic and transformative art, this history contaminated by fiction shows us that it is no different than a historiography that has been socially constructed to attend to the interests of the powerful; neither does it influence our everyday life less. In other words, what Reyes, Borges, Wilcock, and Bolaño do in distinct ways, each transforming the sub-genre of biography differently, could be interpreted as a parody of history when history is understood as what Genette has called "quantitative transposition." I am referring to the capacity to reduce and augment that the parody of historiographical biographies allows for, permitting the omission of certain historical circumstances and emphasizing others, to which it adds details that provoke interruptions in certain historical events in order to magnify them. I am also referring to what Sklodowska called "dinamismo histórico del género novelístico" [historical dynamism of the novelistic genre], alluding to Bakhtin's theory and St. Pierre's concept that connects parody to a "práctica en la cual la historia está explícitamente inscrita" (Sklodowska, 15) [practice in which history is explicitly inscribed].

By conferring on Borges the central place in this practice of inscribing history in parody, Bolaño indirectly recognizes Borges' preponderant role in the transformation of the genre of imagined biographies in Spanish America. Jenckes' *Reading Borges after Benjamin* contributes to this vision of *A Universal History of Infamy*. Jenckes relates Borges's book to Benjamin's definition of allegory, recognizing that "*A Universal History of Infamy* is a book about history itself. The stories take up something that we might call national allegory and allegorize it, parodically and paradoxically telling a history that by its very nature cannot be told, that is *infame*" (68). Jenckes plays here with the double meaning of the word "infame" as both unknown and vile, something that, in any case, traditionally does not deserve to be told because it is insignificant or common. Following the outline of literary genealogy into which Bolaño wishes to insert himself, as well as the connection of his writing with history, one can suggest that Bolaño owes the critical analysis of the socio-political consequences of certain events in certain historical eras to Reyes, and to Borges the inability to speak of certain events, the impossibility of describing with words, and the lack of fidelity to which everything that depends on words is subjected.

In the prologue to *A Universal History of Infamy*, Borges, following Schwob's example, notes the directions that he has followed in elaborating his imaginary biographies. As Bolaño would later do, Borges attributes a literary tradition to himself and clarifies that his tales are the fruit of rereadings of Stevenson and Chesterton, "y aun de los primeros films de von Sternberg y tal vez de cierta biografía de Evaristo Carriego" (Borges, *Cuentos Completos*, 9) [and also from Sternberg's early films, and perhaps from a certain biography of Evaristo Carriego] (Borges, *A Universal History of Infamy*, 13). Borges alludes surreptitiously to Schwob when he mentions one of his principles: "la reducción de la vida entera de un hombre a dos o tres escenas (Borges, *Cuentos completos*, 9) [paring down a man's whole life to two or three scenes] (Borges, *A Universal History of Infamy*, 13), to which he adds the abuse of "enumeraciones dispares y la brusca solución de continuidad" (Borges, *Cuentos Completos*, 9) [random enumerations [and] sudden shifts of continuity] (Borges, *A Universal History of Infamy*, 13)]. Referring to the tales from the section "Etcétera," he mentions the possible superiority of reading in relation to writing since the former "es más resignada, más civil, más intelectual" (Borges, *A Universal History of Infamy*, 13) [is more modest, more unobtrusive, more intellectual] (Borges, *A Universal History of Infamy*, 13). This Borgesian inversion seems to favor the activities and literary genres considered "minor," such as parody and translation through an opportunistic and parasitic reading that feeds on writing. Thus, from very early on, even before the emergence of Pierre Menard, a principle in which authorship is diluted in favor of reading or critical rereading is conferred upon the Borgesian literary task. In the "Prólogo de le edición de 1954" [Prologue to the 1954 Edition], the Argentine writer directs himself more specifically to satirical parody, citing Bernard Shaw, who declares that "all intellectual labor is humoristic" (11), and reinforcing at the same time "menardismo" [Menardism],[7] since he defines his tales as "juego de un tímido que no se animó a escribir cuentos y que se distrajo en falsear y tergiversar ajenas historias (*Cuentos completos*, 11) [the game of a shy young man who dared not write stories and so amused himself by falsifying and distorting the tales of others] (*A Universal History of Infamy*, 12). In addition to writing in the mode of Pierre Menard, Bolaño recovers other Borgesian procedures in his work, such as:

1. The mixture of reality and fiction used as material that feeds literature since language fictionalizes everything, including the author himself when he participates in his narrations as a character;
2. The citation of apocryphal works and authors;
3. The production of literary essays on works that were never written; and
4. Literature as theme and motive of existence of his own fiction.

One of the principal legacies of *A Universal History of Infamy* to *Nazi Literature* is the exploration of the American space as the site of an epic that is different from traditional epic. Some critics, such as Margo Glantz and Marta Gallo, have indicated a relationship between Borges's book and the epic genre. Glantz explores the cinematographic character of Borges' book, while Gallo searches for the meaning of the incidence of this genre in Borges' work. Gallo concludes that the modern heroes of *A Universal History of Infamy*, in contrast to the classics, "establecen un antagonismo con su entorno y al romperse la armonía propia del mundo épico, afirman el coraje ya no en función de una comunidad sino como acto gratuito" (Gallo, 99) [establish an antagonism with their surroundings and upon breaking the harmony proper to the epic world, affirm courage no longer in function of a community but rather as a gratuitous act]. Undoubtedly, there is an impulse toward epic present in all of the tales of the book discussed here, and, in an ostensible way, in the stories that deal with the United States: "The Dread Redeemer Lazarus Morell," "Monk Eastman, Purveyor of Iniquities," "The Disinterested Killer, Bill Harrigan," and "Streetcorner Man," where, in a species of distorted mirage, "The History of Old Time Argentine Underworld" reflects "The History of New York Old Underworld" (*A Universal History of Infamy*, 51).

I would like to dwell on Gallo's proposition that the rupture of harmony in the epic world appears to result from the antagonism between the hero and his world. She suggests that this break is produced by the impossibility of conceiving a non-parodic epic story in the modern world, even if it is serious, as in the case of Joyce's *Ulysses*. Borges, in turn, desires to elaborate a comic parody. It is necessary to recall that these tales from *A Universal History of Infamy* were originally published separately in the newspaper *Crítica* and were designed as Saturday entertainment for a middle-class public (Calvi, 19–21). In this parody, the Borgesian epic hero, mixture of a model that runs the gamut from Hollywood cinema to the recovery of the Gaucho tradition, breaks down faced with the irony that not only separates him from society, but also disarticulates him from life. The epic heroes of most of the stories from *A Universal History of Infamy*, particularly those tales that unfold on North American soil, live in limitless and senseless violence that precedes a banal death whether it is in a hospital bed like Lazarus Morell, or via an anonymous assassination, like Monk Eastman, or by being brought to justice as an enemy of the community, like Bill Harrigan. Those non-heroic deaths are ironically inconsistent with their lives that conferred fame upon them, although the fame was due to illegal or dishonorable actions. The heroes of these parodic epics are thus doubly infamous. They were infamous in their lives, because they were transformed into villains (the first sense of *infame* as vile), and, in their death, they were infamous according to the second meaning of the word, because they became unknown.

Seven tales from *Nazi Literature* take place in the United States and share with Borges's tales the sensation of continuous movement, perceived by the shifting of the masses, or by the travel of the protagonist, in the immense American space. This characteristic connects them to the epic genre since, in general, the protagonists of both Borges's book and Bolaño's book travel. Curiously, among the exceptions to this principle in *Nazi Literature* are two North American authors discussed in the chapter "The Aryan Brotherhood": the so-called Thomas R. Murchison and John Lee Brook spend the greater part of their lives in jail, sharing delinquency and racism with Borges's characters. The latter characteristic belongs to the North American characters whom Borges recreates and, of course, to all the characters in *Nazi Literature*. One can thus say that *Nazi Literature* inherits a special specificity from *A Universal History of Infamy*, whose reality is American, if we consider that, in general, the tales by Borges that possess the most concrete space and time are located on the American continent, in contrast to those dealing with generic abstractions or philosophical inquiry which are independent of the spatial-temporal axis. To the North American tales, we should add "Tom Castro, the Implausible Impostor," who spends a good part of his life in Chile, and the already cited "Streetcorner Man" that portrays the underworld of Buenos Aires.

At the same time, Bolaño owes to Wilcock's *The Temple of Iconoclasts* a formal and political specificity. While Bolaño approaches the world of the ultra-right to caricature the job of writing, Wilcock expands his parody to the arts, science, and technology. Both arrive at a critical parody of Nazism and neo-Nazism, through the dissemination of the figure of Adolf Hitler. Many times, they portray that which is strange, as Darío had done in the nineteenth century,[8] in order to see a glimmer of evil situated sometimes between madness and art or science. One observes in Wilcock's book a connection to Lyotard's critique of the authoritative value of all metanarratives (e.g. philosophy, science, history) that characterizes postmodernity (Lyotard, *The Postmodern Condition*, 34–35). The very title of the work (*The Temple of the Iconclasts*) establishes from the beginning a parodic relationship with history. On the one hand, it recalls the spreading and acceptance of positivism. I am referring to the creation of the "Religion of Humanity" based on Comte's doctrine.[9] It is worth noting the special resonance that such a doctrine acquires in Latin America with the foundation of some secular temples in Brazil and Chile. On the other hand, the term "synagogue," derived from the verb "to congregate" and employed in Wilcock's book with the sense of convoking a meeting, at the same time, is strongly associated with the Jewish faith, a specific religious affiliation. In Wilcock's book, the term "synagogue" ironically groups together the strange ones, the mad ones, and, by opposition, those who are not Jewish, and, frequently, are identified with anti-Semitic associations represented principally by the Nazis in the most varied images.

One of Bolaño's tales dedicated to North American writers is "Harry Sibelius," the author of a monumental historical novel who rescues the forces of the Axis Powers and displaces them to the United States. Among the tale's principal characteristics, the technique of "writing with the phantom of Pierre Menard" stands out, as Bolaño noted in the pro-logue to *Distant Star*, mentioned in a veiled way in this segment. I also associate this tale with the story from Wilcock's *The Temple of Iconoclasts*, "Aaron Rosenblum." Wilcock, in his text, leaves open questions related to the utilization of certain strategies that are associated with the expres-sion of totalitarian tendencies, such as the adoption of an apocalyptic dis-course at the service of a regenerating utopia, as well as the problem of the conceptualization of the forms of contemporary evil. Such tendencies constitute the center of Bolaño's explorations in *Nazi Literature*. In each chapter, a series of generic configurations and of authors associated with fascist ideology is proposed. Moreover, any form of comprehension or plausible explanation of infamy in its diverse forms is also rejected.

In "Harry Sibelius," Bolaño explores the themes of the science fic-tion genre, intercalating them into an exploration of the forms of evil repeated throughout the tale. When we read the texts by Bolaño and Wilcock, we observe that that of Sibelius adds new perspectives to "Aaron Rosenblum." The most important elements delineated are the following:

1. The writing of Sibelius' novel was motivated by the work of two North American authors of science fiction, Norman Spinrad and Philip K. Dick, as well as by a story by Borges;
2. The novel is the black mirror of *Hitler's Europe* by the British his-torian Arnold J. Toynbee;
3. The title of Sibelius' book is *The True Son of Job*, and its prologue repeats the title of the prologue by Toynbee, "The Elusiveness of History";
4. Sibelius' tales are the fruit of chance and reach their narrative cul-mination when they are superimposed on the bureaucratic machine described with perfection; and
5. After publishing his novel, Sibelius retires from the literary cir-cuit only to reappear in the publications of the magazines on war games, writing articles and designing some games.

Philip K. Dick (1928–1982) wrote *The Man in the High Castle* (1962), an alternative vision of the future, had the Nazis won World War II, which presents in its plot another alternative novel, *The Grasshopper Lies Heavy*. In that fictitious novel, President Roosevelt was not assassi-nated in 1933, which is the historical point of reference in *The Man in the High Castle*, and the United States conquered Germany and Japan. The mirage of history in its double sense—the unfolding of reality and in the novel—is diversified, succeeding in parodying literary criticism when, for example, in the seventh chapter a sophisticated Japanese couple, the Kasouras, begin a discussion about the novel *The Grasshopper Lies Heavy*, considering whether it would fit within the science fiction genre. The difficult apprehension of history and reality breaks with a supposed linear time, thus creating a constant possibility of reversibility, since the novel is situated in the present (1962). In addition, it often creates the impression of alternation between the losers and winners, which favors a schizophrenic structure that gradually occupies its space. To this, one can add the paranoia typical of a society dominated by strong structures of power.

Dick is one of the writers of science fiction most admired by Roberto Bolaño. In the prologue to *El espíritu de la ciencia-ficción* (2016) [*The Spirit of Science Fiction*], written in 1984, Christopher Domínguez Michael affirms that science fiction contains an ethical element for Bolaño, "la búsqueda invertida de un tiempo perdido [siguiendo a Ursula K. Le Guin y Philip K. Dick, quienes] moralizaron el futuro como una extensión catastrófica del siglo XX" (11) [the inverted search for a lost time (following Ursula K. Le Guin and Philip K. Dick, who) moralized the future as a catastrophic extension of the twentieth century]. Such moralization supposes a state of alert to the dangers of fascism and its splinter groups after World War II in order to combat a modernity that values these tendencies. This preoccupation crosses all of Bolaño's work and reverberates in the text here commented upon, justifying the inclusion of the two U.S. writers in its first line. Sibelius' novel is presented as the mirror of Dick's work, sometimes even insinuating itself as its parody since both share not only an essential part of the plot, but also the complexity of the narration with its multiple characters and the crossing of plots, as well as the incorporation of elements and characters from U.S. pop culture.

The fundamental difference between the two works is ideological, since Bolaño's apocryphal novelist seems to believe in a fascist victory, while Philip Dick denounces the horrors of Hitler's government. In artistic terms, this difference is established in the opposition between the writer who knows how to manipulate with schizophrenic language to denounce the excesses of real and bureaucratic society through the fictitious world, and the writer who does not know how to act in a manner distanced from the institutions of control. Here, an ideological fragmentation is revealed, created as much by neoliberalism as by the political discourse of the Left in Latin America at the end of the twentieth century and which corrupts the role of the intellectual. In this corruption, the intellectual is placed at the service of the consecration of technocratic models, or at the service of the exaltation and almost sanctification of the figure of the *caudillo* (leader). The parody of the discourse of literary criticism is joined to this depravation of the writer in phrases such as this: "Su fuerte es la administración. Pero cuando sus personajes [e] historias invaden y se superponen a la maquinaria burocrática que con tanto esfuerzo ha levantado es cuando alcanza sus más altas cotas narrativas" (*La literatura nazi*, 134) [Administration is his strength. But it is only when his characters and stories infiltrate and overrun the painstakingly assembled bureaucratic machinery that he reaches the summit of his narrative art] (*Nazi Literature*, 123).

Another science fiction writer mentioned in Bolaño's tale is Norman Spinrad, who wrote *The Iron Dream* (1972), another alternate-history novel composed of three parts. The middle section deals with a novel titled *Lord of the Swastika* written by Adolf Hitler. The alternative history creates a Hitler who emigrated to the United States in 1919, after World War I, and who continues his career as a mediocre artist in this country, at first as an illustrator of science fiction books and, later, as an editor and writer of this same genre. Without Hitler's leadership, there was never an equivalent of World War II. However, the Soviet Union constituted itself as the great power that threatened the world and that took charge of the domination of Jews in Europe in Spinrad's world. In broad strokes, Spinrad's book, like the one by Bolaño, warns how science fiction and the literary institution can help to construct a society of Nazi ideology, since, in the case of *The Iron Dream*, a mediocre book such as *Lord of the Swastika* was acclaimed by the public and by specialized criticism. Spinrad's book is constructed as a parody on various planes:

1. It is a parody of the autobiography of Hitler, as well as the exposition of the national-socialist ideology of *Mein Kampf* (1925–1926);
2. It is also presented as a parody of the language of criticism and of the literary institution that acclaims a mediocre work; and
3. It is constructed as a social satire as well, since beyond the horrendous historical crime that Hitler represents, American society is reproached for its fondness for war and its excessive yearning for power and wealth.

This concern for rethinking science fiction from an ethical position, noted in both novels commented upon here, is due to the malleability of the fascist ideology that science fiction presents, not because the writers of the genre spontaneously agree with this type of politics, but because, as Gomel postulates, science fiction "is the kind of narrative that results from the cross-fertilization of apocalypse and science" (129). Science fiction thus can share the seed of Nazi discourse, in other words, the indistinguishable mixture of narrative, science, and fantasy. From there arises the preoccupation of these great writers of science fiction to bring Nazism to the center of novels that present an alternative vision of reality, in order to demonstrate its horrors and injustices.

For Gomel, *The Iron Dream* as a parody of Hitler's autobiography absorbs Hitler's discourse reproducing "the total impersonality of Hitler's first-person voice [since both narratives] rather than focusing on the psyche of the protagonist... converge on the body of the antagonist" (Gomel, 134). Furthermore, this body possesses the mark of monstrosity since the Nazis saw the Jews as an inhuman species, as individuals barely masked as humans. In any case, what really attracts attention in *The Iron Dream* is not its allegorical character in relation to historical events regarding Hitler's rise to power and the war between races that broke out since then, but "the degree to which these events, insofar as they are shaped by Nazi ideology, correspond to the narrative framework of fantasy" (142).

Bolaño explores this relationship between Nazi ideology and fantasy in *Nazi Literature*. For instance, in *The True Son of Job*, the novel written by Harry Sibelius, a production of fantasy is enacted that distorts what is read through the fragmentation of various stories and of their alternation through a montage of these fragments in a new context. To put it another way, Sibelius' novel distorts not only Dick and Spinrad, but also a story by Borges, which, although barely mentioned, is structurally the black mirror of *Hitler's History*, written by Toynbee. The fictitious novel's introduction is called "The Elusiveness of History," exactly identical to Toynbee's prologue: "La frase de éste 'la visión del historiador está condicionada por su propia ubicación en el tiempo y en el espacio; y como el tiempo y el espacio están cambiando continuadamente, ninguna historia podrá ser nunca un relato permanente'" (*La literatura nazi*, 131) [The following sentence from Toyenbee expresses one of the pivotal themes of Sibelius's introductory text; "the historian's view is conditioned by his own location in time and place, and since time and place are continually changing, no History can ever be a permanent record that will tell the story"] (*Nazi Literature*, 121).

This reflection on history reminds us intentionally of another story, where the narrator interprets history as changing according to context, since Menard, writing identical sentences to those of Cervantes in the twentieth century, "no define la historia como indagación de la realidad sino como su origen. La verdad histórica para él no es lo que sucedió, es lo que juzgamos que sucedió" (*Cuentos completos*, 40) [does not define history as an investigation of reality, but as its origin. Historical truth, for him, is not what took place but what we think took place] (*Ficciones*, 52).

"Pierre Menard, Author of The Quixote" is the work by Borges that speaks of the power of contextualization through a block of space and time that alters meaning. In this way, the fragility of meaning and of our reasoning of reality is revealed. Through the paradox of context and spatial-temporal splitting—Menard writes an infinitely richer text than the original and, at the same time, it is identical to Cervantes' text—Borges alters ideas like that of fixed identity of an original text or author. In this way, he creates what Sarlo refers to as the "scandal of logic" and what Genette calls the "literary utopia" that could be summarized as an infinite identity of texts and writers. In other words, each author is a single writer, each text is a unique text, and, at the same time, all texts are infinitely re-inscribed. However, as Sarlo explains to us, "all texts are read against a cultural background which forms the fleeting course of meaning into a historical pattern" (Borges, *A Writer on the Edge*, 32). The idea that meaning emerges from historical contextualization is precisely that which Roberto Bolaño hopes to explore in his text, although with diverse results. In contrast to Menard—who, by not adding anything, enriches the original text because the new spatial-temporal context perfects the original text on its own—Sibelius impoverishes it, confusing art and bureaucracy since "el novelista virginiano parece creer que en algún lugar 'del tiempo y del espacio' aquel crimen se ha asentado victorioso y procede a *inventariarlo*" (*La literatura nazi*, 131) [the Virginian novelist seems to believe that 'somewhere in time and space' the crime in question has definitively triumphed, so he proceeds to *catalogue it*] (*Nazi Literature*, 121, my emphasis).

Menard's technique, which could be summarized as a constant temporal recontextualization combined with variations of narrative perspective that infinitely multiply the connotative potential of a specific text, reappears, as López Calvo demonstrates, throughout the literary work of Roberto Bolaño. According to this critic, these almost identical paragraphs that Bolaño makes circulate among his novels and short stories confirm his intention of conferring a stylistic and narrative totality to his work, and suggest that "just as Menard rewrites Cervantes's work and Cervantes parodically rewrites the Spanish literary tradition in his masterpiece, Bolaño may be rewriting the denunciatory and liberationist Chilean Literature in exile" (López-Calvo, 44). The parodic rewriting to which Cervantes, Borges and Bolaño recur acquires political connotations in any case, revalidating the connection between parody and ideology. In this sense, amplifying the criticism of Chilean literature in exile, O'Bryen recognizes a restoration of political values in the rewriting of the last chapter of *Nazi Literature*, "Ramírez Hoffman, el infame" [Ramírez Hoffman, the Infamous One], which was eventually transformed into Bolaño's novel *Distant Star*. For O'Bryen, writing with the phantom of Pierre Menard, as Bolaño suggests in the prologue to his novel, shows:

1. The capacity of literature to transform itself into an instrument of violence;
2. The necessity of rethinking the ties between vanguards and neo-vanguards to political authorities in light of the lack of determination of literature; and
3. The complicity of literature with dictatorship and its neoliberal legacy, understood within the double failure of the armed struggle and revolutionary forms of writing.

By appealing to the doubles, twins, and heteronyms that Menard-like writing provokes, Bolaño rethinks ethical political questions such as responsibility and justice (O'Bryen, *Roberto Bolaño, A Less Distant Star*, 24–28).

It is necessary to underscore the differences between the last episode of *Nazi Literature*, and the critical and parodic direction alluding to the relationships between the vanguards and totalitarian regimes, into which the works analyzed here—"Harry Sibelius," as well as the majority of texts of *Nazi Literature in the Americas* and *The Temple of Iconoclasts*—insert themselves. Historically, the most famous case is that of Marinetti, leader of Italian futurism and fascism. Wilcock, throughout the tale

"Llorenç Riber," confronts us with another case of the representative French vanguard polemic, the dramatist, movie director, writer, poet, musician, and designer Jean Cocteau, who came to be seduced by the Nazi regime and by the figure of Adolf Hitler. Various signs of plays and montages suggested in "Llorenç Riber," and of course, parodically modified, leave clues that lead us to the figure of the French artist. Among them, the most notorious is the cinematographic screenplay *Tristan and Isolde*, a mocking reference to Cocteau's screenplay *The Eternal Return* (1943), an adaptation of the classic *Tristan and Isolde*. On the other hand, the greater part of the writers of *Nazi Literature* belong to the historical era of the vanguards and neo-vanguards in Latin America, which does not mean that they all belong to these artistic movements. Thus, like Wilcock, in various of the imaginary biographies created by Bolaño, the fictitious author is connected to one or more real writers by common traits between the real and the apocryphal works. A parodic example is Sibelius' biography, which we have just discussed.

Another question, which is outside the scope of parody, is the specific criticism that Bolaño makes of the Chilean neo-vanguard and its impotence faced with the evils generated by totalitarianism. This is specifically found in the last chapter of *Nazi Literature*. Critics such as O'Bryen and Jenckes, among others, observe that Bolaño anticipates Thayer in rejecting the idea that the Chilean neo-vanguard has altered or perturbed the repressive discourse of dictatorship "since in [Thayer's] view the military regime executed a rupture that effectively absorbed or deflected any other form of rupture" (Jenckes, *Witnessing Beyond the Human*, 64). This observation helps us to better understand why a Nazi poet and pilot composed poems in the skies of Chile in the last chapter of *Nazi Literature* as poet Raúl Zurita had done in the skies of New York. Bolaño seeks to show the uselessness of the act, since any aesthetic radicalism can be surpassed with advantage by an ultra-right-wing psychopath supported by the military regime, or, as O'Bryen explains: "Wilder's [Ramírez's] acts point to uncanny specularity between CADA's [Colectivo de Acciones de Arte (Collective of Art Actions)] avant-garde 'insubordination of the sign' and the fascist state 'avant-garde' anti-institutionalism" (27).[10]

The final episode of Bolaño's book is complex and difficult to classify. Because of its length, it distances itself from imaginary biography and it does not clearly present the characteristics of a parody either.

The exhibition of mutilated bodies of dead women has more to do with "The Part of the Bodies" of Bolaño's novel *2666* than with any other text of *Nazi Literature*, where the anachronism of the literary system is parodied. For example, these other sections parody the language of dictionaries of authors, which portrays a change in the socio-political system. In this system, fascism, although it infiltrates beneath the surface, is no longer dominant, ceding space for its criticism. The same is true for Wilcock's texts. Parody in Borges is explained by the space Borges occupied in Argentine literature, inserted between Gaucho literature and Europeanism. Borges denounces through parody the anachronism of the literary system using quotations, pastiches, translations, and cultural allusions, among other techniques (Piglia, 63–64).

We have already seen how "Harry Sibelius" adopts techniques resulting in writing according to the model of Menard. Wilcock's "Aaron Rosenblum" is connected to Bolaño's tale to form a criticism that encompasses the historic, ideological and aesthetic. Although this last aspect may seem explicit in Bolaño's story, reading both stories in conjunction shows that a neo-Nazi ideology survives, which aesthetically contradicts the more elitist vanguard aesthetics to achieve postmodern artistic manifestations of a more popular character. If, today, it is no longer so certain that neo-Nazism has been aborted, as recent events show us, what does seem correct is that this current has subsisted thanks to popular mythology and the kingdom of the imaginary.

At this point Wilcock's story is instrumental, as is the study by Elana Gomel upon which we have already commented. Gomel explains the permanence of fascism in popular North American literature and cinema through the science fiction genre, demonstrating the presence within Nazi narrative of the same motives indicated by Wilcock and Bolaño in their texts: utopia and apocalypse. Gomel alerts us to the risk that these stories have cast aside: "political clout, neo-Nazism has at its disposal only stories. But these stories are still powerful enough to send a gun-toting loner on a rampage of killing, or insidiously, to sway an electorate. This power must be accounted for" (Gomel, 128). The two writers warn us of these same dangers in an ironic manner, or through an exhaustive redoubling of parody.

In the narrative of Nazism, all apocalyptic phenomena are presented as the paradoxical junction of dual aspects: end and rebeginning, destruction and restoration, extreme suffering and ecstasy. One could then speak of a utopia of Apocalypse that seeks the regeneration of humanity or the recovery of paradise, causing it, first, all evil in order to later "purify it." Enumerating these evils, Wilcock begins the writing of "Aaron Rosenblum":

> Los utopistas no reparan en medios; con tal de hacer feliz al hombre están dispuestos a matarle, torturarle, incinerarle, exilarle, esterilizarle, descuartizarle, lobotomizarle, eloctrocutarle, enviarle a la guerra, bombardearle, etcétera: depende del plan. Reconforta pensar que incluso sin plan, los hombres están y siempre estarán dispuestos a matar, torturar, incinerar, exilar, esterilizar, descuartizar, bombardear, etcétera (Wilcock, *La sinagoga de los iconoclastas*, 23)

> [Utopians are heedless of methods. To render the human species happy, they are prepared to subject it to murder, torture, incineration, exile, sterilization, dismemberment, lobotomy, electrocution, military invasion, bombing, etc. Everything depends on the project. Somehow, it is encouraging to think that even in the absence of a project, men are and always will be prepared to murder, torture, sterilize, quarter, bomb, etc.]. (Wilcock, *The Temple of Iconoclasts*, 27)

This notion of the "utopia of Apocalpyse" is reiterated in the text, in diverse ways, constituting a basis for the conduct of two illustrious Utopians. One Utopian in Wilcock's story is fictional, and his utopia "was unfortunate. The book destined to bring him fame. *Back to Happiness or Joyride to Hell* appeared in 1940, precisely when the intellectual world was busily engaged in defending itself from another, equally utopian project of social reform—total reform" (Wilcock, 27–28). The other "Utopian" is Adolf Hitler. The real character interacts with the fictitious one. On one hand, Hitler seemed to facilitate part of Rosenblum's project of returning England to the sixteenth century, with regard to the elimination of a large part of humanity. On the other hand, the two protagonists differed in some guidelines about their respective plans: while Hitler aspired to suppress the Jews, his English brother proposed other more subtle, sophisticated, and diversified priorities with the same end of extermination, such as the containment of the Turks, the organization of tournaments, the diffusion of syphilis, or the exacerbation of religious disputes. In any case, the plans of the two were based on "the progressive rarefaction of the present" (24 and 30) in order to return to the Elizabethan world of Shakespearean drama, or the Volkish utopia of the eighteenth century, based on nationalism and racism, reflected in the genre of the popular novel.

If Wilcock creates an English double of Hitler, Bolaño achieves the madness of creating Max Mirabelais in another one of his imaginary biographies: "el Pessoa bizarro del Caribe" (Bolaño, *La literatura nazi*, 140) [the Caribbean's bizarre answer to Pessoa] (Bolaño, *Nazi Literature*, 130)—a Haitian bard who simultaneously sings the praises of the magnitude of the Aryan race and the expression of negritude. In all of these cases, the issue is not the proclivity of a certain ethnicity to commit acts of cruelty. The problem that these writers posit upon proposing the theme of fascism centered around the figure of Hitler and his admirers is not that the Germans executed genocide because they are cold and inhuman but, rather, that any human being stimulated by certain ideologies can commit atrocities of this magnitude. This type of multiplication allied to repetition in the history of humanity, of the great crimes committed by this or that socio-political institution in the past, its repetition in the present, and its return in the future, is structured as the backdrop upon which Wilcock organizes his text. In other words, through the repetition of historical events, the almost infallible prediction of the return of the human atrocities that are enumerated in the first paragraph of "Aaron Rosenblum" is assured.

Temporally, from a present situated during World War II, one returns to the Renaissance and concomitantly advances toward a future populated by a terror that heralds biological or chemical wars (through the propagation of processes of contamination), as well as the employment of other subtle techniques of domination, which take advantage of human passions such as racism, sports, and religion. In this way, the presence of the figure of Hitler and his double in the narration forces us to emphasize the twentieth century as the privileged temporal frame of the cruelties mentioned at the beginning of the text, although it is not the only one. We might thus think of Guernica, genocide, the Soviet gulags, Hiroshima and Nagasaki, the Chinese Cultural Revolution, and the Dirty War in the countries of the Southern Cone of America to enumerate some of the somber episodes of recent history. The tactic employed by Wilcock—that of ostensible repetition of content and form—emphasizes the cyclical return of such atrocities, encompassing the past as well as the future, to situate us in the center of the problem upon which the text constructs itself.

In its totality, "Aaron Rosenblum" reflects on the difference between current forms of evil on two dimensions. The first relates forms of evil to ancient forms, the second to current ones. On the one hand, it becomes very difficult to compare institutions such as the Inquisition, slavery, and torture with the generalized surveillance of all sectors of life, the division of labor, and torture that takes place in modern societies, just to cite a few examples. On the other hand, all political systems of the twentieth century—Nazism, Communism, liberal democracy—were involved in cases of mass extermination. However, one cannot affirm that those crimes were equivalent. A common element that seems to act as a distinction between past and present forms of evil, as well as an equalizer in the cases of mass extermination during World War II, is the technological development that made possible a degree of destruction never before achieved or imagined. With regard to the first dimension of this difference, which contrasts the forms of contemporary evil to others past, various philosophers admit that there is a similarity between them. That is, basically, the totalitarian regimes of the past century did not invent but, rather, adapted already existing cruelties, making them more sophisticated through technology to create more terror.

In *The Origins of Totalitarianism*, Arendt explains that, upon constituting new forms of domination, totalitarian structure transcends the principle of nihilism based on the formula that "everything is permitted" in order to create another until then unknown principle, that postulates that "everything is possible," even that which surpasses reality. This disassociation between the real and the possible to which philosophy refers, although indirectly, when questioning the meaning of the concept of assassination in the face of the mass production of cadavers, has to do with technological development, which permits the death of millions within a very short time. Here, we have already entered the sphere of difference that contemporary forms of evil establish among themselves, adding to technology other methods whose objective is the destruction of the spirit, the psyche, and the character of the victim. Among them stand out the creation of patrols comprised of Jewish prisoners responsible for the execution of their companions (the *Sonderkommando*) and the total domination of chance, reigning absolute over all human actions (*Origins of Totalitarianism*, 345–346).

Upon connecting the repetition of forms of evil to the figure of Hitler, who is associated with the incarnation of ignominy *par excellence*, Wilcock explores in his text an aporia that joins that which we do not dare express with that of which we cannot conceive. Such an aporia is related to experimentation with military artifacts, because the possibility of the repetition of a war is the equivalent of the danger of destruction of life on the planet through new nuclear arms. The great wars of the twentieth century created this technological terror. However, the atrocity that the figure of Hitler evokes is Auschwitz as the representation of forms of contemporary evil because, as Neiman explains, it makes unviable any possibility of an intellectual answer in the sense that the tools of civilization could not impede or prevent it (*Evil in Modern Thought*, 256). The industrialization of the concentration camps is connected to the technical implementation of the forms of contemporary evil and their capacity for mass destruction. An example of this powerful infernal machine in action is offered by Didi-Huberman when he records that "In the summer 1944, 435,000 Hungarian Jews were deported to Auschwitz between May 15 and July 8. In a single day 24,000 Hungarian Jews were exterminated" (*Images in Spite of All*, 7).

The irony that closes Wilcock's text proposes a terrifying inversion after Rosenblum is killed by an aerial attack by the German army. The narrator explains Rosenblum's plans to eliminate a considerable part of the English population and return to the sixteenth century, and that these plans are being executed meticulously by Hitler, the other Utopian, warning that if "La utopía de Hitler ha caído en descrédito. La de Rosenblum, en cambio, reaparece periódicamente, bajo disfraces diferentes" (26) [Hitler's utopia, meanwhile, fell into extreme discredit. Rosenblum's, in contrast, resurfaces periodically in different guises] (31). The title of the book by Harry Sibelius, *The True Son of Job*, highlights the same theme of evil in modern times, contrasting it, ironically, with the beliefs of the past. The story of the biblical character refers paradigmatically to reflections about the origins of evil, a concern that is connected to the works we discussed in this section, although, contrary to what is usual, this problem is treated with irreverence and humor, albeit black humor. When mentioning a work that narrates Hitler's victory in World War II and his subsequent domination of the United States referred to as a descendance of Job, the justification of extreme suffering is vindicated (the discourse of the friends of Job), the irrevocable separation of virtue and happiness, virtue being the only recompense for itself. The biblical figure also evokes a necessity to confront and understand evil in the world without falling into desperation (Job's discourse). Finally, being a descendant of Job implies becoming aware that the human condition is governed by chance, especially in totalitarian regimes where the abuses of power disseminate moral evil leading the human being to abandonment. Harry Sibelius, the author of the book, in turn, is a mere office worker occupied in describing the functioning of the administration, a bureaucrat. Sibelius echoes the copyist, the translator, the plagiarist, in recycling already explored materials, producing minor texts and a second-hand literature. In sum, he is a throwback to producers of a minor literature such as Menard and to the idiotized geniuses that populate Borges' literature.

Oscillating the pendulum between different degrees of infamy, the followers of Schwob in Latin America seek the apprehension of the unique in different ways, selecting the most representative individuals, among the available human material, according to their intentions. What we notice in the creative diversity presented in biographical style refers, rather, to a variety of tones, styles, and genres associated with parody that resist any fixed form of classification. Parody denounces anachronisms at the same time that it accompanies the changes in social and ideological conditions. Parody also heralds a critical vision of literature and reality that many times breaks limits and confuses spheres. In this way, each of these writers adapts his own production—according to his particular aesthetic and ideological aspirations, variable in time—to various ideas. Borges created his work based on the power of language to alter reality, turning his surroundings into fiction, including the idea of the author and the reader, as well as basing himself on the permeability of texts. His parodic instruments mainly derive from taking the lack of harmony between thought and reality, or the mistakes and exaggerations of logic, to their final consequences. Wilcock transforms parody into an instrument equivalent to dissonance, re-duplicating it, in order to denounce the crisis of his era. Bolaño turns it into skepticism of reality, of literature, of any power that has the ability to change reality.

If, as Borges proposes, texts communicate among themselves, or one is always re-writing the same text, perhaps every literary text is already a parody of another text. Humoristic parody is an intellectual labor. Laughter induces us to think, as Benjamin himself proposes when he interprets *Brecht*'s epic theater.[11] However, as Borges himself warns us, one always runs the risk that "la obra ya [sea] su propia parodia y el parodista no [pueda] exagerar su tensión" [the work was already its own parody, and the would-be parodist was unable to go beyond the original text] (*A Universal History of Infamy*, 11). This series of artifices serves to define and illustrate the use of parody in Latin American postmodern literature since the two writers—Borges and Bolaño—upon founding their own genealogy, connect it directly to this genre. Borges is considered one of the most illustrious precursors of Latin American postmodernity, while Bolaño is one of its greatest exponents. By liberating the critical capacity that all parodic exercises contain, Borges reveals to us that neither language, nor anything related to it, deserve to be considered trustworthy. Bolaño, in the same vein, stresses the fragility of institutions. I hope to have demonstrated throughout these reflections that *La literatura nazi en las Américas* does not claim to prove that literature in the Americas allowed itself to be contaminated by Nazi ideology. The fundamental fact regarding *La literatura nazi en las Américas* is that it criticizes Nazism, and that neo-Nazism reveals one of the most prevailing aspects of postmodernism, which is that of self-questioning, investigating the very validity of the literary task, and of literature and its institutions.

NOTES

1. Enrique Schmukler in "La littérature nazie en Amérique, de Roberto Bolaño: parodier l'auteur et le système littéraire à l'aide du détournement du mode biographique" also considers the text by Bolaño parodic, based on the idea of transformation "porque escribiendo a la manera de un diccionario de autores literarios, Roberto Bolaño encuentra un modo no sólo de transformar, sino que sobre todo de deformar y de degradar las figuras de ciertos autores, nombres de instituciones y actores de la órbita literaria, metiendo también en la obra una representación igualmente paródica del género biográfico" (408) [because writing in the style of a dictionary of literary authors, Roberto Bolaño finds a way to not only transform, but above all to deform and degrade the figures of certain authors, names of institutions and actors in the literary orbit, also infusing into the work an equally parodic representation of the biographical genre].

2. I am specifically referring to the following articles compiled in *Between Parentheses: "Advice on the Art of Writing Short Stories,"* where one reads, "Read Petrus Borel, but also read Jules Renard and Marcel Schwob, especially Marcel Schwob and after that Alfonso Reyes, and then Borges" (351) and to "The Brave Librarian," where Bolaño insists again on the connection between the imaginary biographies of Reyes and Borges with that of Schwob "whom they both loved" (313).

3. All translations, unless otherwise noted, are mine.

4. Although fascism emerged first in Italy, the socio-political movement extended to other countries. It is in this ample sense that I use the term.

5. Note that all translations of *La literatura nazi en las Américas* come from *Nazi Literature in the Americas*. Translated by Chris Andrews. New York: New Directions Publishing, 2008.

6. Adolf Hitler's biographical events allow for both approaches: the two censures in the School of Art of Vienna, his professional identification as a painter, the sale by third parties of his paintings on the street, the Bohemian life before World War I.
7. Pierre Menard is the character created by Borges who is alleged to have written *Don Quixote* in the twentieth century. Although the words of the novel are the same of those penned by Cervantes in the seventeenth century, the meaning is entirely different as the novel is now "re-written" (read) in a new context. This concept of manipulation of another's texts or reading as a form of authorship is what is meant by the term Mendardism in this chapter.
8. I am referring to the book *Los raros* [The Strange Ones] published in the same year as Schwob's *Imaginary Lives*.
9. Comte's "Religion of Humanity" is a secular religion that led to the creation of humanistic or ethical churches that were not associated with any particular religious affiliation.
10. CADA (Colectivo de Acciones de Arte) [Collective of Art Actions] refers to a group of Chilean artists integrated by the visual artists Lotty Rosenfeld and Juan Castillo, the writer Diamela Eltit, the poet Raúl Zurita, and the sociologist Fernando Balcells. This group was operative between 1979 and 1985 with a series of acts of opposition to the military dictatorship headed by General Augusto Pinochet. In one of these acts, Zurita hired planes to sky-write passages from his anti-Pinochet poem "The New Life" over Manhattan in the 1980s.
11. Consult Walter Benjamin, *Understanding Brecht*, 100–101.

Works Cited

Arendt, Hannah. *The Origins of Totalitarianism.* Orlando: Harcourt, 1976. Print.

Bakhtin, Mikhail. *Rabelais and His World.* Translated by Helene Iswolsky. Indianapolis: Indiana University Press, 2008. Print.

Bolaño, Roberto. *La literatura nazi en América.* Barcelona: Seix Barral, 1996. Print.

———. *Distant Star.* Translated by Chris Andrews. New York: New Directions Publishing, 2004. Print.

———. *Nazi Literature in the Americas.* Translated by Chris Andrews. New York: New Directions Publishing, 2008. Print.

———. *Between Parentheses. Essays, Articles and Speeches, 1998–2003.* Edited by Ignacio Echevarría and translated by Natasha Wimmer. New York: New Directions Books, 2011. Print.

———. *Bolaño por sí mismo: Entrevistas escogidas.* Edited by Andrés Braithwaite. Santiago, Chile: Ediciones Universidad Diego Portales, 2011. Print.

Borges, Jorge Luis. *Ficciones.* New York: Grove Press, 1962. Print.

———. *A Universal History of Infamy.* New York: E.P. Dutton, 1972. Print.

———. *Biblioteca personal: prólogos.* Buenos Aires: Emecé, 1998. Print.

———. *Cuentos completos.* México: Debolsillo, 2014. Print.

Calvi, Pablo. "La construcción de un lector democrático de masas. Borges en el diario *Crítica* de Buenos Aires y la historia universal de la infamia." *Revista Famencos* n. 23 (2016): 1–23. Print.

Darío, Rubén. *Los raros.* Ed ediciones, S.L., 2016. Print.

Dick, Philip K. *The Man in the High Castle.* New York: Popular Library, 1962. Print.

Didi-Huberman, Georges. *Images in Spite of All: Four Pictures from Auschwitz.* Chicago and London: Chicago University Press, 2012. Print.

Domínguez Michael, Christopher. "El arcón de Roberto Bolaño." In *El espíritu de la ciencia-ficción* by Roberto Bolaño. Barcelona: Penguin Random House Grupo Editoria, 2016. Print.

Gallo, Marta. "Historia universal de la infamia: una lectura en clave épica." *Variaciones Borges* (2001): 81–101. Print.

Genette, Gérard. *Figures: Essays.* Paris: Editions du Seuil, 1966. Print.

———. *Palimpsests: Literature in the Second Degree.* Translated by Channa Newman and Claude Doubinsky. Lincoln: University of Nebraska Press, 1997. Print.

Glantz, Margo. "Intertextualidad en Historia Universal de la Infamia." In *Borges Múltiple.* Edited by Pablo y Laura Zavala Brescia. Mexico: UNAM, 1999, 233–243. Print.

Gomel, Elana. "Aliens Among Us: Fascism and Narrativity." *Journal of Narrative Theory* 30.1 (2000): 127–162. Print.

Hutcheon, Linda. *A Theory of Parody: The Teachings of Twentieth-Century Art Forms.* London: Routledge, 1991. Print.

Jenckes, Kate. *Reading Borges After Benjamin: Allegory, Afterlife, and the Writing of History.* Albany: State University of New York Press, 2007. Print.

———. *Witnessing Beyond the Human: Addressing the Alterity of the Other in Post-coup Chile and Argentina.* Albany: State University of New York Press, 2017. Print.

López-Calvo, Ignacio. *Roberto Bolaño, a Less Distant Star: Critical Essays.* New York: Palgrave Macmillan, 2015. Print.

Lyotard, Jean-François. *The Postmodern Condition: A Report on Knowledge.* Minneapolis: University of Minnesota Press, 1984. Print.

Mann, Thomas. "That Man Is My Brother." *Esquire* XI.3 31 (1939): 31, 133. Print.

Neiman, Susan. *Evil in Modern Thought: An Alternate History of Philosophy.* Princeton: Princeton University Press, 2002. Print.

O'Bryen, Rory. "Writing with the Ghost of Pierre Menard: Authorship, Responsibility, and Justice in Roberto Bolaño's Distant Star." In *Roberto Bolaño, A Less Distant Star: Critical Essays*. Edited by Ignacio López-Calvo. New York: Palgrave Macmillan, 2015, 17–33. Print.

Parra Triana, Clara. "La fábula histórica en Alfonso Reyes." *Revista Valenciana* 16 (2015): 215–231. Print.

Piglia, Ricardo. *Crítica y ficción*. Buenos Aires: Anagrama, 2006. Print.

Reyes, Alfonso. *Retratos reales e imaginarios*. México: Lectura Selecta, 1920. Print.

Sarlo, Beatriz. *Jorge Luis Borges: A Writer on the Edge*. London: Verso, 1993. Print.

Schmukler, Enrique. "La littérature nazie en Amérique, de Roberto Bolaño: parodier l'auteur et le systeme littéraire a l'aide du détournement du mode biographique." In *L'Epuisement du biographique*. Edited by V. Broqua, G. Marche, and F. Dosse. Newcastle upon Tyne, UK: Cambridge Scholars, 2010, 407–417. Print.

Schwob, Marcel. *Imaginary Lives*. Translated by Hammond Lorimer. New York: Boni & Liveright, 1924. Print.

Sklodowska, Elzbieta. *La parodia en la nueva novela hispanoamericana (1960–1985)*. Amsterdam: John Benjamins Publishing Company, 1991. Print.

Sorrentino, Fernando. *Seven Conversations with Borges*. Translated by Clark M. Zlotchew. Philadelphia: Paul Drybooks, 2012. Print.

Spinrad, Norman. *The Iron Dream*. New York: Avon Publications, 1977. Print.

Ulrich, Volker. *Hitler Ascent, 1889–1939*. Translated by Jefferson Chase. New York: Alfred A. Knopf, 2016. Print.

Wilcock, J. Rodolfo. *The Temple of Iconoclasts*. Jaffrey, NH: David R. Godine, 2014. Print.

Zonana, Víctor Gustavo. "De viris pessimis: Biografías imaginarias de Marcel Schwob, Jorge Luis Borges y Juan Rodolfo Wilcock." *Revista de Filología Hispánica* 16.3 (2000): 673–690. Print.

CHAPTER 7

Claudia Piñeiro's *Elena Knows*: How Parody in the Crime Novel Explores Disability and Feminism

Patricia Varas

Parody is a rhetorical device that has received special scholarly attention over recent decades due to its important role in the politics of representation and theorization of postmodernity. This device has become a key feature of postmodern thought and culture because it makes us aware that there are no seamless, unified narratives or representations. Parody in a literary text makes the reader conscious, in a self-reflexive manner, of the text's workings, denaturalizing what has come to be considered natural and is, indeed, cultural (Hutcheon, *Politics*, 2). Linda Hutcheon calls this awareness a "complicitous critique" (*Politics*, 13) since it undermines at the same time that it inscribes. In her book devoted solely to parody, Hutcheon emphasizes the doubled-voiced quality of this discourse, stating that "the ideological status of parody is a subtle one: the textual and pragmatic natures of parody imply, at one and the same time, authority and transgression, and both must be taken into account" (*A Theory*, 69).

P. Varas (✉)
Willamette University, Salem, OR, USA
e-mail: pvaras@willamette.edu

© The Author(s) 2018
H. C. Weldt-Basson (ed.), *Postmodern Parody in Latin American Literature*, Literatures of the Americas,
https://doi.org/10.1007/978-3-319-90430-6_7

149

In Latin American literature, particularly regarding the detective genre, this parodic or double-voiced complicity has had the most impact on the "appropriation" and acceptance of the genre. There are many terms used to denote parody: "artistic recycling," "trans-contextualization," "intertextuality," 'ironic quotation," "pastiche," and "appropriation," among others. The last is perhaps the concept that best articulates the subversive intention of double-voicing that parody has implied in Latin American letters.[1]

Bernardo Subercaseaux has defined appropriation as a way to understand the relationship between Latin American and Western thought and culture. For the Chilean thinker, this model takes into consideration the complex nature of this relationship and emphasizes the idea of "fertility," of "un proceso creativo a través del cual se convierten en 'propios' o 'apropiados' elementos ajenos" (130) [a creative process through which alien elements are 'appropriated' or become one's own].[2] Appropriation implies agency, adaptation, transformation, and an active reception that takes into account, in an organic fashion, the existent and original artistic and intellectual expressions, and is not merely an adoption or reproduction of exogenous or alien ones (130–131). Furthermore, appropriation has the potential for presenting culture and thought as a process in the making: "Lo latinoamericano no sería algo hecho o acabado, sino algo que estaría constantemente haciéndose" (Subercaseaux, 132) [Latin American culture would not be something completed or a finished product, but something that would be constantly in the making]. Finally, appropriation means that Latin American culture is part of a universal one, partaking of the right to be cosmopolitan without "complexes" or "guilt" (Subercaseaux, 133).

The appropriation model is particularly felicitous when discussing parody because it is more open to hybridity, to syncretic thought, and to "los rasgos y matices que se van configurando en el proceso de hacer propio lo ajeno" (Subercaseaux, 133) [the features and nuances that are being configured in the process of making the alien one's own]. It is no coincidence that Jorge Luis Borges, the creator of the great armchair detective Don Isidro Parodi (1942), actively reclaims the right for Argentines to appropriate other cultures and to become citizens of a wider world:

> ¿Cuál es la tradición argentina? Creo que podemos contestar fácilmente y que no hay problema en esta pregunta. Creo que nuestra tradición es toda la cultura occidental, y creo también que tenemos derecho a esa tradición, mayor que el que pueden tener los habitantes de una u otra nación occidental. (Borges, n.p.)

> What is the Argentine tradition? I believe that there is no issue with this question and that we can easily answer it. I believe that our tradition is all Western culture, and I believe as well that we have the right to this tradition, even more so than the inhabitants of any other Western nation do.

Although Borges is solely referring to Argentine culture and to the Western world, the idea of the right to take and partake of the exogenous echoes Subercaseaux's appropriation.

Parody is a vital device in which appropriation can take place because sheer imitation or the mirroring of the colonial culture as role model or as the goal to achieve is no longer adequate or desirable. Thanks to parody, Latin American artists and thinkers gain agency, and can become active seekers and doers. At an ideological level, it is obvious the advantages parody brings because it is essentially democratic (Hutcheon, *A Theory*, 81). Parody questions all aesthetic and paradigmatic norms, and there is "an exchange value in relation to literary norms" (Hutcheon, *A Theory*, 77).

However, the reader must recognize or actualize parody for it to continue having this egalitarian effect. In other words, the reader has to complete the rules, the texts, and the difference. If the reader misses the decentering discourse—that is, the parodic wink, or the alternative dialogue with tradition—parody gets lost and an elitist art with limited access replaces the democratic text (Hutcheon, *The Politics*, 2–7).

For some critics, a formula that relies on the parodic constructs the detective genre. Detective novels are a double-coded message in which a repetition with a difference is actively playing out the characters, the investigation, the clues, and the sidekick, among other features. For example, the detective must re-enact the criminal's actions and thinking; red herrings are mocking clues; the bumbling sidekick emulates the reader as he or she struggles to understand and arrive at the truth, and so forth. Furthermore, the apparent realism that dominates the genre is a constructed artifice; it is a parodic representation that "despite the illusion of plausibility which authors strive to create, mimetic reality is neither their intention nor their effect" (Klein, *The Woman*, 224). Thus, parody is at the heart of the genre.

Moreover, parody is a particularly important device in Latin America when it comes to genre and gender matters in crime fiction. Several critics of detective fiction in Latin America have remarked on its foreignness. Because of its strange expectations of justice and order, Diego Trelles Paz convincingly argues that, since its inception, the detective novel was an imported and incompatible product "en sociedades pauperizadas en donde la gente había perdido credibilidad en la ley y desconfiaba de las fuerzas del orden" (81) [in poverty stricken societies where people had lost their belief in the law and distrusted the forces of law and order]. David Lagmanovich has demonstrated how the genre in Argentina started as an imitative practice and then developed its own characteristics (55). Thus, the first step in the adoption of the genre has been to imitate the formula, absorbing its exogenous features, in order then to slowly develop and incorporate characteristics that strongly identify the detective novel with the local context and tradition. We could summarize the process of the development of the detective fiction in the region succinctly: first, imitation takes place, which can be shallow stereotyping with no assessment or self-awareness; and, second, a distancing follows and a "repetition with difference," which we call parody, takes place (Hutcheon, *A Theory*, 32).

In terms of gender, feminist critics have carefully studied detective fiction, especially the hard-boiled variety. Kathleen Gregory Klein has argued that hard-boiled fiction follows "a macho credo" ("Women Times," 4) and calls for a thorough revision of the formula that will also address the implied reader who should no longer be male (12). Klein also maintains, in a narrow reading of the parodic, that the woman detective is an intruder because female detective novels are a parody in which only one significant change has been made (*The Woman*, 174–175). Priscilla Walton and Manina Jones warn against turning the male detective into a drag performance with the female detective (99), emphasizing the aesthetic and ideological importance of ironic distancing in an askew manner. Maureen Reddy sees a parallelism between the development of female detective fiction and feminism or gender politics (195) and pinpoints how generic conventions are turned topsy-turvy in the female detective series of the 1980s (198–199). In effect, female detective fiction appropriates features of the male detective story in a self-aware manner. Sally Munt, like Reddy, establishes a parallel development between the female detective genre and the Women's Movement (19). Munt explains feminist reaction against postmodernism and its parodic stance "as a luxury only men can afford" (170), and stresses the importance of situating discussions on diversity "within political contexts" (171). However, she is able to see the potential of parody as much more than a reflective mirror to male crime fiction: "But it is precisely this structural mutability of the form to parody which substantiates my claim that these [female] writers are implicated within it, not adjunctive to it" (Munt, 26).

Parody is, without doubt, of vital importance in re-inscribing women's experience and agency in the detective genre. The generic formula is recognized as particularly flexible and adaptable to place, time, race, ethnicity, sexuality, and gender, among other variables. However, feminist critics, in one way or another, bring to our attention the relevance of understanding the ideological and aesthetic importance of the ironic distancing of parody. To feminize the genre is more than substituting the female for the male detective, or rewriting its conventions; it is about capturing women's identity and experience in a world that has systematically oppressed and diminished women as inconsequential. The parodic in the female detective genre must be subversive of patriarchal values and institutions.

Parody has one more important role to play in the detective genre at the epistemological or hermeneutical level. There is a new alteration of the formula with the so-called "metaphysical" detective, crime fiction, or anti-detective novel. This postmodernist genre actively questions and challenges the rules of detective fiction. There may be no detective, and the crime and its solution take second place to other discoveries of an epistemological or ontological nature. In these stories, knowledge is uncertain and the mystery, in a manner of speaking, is unsolvable. If the emphasis of the detective genre is not the existence of an enigma, but the "*expectation* of a solution" (Grossgovel, 41, emphasis in the original), the metaphysical detective novel foils it. This alteration to the formula creates a new narrative that:

> Does not have the narcotizing effect of its progenitor; instead of familiarity, it gives strangeness, a strangeness which more often than not is the result of jumbling the well-known patterns of classical detective stories. Instead of reassuring, they disturb. They are not an escape, but an attack... If, in the detective story, death must be solved, in the new metaphysical detective story it is *life* which must be solved. (Holquist, 173, emphasis in the original)

Parody is an essential instrument in the creation and the subversion of the genre. Parody systematically dismantles the generic conventions; yet, the reader must be able to perceive this parodic effort. As Stefano Tani asserts, the writers cultivating the metaphysical detective novel exploit the conventions by deconstructing "the genre's precise architecture into the meaningless mechanism without purpose; they parody positivistic detection" (34). If the reader does not recognize the action of disassembling the beloved detective genre, the crime fiction falls flat, becoming an intellectual or arcane game at best.

As Maggie Humm points out, literary genres carry aesthetic and ideological messages, and women writers are constantly pushing the limits, violently disrupting genre boundaries (4). The masculine conventions in the detective genre are easily recognized and relied upon by popular culture; these "parodic and circumscribed embodiments" (Humm, 202–203) are destabilized and rewritten by women writers who initiate their own tradition. Women writers practicing the genre are, in effect, interfering with a male tradition that overvalues a hyper-masculinity and that has denied women entry into this "men's only club." By inscribing female paradigms, the women writers are fully aware of their predecessors (male and female), enriching their practice by absorbing all possibilities and denying none. Because the masculine development of the genre has been particularly aware of a patrilineal legacy à la Harold Bloom, "where each writer is fully aware of writing within the shadow of his predecessor, but revises his text to push out the form and relate it to his particular milieu" (Munt, 304), a women's practice of detective fiction requires innovation and the incorporation of new values and approaches.

In this chapter, I will study a crime novel by the Argentine Claudia Piñeiro, *Elena sabe* (*Elena Knows*, 2007). I prefer the term "crime novel" to "anti-detective" or "metaphysical detective novel" because it opens up the generic and gendering implications of this work. While the crime novel can have the characteristics of the anti-detective story, this genre further explores certain features—such as, evil, suspense, thoughts, and emotions, and deals more in depth with the characters' psychology and their motives. The crime novel constantly manipulates and misdirects the reader, and thwarts the expectation of a solution of the crime, since there is a lack of pronouncement because guilt and justice or retribution are no longer as important as in the detective narrative. In general, due to the lack of a detecting authority and a plot closure, crime fiction, as in the case of Ruth Rendell's fiction, raises "questions about crime, desire and society without limiting the responses of the reader" (Rowland, 49). Feminist crime fiction captures the social chaos while commenting on the patriarchal institutions that have oppressed the female characters and the vicissitudes encountered by them that are a manifestation of this inequality.

Elena Knows received the German *LiBeraturpreis* in 2010. This novel actively questions and subverts the rules of detective fiction: there is no detective or assassination; what is of primary importance are discoveries of an epistemological and ontological nature that take place through the depiction of the mother–daughter relationship. In *Elena Knows*, knowledge is uncertain, as Mónica Flórez has remarked in her fine study (44), and the crime is unsolvable. The narrative structure is innovative and an aesthetic challenge. It is ironic, parodic, and highly allegorical—all characteristics of the metaphysical story, as Merivale and Sweeney argue (4)—while trying to capture the thought and physical patterns of Elena, who has Parkinson's disease. The novel is divided into three sections defined by the passing of time and the effect of the medicine (levodopa) she needs to take to be able to move through the day—morning, noon, and night.

Elena decides that she must discover her daughter's killer. Rita is found hanging from the church bell tower on a stormy day. The police have determined that Rita committed suicide, an unacceptable conclusion for Elena. The reasons for Elena's inference are simple enough, as a good detective would understand: Rita, a devout Catholic, would not contaminate the Church with such a crime. Besides, she feared storms and therefore lightning would have kept her away from the bell tower.

Gearing up for a long day, made painfully difficult due to Parkinson's, Elena carefully and methodically takes her medicine and prepares for the trip from the suburbs to the city, Buenos Aires. She is determined to collect a debt: Isabel owes her and Rita much because they stopped Isabel from having an abortion when she was young and now she is the happy mother of a young woman. Elena believes that Isabel will be her ally and help her find the assassin. However, this is all a misconception. Isabel never wanted to be a mother; her husband raped her and forced her to have the child; her life and marriage are a sham and, instead of gratitude, she is full of hatred for Rita. In the end, Elena must accept what she knows, what she has found out, and has to live with it. Throughout the novel the phrase "Elena knows" is repeated constantly with several variations that reflect the certainty of what she knows, as well as the growing doubts of what she does not. In addition, there is the play with tenses, which in Spanish convert the verb "to know" (*saber*) into "to find out" (*supo*). Elena's voyage is one of knowledge and acceptance of the sad truth: Rita did commit suicide because she could not cope with Elena's illness. Did she fear being her mother's caregiver and having to become Elena's mother, or did she fear the illness? Was it fear of what it did to Elena's body, or maybe of inheriting Parkinson's? (Piñeiro, 172–173). As a corollary of this discovery, Elena finds out yet one more thing: "Yo sí quiero vivir...a pesar de este cuerpo, a pesar de mi hija muerta...sigo eligiendo vivir" (173) [I do want to live...in spite of this body, in spite of my dead daughter...I choose to live].

The first parodic element in *Elena Knows* is the adaptation of the crime narrative to Argentine society. As Piñeiro remarks on her work: "Son novelas donde claramente es un país que pasó por la dictadura. La dictadura no está presente...pero esa gente es producto de haber tenido una dictadura militar en su país" [these are novels where clearly there is a country that went through a dictatorship. The dictatorship is not present...but the people in them are the product of a military dictatorship in their country] (Personal Interview). Piñeiro in the same interview refers to "comportamientos antiéticos" [antiethical behaviors], which are responsible for tensions, oppression, unequal treatment, and deplorable conducts that drive the plot and explain the social malaise that affects the characters. Later, we will see how these behaviors converge on the discourse of disability.

Elena and Rita live in the suburbs of Buenos Aires, and belong to a lower-middle class that is continuously losing ground. In the novel we see the small savings, the decisions made to economize, and the struggle to continue living decently. In *Elena Knows*, Piñeiro moves away from the life in the exclusive gated communities or "country" of her other novels and perambulates the city with Elena in a parody of the gumshoe detective.

Elena must travel to Belgrano, the upper-middle class well-to-do and long-established neighborhood where Isabel lives. She must make the trip while the levodopa works and ensures her mobility. Yet, she prefers to take the train, subway, and a cab, and figure out the journey on her own instead of taking a *remis* or taxi service, which would be easier for her because "era mucho viaje, mucho gasto" (18) [it was a long trip, too expensive]. Elena's decision not only reflects her intense will to do things on her own terms, a defining trait of hers, but also sets up the parodic trip to the city that defines the gumshoe detective. Known for his mobility and *flâneur* qualities, the gumshoe investigator moves around the city, stealthily searching for clues.

Elena and Rita's social standing contrasts with Isabel's. She not only might support Elena's search with her younger and abled body, but also has the means to do so as she lives in a beautiful house and neighborhood, "en una vieja casa en Belgrano, con puerta de madera pesada y herrajes de bronce" (17) [in an old house in Belgrano, with a heavy wooden door and bronze fittings]. There is no doubt that Isabel has the capacity to aid Elena if she joins her in her search, potentially becoming her sidekick. These parodic elements are thwarted, nevertheless, as Isabel confesses, "no la puedo ayudar porque a su hija la maté yo...La maté de tanto desearle la muerte" (147) [I cannot help you because I killed your daughter...I killed her by wishing her death so much].

With this emotionally charged confession, Isabel obliterates the detective novel formula: there is no sidekick to help Elena; and, since there is no actual assassination, there is no need for a detective. Unlike the traditional detective story, exaggerated feelings, not cerebral ruminations, dominate, creating new meanings for the crime narrative.[3] The dominance of emotions, relationships, behavior, and social identities, as well as the precariousness of social norms and their expression of power, provoke anxiety in the reader that contrasts with the sense of fulfillment of the detective story. The anti-detective novel promotes "the decentering and chaotic admission of mystery, of nonsolution" (Tani, 41).

In an interview, Piñeiro declares: "El suspenso es clave incluso para contar otras cosas (que no sean de la novela negra)" [suspense is the key for even telling other things (that are not detective stories)] (Personal Interview). For Piñeiro, suspense is a manner of seducing the reader; it is part of the art of conversation as well, and it must never be a lie. In her novels, suspense is a powerful tool used to awaken affect in the form of anxiety, pity, fear, even guilt in the reader. Elena's search for Rita's assassin eerily echoes the search for the disappeared children of the Mothers of the Plaza de Mayo. As the author states, "de afuera la búsqueda de cualquier madre se ve como [que] es una loca" [to an outsider the search of any mother is seen as if she were crazy] (Personal Interview).[4] Michele C. Dávila Gonçalves has observed that the police's lack of support in Elena's search "reminds us of the mothers of the 'Plaza de mayo'" and their "consuming desire to know and understand what had happened to them [their children]" (69).

Elena's investigation mirrors with a difference the Mothers' in many moments.[5] In effect, any discourse dealing with motherhood in Argentina inevitably leads us to the Mothers of the Plaza de Mayo.

In *Elena Knows*, there are several instances that can refer to them: Elena says, "tenía una hija pero la mataron" (115) [I had a daughter, but she was killed]; "la maternidad Elena piensa, garantiza ciertos atributos, una conoce a su hijo, una madre sabe, una madre quiere...¿Seguirá siendo una madre ahora que no tiene una hija?...¿Qué nombre tiene ella sin su hija?" (66) [motherhood, Elena thinks, guarantees certain qualities, a mother knows her son, a mother knows, a mother loves...Will she continue being a mother now that she doesn't have a daughter?...What name does she have without her daughter?]. Elena's illogical refusal to accept Rita's suicide and her stubborn search for the truth may also be seen as references to the Mothers of the Plaza de Mayo: "Hoy va a jugarse la última carta para tratar de averiguar quien mató a su hija" (16) [today she will play her last card to try to find out who killed her daughter]. Moreover, her antagonism against the police with its ironic distancing reflects the Mothers' ongoing search for their disappeared children with an important difference: "Alguien la mató aunque todos digan otra cosa" (31) [somebody killed her even though everybody says something else]. Although Elena's narrative would also appear unsolved, it finds a solution in the end unlike the Mothers' quest. However, the strong love for the lost ones gives sense to the Mothers' grief and search, and is what will also advance the plot in *Elena Knows*. The infinite sadness and the desperation of Elena's search for understanding and justice moves the reader, and produces conflictive emotions that relate to the here and now, as well as to historical forces that defined motherhood in Argentina.

The end of Elena's search results in a discovery—not of who killed Rita, but of a finding of an epistemological nature: What Elena knows. On the last page (173), Elena confesses that she will live in spite of everything, and that she will learn to accept day by day, marked by the pills she takes, and by the knowledge that Rita feared something more than lightning and God: Her own mother and her impaired body. This is what Elena knows. Rita has committed suicide, fearful of the demands her mother's illness will make on her, fearful of becoming her mother's mother:

> Mi madre no puede ser un bebé, un bebé es lindo, un bebé tiene la piel suave y blanca, y la baba clara ... y yo estoy condenada a ver cómo su cuerpo va muriendo sin que ella muera. Rita, por primera vez en mucho tiempo, lloró. No doctor, mi mamá no va a ser un bebé, y no creo que yo pueda ser esa madre que usted me pide. (164)

My mother can't be a baby, a baby is beautiful, a baby has soft and pale skin, and his drool is clean ... and I am condemned to see how her body dies without her dying. Rita for the first time in a long time, cried. No, doctor, my mother is not going to be a baby and I don't think that I can be that mother that you are asking me to be.

This novel is as much about solving a mystery as about the female body: "Es la novela [mía] más femenina, más feminista y que más tiene que ver con la maternidad" [it is the most feminine, most feminist novel (of mine) and the one that has primarily to do with motherhood] (Personal Interview). In a feminist parodic twist, the crime novel presents the family as the claustrophobic unit where motherhood is examined. Piñeiro claims, "la novela trabaja sobre el cuerpo (femenino)" [the novel is about the (female) body] (Personal Interview). In the beginning, Piñeiro had thought of titling her work "El cuerpo de los otros" [The Body of Others] because doctors abuse and opine about ill bodies, especially women's, to the point they no longer belong to the diseased. According to Piñeiro, abortion is another example in which everybody pronounces about the female body, taking away her agency to make decisions; it is the abuse of the body of "the other" (Personal Interview).

Elena portrays the disabled body with a courage and compassion rarely seen in Latin American fiction. Long paragraphs present Elena's trip to Buenos Aires, her voyage of discovery, some of them five pages in length, parodying the painful effort Elena makes to discover her daughter's assassin. The narrative, told in an omniscient voice with some dialogue and run-on sentences, depicts Elena's struggle with her illness, such as her need to measure her pills to make sure she will not "freeze" while on the train or taxi. Claudia Piñeiro actively inscribes the disabled female body in a manner that refuses conventions and does not reduce the body to judgments of normalcy; the narrative is not loving or humorous. The form that the author chooses to grapple with Elena's disability shuns common "normalizing devices of plot" (Davis, 15), which turns the deviant character into an evil being, preferring instead to depict disability as central to the novel. Piñeiro portrays the social attitudes that develop the impairment into a disability while describing in much detail the actual impact Parkinson's has on Elena's body, which is undeniably suffering and losing the ability to function without medicine and Rita's care. In this manner, with a realistic style, the author makes the invisible

visible, running the risk of making the broken body more fearful than the abled one.[6]

Elena is strong, opinionated and, at times, abusive. She cannot emblemize the "mother of the nation" through her motherhood because Piñeiro subverts the allegory of disability or illness as evil and refuses to continue imprinting the female body with the traditional constructions of nationhood that prescribe specific gender concepts of masculinity and femininity. Elena's main victory is that, through sheer determination, not essentialism or duty, she fulfills her role as mother and constructs a narrative that will make sense of her life and of Rita's death. By personifying the disease, making it into an "Ella" [She], Elena creates a textual space, which is not a mere abstraction, but actualizes itself in the narrative that creates the novel. Piñeiro, as a novelist, has chosen a difficult topic that confronts humanist suppositions that silence disability because it perceives it as debilitating, as an abnormality, which needs correction. Yet, Elena is saved from this perception by an element that defines her and which is of vital importance for the narrative: Her stubbornness. As Kralic et al. explain, coping is a state of being, characterized by tolerating or minimizing what cannot be mastered, while "'self-management,' however, makes reference to the activities people undertake to create order, discipline and control in their lives" (260).

Elena represents this effort of "self-management" during the novel. Her refusal to abdicate her search for Rita's assassin reflects her obstinacy to not resign her body to "She," Parkinson's. A combative language depicts Elena's obstinacy. Descriptions of her are full of repetitions marked by the slow rhythm of someone who is grappling with the disease: "Allá va, un pie delante del otro, a pesar de que ya nadie puede devolverle al rey su corona, ni a su hija la vida, ni a ella su hija muerta" (67) [there goes Elena, one foot in front of the other, even though nobody can return to the king his crown, nor to her daughter her life, nor to Elena her dead daughter]. Piñeiro depicts the disabled person's struggle for a script, for agency. If in the postmodern age we acknowledge the self in flux, people with impairing illnesses seek the contrary; to stabilize themselves: "It is precisely because their hold on themselves and language is fast becoming tenuous—and thus *too* fluid—that the need to fix themselves and loved ones becomes imperative" (Ramanathan, 69, emphasis in the original). Thus, we must read Elena's unpleasantness with Rita and others as part of her narrative, and of an identity that actively inscribes motherhood and disability in her terms.

Piñeiro, through Elena's narrative, continues to subvert and demystify the female body: "¿Se puede ser algo sin cuerpo que obedezca?" (94) [can one be something without a body that obeys?], while opening up new readings and actively questioning obsolete ones in Argentine culture. Just as she has questioned Elena's motherhood and alluded to the ongoing search of the Mothers, she discusses sterility and abortion. The female characters are all different kinds of mothers. Elena, Isabel, and even Rita grapple with the obligation of being or becoming a mother. Thus, there is a constant struggle to recover the female body and to make women's experience count in the construction of their subjectivity. Elena is the most successful character, ironically, in exercising her agency, while Rita's and Isabel's bodies are imprisoned (or disciplined) by scientific and social norms. Rita's body is "defective" and, coincidentally, so is that of her boyfriend, Roberto, who has a hunched back. Elena, with a mordant lack of compassion, constantly remarks on his and other people's appearance, without any critical consideration, saying things as she sees them, making Rita exclaim, "Mamá, ¿te gustaría que hablaran así de vos?" (103) [Mother, would you like it if people talked about you like that?]. It would appear that Elena is the mouthpiece of Argentine society where discriminatory language is still the norm. That the body is discursively constructed is unquestionable, and, as we read the offensive language, our awareness of its power to name and evaluate increases. At the same time that Elena is empowered by this act of naming, because we react critically to her prejudices, her power as a grieving mother decreases.[7]

Elena has always been uncertain of Rita's fertility. This fact diminishes her body's value socially and privately. Elena pejoratively refers to Rita's "reglas amarretas" [stingy periods] and expresses her doubts that her womb functions (78 and 79). On the one hand, the female body as a reproductive machine is highly valued by Rita and Elena, following their Catholic upbringing. On the other hand, its abject meanings are constantly emphasized. Rita refers to menstruation as something that makes her "dirty" (78). The female body is an object of ridicule and disgust. For example, Elena forces Rita to undergo an exam to see whether she has a uterus. The description of the exam resembles a medieval torture; and, what is worse, both Elena and the doctor laugh at Rita's discomfort and moans of pain, exhibiting a lack of empathy: "No podés decir que eso te duele, Rita, le dijo el doctor Benegas. Y ella no contestó, sino su madre, claro que no le duele doctor, lo hace para hacernos sentir mal a nosotros" (80) [you can't say this is hurting you, Rita, Doctor Benegas said. And she didn't answer, but her mother did, of course it doesn't hurt her, doctor, she does it (cry) to make us feel bad]. The scientific discourse and the authority of the male doctor who had been "médico de Elena de toda la vida, que también había sido médico de la madre de Elena. Y de sus tías" (79) [Elena's doctor all her life, who had also been Elena's mother's doctor. And her aunts'] dictate the painful, scary, and shameful experience that scars Rita for life.

Abortion is also alluded to as one more intervention that determines the female body and woman's experience. If the female body is valued for having children (Elena's dream is to have a grandson), under a Catholic perspective the termination of a pregnancy is the end of a life. Isabel is not able to exercise agency over her own body and her husband forces her to have an unwanted child that will tie her for life to an abusive man. By embodying the law of the father, Rita and Elena intervene and obstruct Isabel's agency.

In this crime novel, a parody of detective fiction, Piñeiro uses the female body as the site where social crimes converge and multiple abuses take place. By recovering and exploring the materiality of the female body, the female characters can express new ways of being. Rita confronts her religiosity and her God by committing suicide in a Church; Isabel expresses her anger for being forced to be a mother; and Elena articulates her will to continue to live against all odds. These women refuse to normalize their bodies as objects of pleasure for men, or as protective and caring environments for others. Instead, they become subversive and disrupt patriarchal order. Their bodies are the abject; they inspire revulsion and horror to others and themselves. Yet, they have managed to keep honest with themselves by rebelling against their destinies, thereby showing determination and strength of character.

If, for Adrienne Rich, "the loss of the daughter to the mother, the mother to the daughter, is the essential female tragedy" (237), *Elena Knows* reworks this feminist truth. In this crime novel, we can see the effort of the mothers and daughters to accept and define new realities and relationships where no role models or idealized stereotypes dominate, where fragmented female identities exist, and where women must strive for a world in which their agency is valued as much as the building of community. For parody to have subversive value, it must help create new worlds that do not mirror the ones we know but, instead, present risky options in which we recognize and appropriate reality, only with a difference.

Notes

1. It is worth clarifying that the appropriation Subercaseaux defines is the opposite of the "cultural appropriation" that is being debated today, which supports a "misappropriation" or borrowing of "others" cultures by a dominant culture with the intention to maintain colonial or hierarchical cultural values. The result can be offensive, a distortion, a desecration or even exoticization. Subercaseaux is advocating for a Latin American identity that is always being articulated, always in the making. As a consequence, "cultural heterogeneity" is embraced (see José Joaquín Brunner, 40). The appropriation that Latin American culture enacts turns the tables on power, by questioning the "universalizing paradigm of the Center: dependency and imitation as colonialized inflections, but also parody and recycling as decolonizing strategies" (Richard, 219). Richard warns us, however, against complacency. She claims that, to find true empowerment, Latin Americans must demand, "to know why the identity/difference conflicts continues to be arbitrated by the discursivity of the First World" (222).
2. This translation and all others, unless otherwise noted, are mine.
3. In "New Latin American Crime Fiction: *Elena sabe* by Claudia Piñeiro," I argue that the actual crime in *Elena Knows* is the destruction of the mother–daughter relationship.
4. The Mothers of the Plaza de Mayo were contemptuously called "las locas" (crazy ones) and dismissed by the military dictatorship in Argentina (1976–1983).
5. Piñeiro, in an interview, acknowledges that she had not thought of that connection with the Mother's directly or strictly, but she does not discard it because the novel is about motherhood (Personal Interview).
6. Tobin Siebers warns about employing realism to represent the body of "the sufferers of disability" (179–180).
7. Simi Linton's essay "Reassigning Meaning" explains the importance of language and conventions to denote and connote disability in a negative or empowering manner (161–172). There is an ironic acknowledgement of the importance of language in the novel. Rita and Elena must go to the "Servicio Nacional de Rehabilitación y Promoción de la Persona con Discapacidad" [National Service for Rehabilitation and Promotion of the Disabled] or "el antiguo Instituto del Lisiado, al que madre e hija seguían llamando por su viejo nombre, a pesar de que desde hace años lleva otro que en su extensión intenta no ofender a nadie pero cansa" (101) [the former Institute for the Handicapped, which mother and daughter continued calling by its old name, even though for many years now it has another one, whose length tries to not offend anyone but it is tiring].

WORKS CITED

Borges, Jorge Luis. "El escritor argentino y la tradición." Versión taquigráfica de una clase dictada en el Colegio Libre de Estudios Superiores y reproducida en el libro Discusión. In *Contratiempo. Revista de pensamiento y cultura*. Edited by J. L. Borges. Madrid: Alianza, 1997. http://www.revistacontratiempo. com.ar/borges_tradicion.htm. Web.

Brunner, José Joaquín. "Notes on Modernity and Postmodernity in Latin American Culture." In *The Postmodernism Debate in Latin America*. Edited by John Beverley, Michael Aronna, and José Oviedo. Durham: Duke University Press, 1995. 34–54. Print.

Dávila Gonçalves, Michele C. "Subversions of Motherhood: The Sleuth in Claudia Piñeiro's Crime Fiction." In *Twenty-First Century Latin American Narrative and Postmodern Feminism*. Edited by Gina Ponce de León. Newcastle-upon-Tyne, UK: Cambridge Scholars Publishing, 2014. 53–74. Print.

Davis, Lennard J. "Constructing Normalcy. The Bell Curve, the Novel, and the Invention of the Disabled Body in the Nineteenth Century." In *The Disability Studies Reader*. Edited by Lennard J. Davis, 2nd ed. New York: Routledge, 2006. 3–16. Print.

Flórez, Mónica. "*Elena sabe* y los enigmas de la novela policiaca antidetectivesca/ metafísica." *Lingüística y literatura* 58 (2010): 41–50. Print.

Grossgovel, David I. *Mystery and Its Fictions: From Oedipus to Agatha Christie*. Baltimore: Johns Hopkins University Press, 1979. Print.

Holquist, Michael. "Whodunit and Other Questions: Metaphysical Detective Stories in Postwar Fiction." In *The Poetics of Murder. Detective Fiction and Literary Theory*. Edited by Glenn W. Most and William W. Stowe. New York: Harcourt Brace Jovanovich Publishers, 1983. 149–174. Print.

Humm, Maggie. *Border Traffic. Strategies of Contemporary Women Writers*. Manchester: Manchester University Press, 1991. Print.

Hutcheon, Linda. *A Theory of Parody*. New York: Methuen, 1985. Print.

———. *The Politics of Postmodernism*. New York: Routledge, 1989. Print.

Klein, Kathleen Gregory. *The Woman Detective. Gender and Genre*, 2nd ed. Urbana: University of Illinois Press, 1995. Print.

———. "Women Times Women Times Women." In *Women Times Three: Writers, Detectives, Readers*. Edited by Kathleen Gregory Klein. Bowling Green: Bowling Green State University Popular Press, 1995. 3–13. Print.

Kralic, Debbie, Tina Koch, Kay Price, and Natalie Howard. "Chronic Illness Self-Management: Taking Action to Create Order." *Journal of Clinical Nursing* 13 (2004): 259–267. Print.

Lagmanovich, David. "Evolución de la narrativa policial rioplatense." *Revista de Crítica Literaria Latinoamericana* 27.54 (2001): 35–58. Print.

Linton, Simi. "Reassigning Meaning." In *The Disability Studies Reader*. Edited by Lennard J. Davis, 2nd ed. New York: Routledge, 2006. 161–172. Print.

Merivale, Patricia and Susan Elizabeth Sweeney. "The Game's Afoot: On the Trail of the Metaphysical Detective Story." In *Detecting Texts. The Metaphysical Detective Story from Poe to Postmodernism*. Edited by Patricia Merivale and Susan Elizabeth Sweeney. Philadelphia: University of Philadelphia Press, 1999. 1–24. Print.

Munt, Sally R. *Murder by the Book? Feminism and the Crime Novel*. London: Routledge, 1994. Print.

Piñeiro, Claudia. *Elena sabe*. Buenos Aires: Alfaguara, 2007. Print.

———. "Personal Interview." March 26, 2017.

Ramanathan, Vaidehi. "Texting Doppelgangers: Repetition, Signs, and Intentionalities in (Auto)biographical Alzheimer Writing." *Journal of Literary and Cultural Disability Studies* 3.1 (2009): 67–84. Print.

Reddy, Maureen. "Women Detectives." In *The Cambridge Companion to Crime Fiction*. Edited by Martin Priestman. Cambridge: Cambridge University Press, 2003. 191–207. Print.

Rich, Adrienne. *Of Woman Born: Motherhood as Experience and Institution*. New York: Norton, 1986. Print.

Richard, Nelly. "Cultural Peripheries: Latin America and Postmodernist De-centering." In *The Postmodernism Debate in Latin America*. Edited by John Beverley, Michael Aronna, and José Oviedo. Durham: Duke University Press, 1995. 217–222. Print.

Rowland, Susan. *From Agatha Christie to Ruth Rendell. British Women Writers in Detective and Crime Fiction*. New York: Palgrave, 2001. Print.

Siebers, Tobin. "Disability in Theory: From Social Constructionism to the New Realism of the Body." *The Disability Studies Reader*. Edited by Lennard J. Davis. 2nd ed. New York: Routledge, 2006. 173–183. Print.

Subercaseaux, Bernardo. "La apropiación cultural en el pensamiento y la cultura de América Latina." *Mundo* 1 (1987): 125–135. Print.

Tani, Stefano. *The Doomed Detective. The Contribution of the Detective Novel to Postmodern American and Italian Fiction*. Carbondale: Southern Illinois University Press, 1984. Print.

Trelles Paz, Diego "Novela policial alternativa hispanoamericana (1960–2005)." *Aisthesis* 40 (2006): 79–91. Print.

Varas, Patricia. "New Latin American Crime Fiction: *Elena sabe* by Claudia Piñeiro." *From Noir to Gris: Spanish and Latin American Women's Crime Fiction in the New Millennium*. Edited by Nina Molinaro and Nancy Vosburg. Newcastle-upon-Tyne, UK: Cambridge Scholars Publishing, 2017. 89–105. Print.

Walton, Priscilla L. and Manina Jones. *Detective Agency. Women Rewriting the Hard-Boiled Tradition*. Berkeley: University of California Press, 1999. Print.

CHAPTER 8

No Laughing Matter: Post-Soviet Cuba in the Orbit of Postmodern Parody

Elzbieta Sklodowska

That our lives in a postmodern world have been suffused with parody is no news. That on November 16, 2016, Oxford Dictionaries announced "post-truth" as its 2016 International Word of the Year is bad news. However, when I first began to reflect on the role of parody in post-Soviet Cuba, I immediately conceded not only the ubiquity of parodic activity on the island, but also the degree to which so many of its manifestations—from the most aesthetically focused to the mundane— are tenaciously political. And Cubans are quite fond of enlightening visitors that, in Cuba, nothing is what it seems—a sure sign of an over-arching (self)ironic *modus operandi* galvanized by the exigencies of a daily existence no longer in the Soviet orbit, but still under a spectral threat from across the Florida Straits. My initial exhilaration at what appeared to be a treasure trove of diverse materials for this project quickly gave way to the sense of suspicion that, when *everything* begins to present itself with a parodic gesture of a highly codified *double entendre*, some basic taxonomies need to be revisited.

E. Sklodowska (✉)
Washington University in St. Louis, Saint Louis, MO, USA
e-mail: esklodow@wustl.edu

H. C. Weldt-Basson (ed.), *Postmodern Parody in Latin American Literature*, Literatures of the Americas,
https://doi.org/10.1007/978-3-319-90430-6_8

In order to minimize confusion and ambiguity, the keywords announced in my title—post-Soviet, postmodern, parody—will be brought into sharper focus, both separately and as a constellation. To further anchor my study and recalibrate my lens, I will rely on sources from a variety of disciplines (literary and cultural studies, anthropology, history and art history, sociology) in an effort to provide a cross-section of parodic activity in contemporary Cuba. And, finally, I will concentrate on an in-depth analysis of parodic registers in the groundbreaking book by Margarita Mateo Palmer (b. 1950) *Ella escribía poscrítica* (*She Wrote Post-Criticism* 1995). Conceived and published amidst the everyday drudgery of the early post-Soviet era, *Ella escribía poscrítica* engages with the fundamental tenets of "western" postmodernism by means of irreverent (re)production of its metadiscourse and a dizzying amalgamation of fiction and academic criticism, testimony and (pseudo)autobiography, letters and interviews, footnotes and lecture notes.

As we shall see, Mateo Palmer—or, rather, her utterly unreliable narrator—teases fresh insights out of a seemingly infinite array of texts (and lives) of others, suffuses her own style with echoes of other voices and, by some sleight of hand, unleashes the forces of metamorphosis of the overly familiar into the surprisingly novel. Her bid for originality—presumably unsustainable once we have crossed the threshold of postmodernity—plays out as a *tour de force* gendered performance of her own, and strictly on her own terms. Hovering between remixing, sampling, cutting, pasting, recycling, and (re)creating, and steeped in a most radical (self)parody like no other text of Cuban literature, *Ella escribía poscrítica* both merits and fiercely resists critical scrutiny. In spite of its relentless foregrounding of textual artifice, the book is also replete with contextual references to post-Soviet Cuba, thus undermining Jacques Derrida's axiom that there is nothing outside the text.

The designation "post-Soviet" (Casamayor-Cisneros; de Ferrari; Hernández Salván)—albeit unappealing to many scholars and uncongenial to some Cubans—is the most straightforward of the three problematic terms in my title insofar as it denotes a temporal arc of almost three decades, whose watershed beginning was marked by the fall of the Berlin Wall (1989) and the subsequent obliteration of the global Soviet system. In the early 1990s, the abrupt withdrawal of USSR sponsored massive subsidies plunged Cuba into a profound socio-economic crisis of unprecedented proportions known as the "Special Period in Time of Peace" (Sklodowska, *Invento luego resisto*; Hernández-Reguant).

The Special Period unmasked the Soviet-style economic model as a hoax and exposed Cuban leaders as impostors whose thirty-year rule amounted to nothing more than a simulacrum of a socialist utopia. The phantom pains of this traumatic era—which brought no alteration to the Cuban political system and only some tweaks to the economic one—continue to reverberate in the memories and post-memories of Cubans who find themselves "on hold" amidst the perpetually deferred "transition" of the post-Fidel/post-Obama era. Meanwhile, material and ideological vestiges of the Soviet-dominated times function both as a reminder and a remainder of a thwarted utopian quest for a socialist alternative to the capitalist blueprint of modernity. In Cuban imaginary, "what the Russians left behind" (Yoss)—often reframed by the defamiliarizing grip of italics, quotations, and notoriously misspelled transliterations of Cyrillic script—has been subjected to the entire range of parodic activity, from open travesty to nostalgic reverence (Loss; Loss and Prieto; Puñales-Alpízar; Muguiro Altuna; Yoss; Cabrera et al.). Even though the "post" in "post-Soviet" is not synonymous with various "posts" associated with "the so-called postindustrial consumer society that cultural analysts acknowledge to be the heartland of postmodernism" (Coombe, 49), it is undoubtedly an offshoot of the "post" family tree.[1]

As to the postmodern, if we were to agree with John Beverley's assertion that "[o]ne of the things that could be said to define postmodernity as such is the collapse of communism" (47), the alignment between the postmodern and the post-Soviet would appear (almost) unequivocal. On the other hand, Cuba's geopolitical and economic isolation from the post-industrial, consumerist, and transnational capitalism made it an unlikely breeding ground for postmodernism as a purported byproduct of "late capitalism" (Jameson).[2] What remains clear, however, is that, amidst the full-blown crisis of the Special Period, Cuban writers and intellectuals (Araújo; De la Nuez; Ichikawa; Mosquera; Ravelo Cabrera; Cano and García; Hernández Busto; Sánchez Aguilera; Zurbano; Benítez-Rojo; Mateo Palmer, "Postmodernismo y Criterios")—always short on resources and long on resourcefulness, whether on the island or in the diaspora—made a concerted effort to generate their own terms of engagement with the politics and poetics of postmodernism and its avatars.[3]

By looking more closely at Cuban (in)versions of Jean-François Lyotard's "incredulity toward metanarratives" (xxiv), we may be able to ascertain how and why some form of the postmodern could play out at such a jarring remove from the material excess of the post-industrial world and in direct contradiction to Jamesonian "cultural logic of late capitalism." Román de la Campa's assertion that Cuba's *sui generis* postmodernity is a variation of "Third World postmodernity in which politics plays as great a role as aesthetics or philosophy" (96) dramatizes quite pointedly the distance between Jameson's theory, and the reality of living and creating in a politically charged "periphery" where the scarcity of material things seems to be overcompensated by creative imagination and a neo-baroque wealth of words. The paradoxes of Cuban postmodernity can only be captured, as Catherine Davies has done, by acknowledging "the significance of the 1959 Revolution in terms of modernity/ postmodernity" as a caesura when "the Cuban collectivity opted to switch from the narrative of late capitalism to a Marxist/nationalist alternative" (117). Consequently, according to Davies, post-Soviet Cuban postmodernity needs to be situated at the intersection of the "delegitimation of the Marxist grand narrative of emancipation" (116) brought about by the collapse of the Soviet system and "a replay of a half-forgotten endogenous postmodernity" (117).

Davies also addresses, albeit briefly, the interface between parody and postmodernity in Cuba. She remarks that post-modern cultural expressions involve "varying degrees of deconstruction, irony, parody, and pastiche; all efface the line that separates art from life" (106). But what is parody? Is it an artistic technique, a genre, an attitude, a consort of irony and satire, the dialectical force propelling the processes of literary evolution, or perhaps a repertoire of all of the above and much more? Notwithstanding a rather voluminous bibliography on the topic, the answer to this question has proven elusive or, at best, muddled by ambiguity (Bakhtin; Chatman; Dentith; Duvall; Genette; Hutcheon; Rose; Mendand; Waugh). Since it is impossible to reduce parody to a conclusive definition that would satisfy all scholars across various disciplines, for the purpose of this chapter I have adopted Linda Hutcheon's widely-acclaimed demarcation of the contours of parody as "imitation with critical ironic distance, whose irony can cut both ways. Ironic versions of 'trans-contextualization' and inversion are its major formal operatives, and the range of pragmatic ethos is from scornful ridicule to reverential homage" (*A Theory of Parody*, 37). It is a succinct description, yet flexible and capacious enough to encompass a wide range of everyday experiences and aesthetic discourses across time and cultures. It should suffice as a working definition as long as we bear in mind, as I will in the case of Cuba, that discrete manifestations of parodic activity are emphatically idiosyncratic. Consequently, I believe that my primary focus on parody as textual and performative practice will benefit from careful considerations of some of the many contextual variables, such as time, place (urban/rural), politics, cultural traditions, gender, ethnicity, sexuality, education, technology, infrastructure, living conditions, and so on.

If we wish, as we should, to contemplate parody in action, one way of beginning to do so in Cuba's case might by focusing on the performative mechanisms of *choteo*. The practice of *choteo* on the island has endured throughout many socio-political upheavals, including the Revolution of 1959, ever since Jorge Mañach identified it in *Indagación del choteo* [*Inquiry into el choteo*] (1928) as a self-conscious propensity of his countrymen to engage in irreverent mockery aimed at upending the authority of any normative order. If *choteo* seems to pervade daily existence in Cuba, it is because of its chameleonic nature. Similar to parody, *choteo* is easily observable as it morphs into an array of guises and disguises: from political jokes (Tanuma; Prieto) to the playfulness of carnivalesque excess, from (self)ironic ridicule to the subtle intricacies of word games, from the Aesopian code known only to the insiders to the elusive glimpses of outright defiance. Cuban *choteo* is also on full display in the mock epic of hastily scribbled graffiti, which engage in parodic games with the foundational metanarrative of anti-imperialist zeal and the prevailing rhetoric of heroism, sacrifice, and martyrdom. In a country whose national anthem proclaims that to "die for the motherland is to live" the invitation to mockery appears to be permanently open.

To a foreign visitor, the outward appearance of *choteo* might seem quaint or outmoded because Cuba's everyday experience is not as technologically mediated as it tends to be among many other communities around the world, including the Cuban diaspora. Consequently, my initial conjecture about the ubiquity of parodic activity requires a caveat or two. The population of the island is hardly (over)exposed to myriad forms of parody generated by the twenty-first-century social media and digital technologies. For better or worse, and in spite of various "openings" and "transitions" of the post-Fidel/post-Obama era, *Twitter*, *Facebook*, or *YouTube* do not yet have the same grip on Cuban popular imaginary as they do in the larger context of the presumably interconnected globalized world. Access to the internet remains severely restricted (Grenier, "Cultural Policy"; Venegas; Nelson), and even in Havana it would be difficult and uncommon to log into a parodic website akin to whitehouse.org, follow the torrent of news satire shows, or partake of the dizzying punditry of "fake" news gone viral (Baym and Jones; Knapp; Coombe). And, while legal experts in many parts of the globe engage in controversies and lawsuits over the status of parody and satire under the "fair use principle" as defined by Section 107 of the Copyright Act (Coombe, passim), in Cuba even the most blatant infringements of intellectual property laws are seldom frowned upon, let alone persecuted (Marcus; Johnson; Pertierra; San Pedro; Schur; Smith; Hernández-Reguant, "Copyrighting").[4]

In today's Cuba, this *laissez faire* attitude toward the rules of appropriation—which, in different guises, underlies a whole spectrum of discourses, from plagiarism to *bona fide* parody—is considered to be borne out of scarcity. Necessity, indeed, is the mother of invention, as exemplified by the free-wheeling creativity of Claude Lévi-Strauss' *bricoleur* whose knack for making do with "whatever is at hand" is probably as ancient as civilization. In contemporary Cuba, *bricolage* is propelled by the almost legendary grassroots ingenuity as it coalesces into what scholar, artist, and collector Ernesto Oroza (b. 1968) calls "technological disobedience."[5] With its interlacing of transgression and creativity, improvisation and cunning, precariousness and reinvention, this attitude—poignantly illustrated by Oroza's ever-expanding physical and virtual archive of self-made/"hacked" objects—highlights both the resistance to normativity and a heterogeneous layering of influences, some of them camouflaged, some completely erased, some playfully transfigured. Oroza, who traveled throughout Cuba in the early 1990s gathering objects as diverse as aluminum cafeteria trays turned into TV antennas, lanterns made of glass containers and toothpaste tubes, shoes crafted from melted plastic bags, or fans propelled by motors extracted from Soviet washing machines, now uses the internet to display his collection (http://www.ernestooroza.com/; PBS, "The Bizarre"). This virtual "museum" of the material culture of the Special Period evokes a true sense of "wonder," a term coined by Stephen Greenblatt that is somewhat akin to the defamiliarizing effect captured in Victor Shklovsky's time-honored notion of *ostranen'e* ("estrangement"). Occasionally, as Oroza explains in his essays and interviews, "technological disobedience" is tacitly endorsed by Cuban authorities, or it may require an act of *canibaleo*, which consists in dismantling, often illegally, one piece of machinery in order to acquire spare parts for reassembly into another functional unit or system. The symbolically charged meaning of *canibaleo* is not lost

on me in the Latin American/Caribbean context; however, in an effort
to avoid the common trap of Cuban "exoticism," I wish to emphasize
that, while many of the artifacts from Oroza's collection are idiosyncratic
in terms of materials and design, they also respond to the "universal
interpellation" of fundamental human needs and the combined exigencies of scarcity, thrift, and improvisation.[6]

The interpretation of the various manifestations of *choteo*, *canibaleo*,
or "technological disobedience"—and, ultimately, the decoding of their
subversive/transgressive effects—is triangulated by the forces of text,
pre-text, and context. Just as in the case of literary parody, "the relation between text and pre-text is of functional necessity for the text
and therefore has to be noticed by the reader" (Müeller, 48). Parody—
whether mundane or artistic—might be in the eye of the beholder,
but it is never a solitary game and, as Mikhail Bakhtin famously determined, it can only be fully realized in a dialogic interaction between
people and discursive structures. A foreign visitor to the post-Fidel/post-
Obama Cuba is likely to miss the proverbial boat of *choteo*'s purposefully
deployed parody, while, at the same time, s/he might misread Cuban
reality through a distorting lens of exoticism. Parody and its frequent
companions irony and satire, easily get lost in cross-cultural communication, or acquire unintended registers. What invariably catches the eye
of foreign visitors to Cuba is the already mentioned ubiquity of murals
and billboards (*vallas*) devoted to political propaganda. However, what
is ultimately brought into relief in travelogues, blogs, videos, and even
some scholarly publications is not the engagement with the palimpsest
of slogans, quotes, allusions, and word games but, rather, an emphasis
on the aesthetic crudeness of the billboards, which relegates them to
the obsolete category of a post-utopian cabinet of curiosities. For many
foreign visitors, both political graffiti and official propaganda might also
read as clumsy parodies, or perhaps pastiche, of the glamorous commercial advertising so rampant in the consumer societies they come from.

One could easily chalk up these attitudes and blind spots of foreign-
ers to the iterations of Saidian Orientalism, a purported ethnocentric proclivity of the "West" to fantasize itself against inexorably exoticised (mis)
representations of "others." Post-Soviet Cuba lends itself to such com-
pulsive "othering" particularly well, perceived as it might be as a geopolitical anachronism from the perspective of the United States, just at mere
ninety miles away, or as a jarring anomaly in the broader context of the
post-Cold War era. Viewed from the outside, as scholars José Quiroga

and Ana Dopico have shown, post-Soviet Cuba is thus staged as a *tableau* frozen in time, a bizarre theme park left in the wake of defeat and marred by its anachronistic distance from the "(post)modernity" of the rest of the world. Dopico furnishes some particularly succinct and perceptive insights into the pictorial representations of Havana which, as she contends, serves as a "tourist synecdoche" for the entire country: "The gaze of the lens in Havana has accompanied the eye of the market, reflecting the fashionable status and historical exceptionalism of the city as living ruin, and the allure of a scarcity still set apart from the flawed and normative narratives of development, democratization, or global economic integration" (451). To the degree these "doctored" images of Havana get "reintegrated into the global image market" they become, in a way, "defanged" of their critical bite and can no longer play the role of witnesses to the socio-political and economic realities of post-Soviet Cuba: "As images of Havana circulate, they appear to normalize the island's status in a post-Cold War secular order, literally keeping 'out of sight' political conflicts that cannot be assimilated by the narratives of tourism and foreign investment, symbolic or otherwise" (452). I might add that, due to the increasing participation of Cuban artists and writers in global publishing and art circuits, some of them have also been accused of "selling out" when, guided by the invisible hand of the market, they opt to perpetuate the best-selling stereotypes of post-Soviet Cuba (Sklodowska, *Invento*; Price; Garrido Castellano; Fornet; Camnitzer).

Even if we take to heart Judith Butler's admonition (365) not to accept at face value Fredric Jameson's contention that pastiche—as humorless parody "defanged" of its critical acumen—is a quintessential feature of postmodernism (65), we would have to admit that the gratuitous excess of endlessly reposted and replayed *collages* of vintage cars, decaying colonial buildings, and rustic "do it yourself" inventions ends up flattening the purportedly "genuine" Cuba into an Orientalist pastiche. In its desire to "sell" Cuba, the nominally socialist regime of Raúl Castro has no qualms in repackaging, albeit selectively, some of the very same banalities and clichés that abound in foreign blogs and travelogues, and (re)scripting Cuba's "authentic" tropicality with the predictable mix of erotic, sexist, and racialized overtones (the trope of the *mulata*).[7] I would venture that the distortions that occur in the process of refashioning post-Soviet Cuba build up to a pastiche of magical realist "otherness." Viewed more broadly, these representations of Cuba constitute a variation of a phenomenon identified by Graham Huggan as an over-arching feature of the Global South: the marketing of the peripheral exotic from the margins/as the margins. In an endless masquerade of simulacra, the artfully staged vintage cars and the painstakingly restored mansions, monasteries, churches, and squares of colonial Havana stand in for post-Soviet Cuba as much as the open entrails of hundreds of dilapidated buildings that still surround the postcard-like artifice of Plaza Vieja. Nowhere is the postmodern dimension of Cuba more visible than in Old Havana's architectural restoration endeavor. The reconstructive salvaging of the past is, of course, a "repetition with a difference," a *tour de force* of transmutation of ruin into monument, of mansions and palaces into hotels, clubs, and restaurants catering to foreign tourists. Everything seems *as if* it were real, a semantic construct that in Spanish (*como si fuera*) requires the use of the subjunctive, forever imperfect, and signals the fade-out of the original.

As important as this palimpsest-like backdrop might be for tracing the contours of parody in contemporary Cuba, I do not intend to limit myself to everyday practice of *choteo* or the iterations of post-Soviet simulacra throughout global commodity culture. In order to further delineate the parameters of parody as a dual force of artistic creativity and radical ideological critique, I will delve beyond the realm of the quotidian, and into the sphere of artistic, literary, and intellectual production. When revisiting my earlier research on parody in Spanish American narrative (Sklodowska, *La parodia*) and, more specifically, attempting to retrace Cuban literary production of the twentieth and twenty-first centuries, the works of Virgilio Piñera (*La carne de René, Electra Garrigó*), Alejo Carpentier (*El recurso del método*), Guillermo Cabrera Infante (*Tres tristes tigres*), Severo Sarduy (*De donde son los cantantes, Cobra, Maitreya*), Reynaldo Arenas (*El mundo alucinante, La loma del ángel, El color de verano*) and, more recently, Leonardo Padura, Ena Lucía Portela (*Cien botellas en la pared*), Senel Paz (*El lobo, el bosque y el hombre nuevo*), Ana Lydia Vega Serova (*Ánima fatua*) or Alberto Guerra Naranjo (*La soledad del tiempo*) offer compelling evidence that Cuban writers thrive on harnessing the defamiliarizing power of pitch-perfect parody and deploying it both in the service of satiric critique and for the sake of aesthetic virtuosity.[8] A cursory glance at Cuban visual arts confirms that this area, too, is irresistibly drawn toward the parodic mode (Fusco; Lightbody; Santana; Segre; Snyder; Weiss; Zeitlin). As to the domain of the cinema, I could hardly think of a single iconic Cuban film that would not bear an imprint of a parodic gesture: *Memorias del subdesarrollo, Plaf! O demasiado miedo a la vida, La muerte de una burócrata, La última cena, Alicia en el pueblo de maravillas, Fresa y chocolate, Guantanamera, Lista de espera, La película de Ana, Juan de los muertos,* to mention just the most obvious.

It is difficult, of course, to measure the political impact of artistic or literary works that hinge on parody. For one, due to the ephemeral nature of some events, precarious documentation and the interventions of Cuban state censorship, it is almost impossible to assess the full aesthetic force and political ramifications of myriad art collectives, exhibitions, installations, performances, and intellectual projects of the 1980s and 1990s, including *Puré, Grupo Provisional, Arte Calle, Castillo de la Fuerza* and *Paideia,* well-known for their intransigent aesthetic and ideological confrontations with Castro's regime. In his study of Cuban writers of the so-called "Generation O," who started publishing after the crisis of the 1990s, Rafael Rojas claims that "neither the art revolt of the 80s nor the intellectual essayism of the 90s, with its postmodern civism or its erudite archaeologies, negated power to the degree that one can observe or read among younger writers and artists today." As I turn my attention to *Ella escribía poscrítica*, I will argue, however, that its daring distinctiveness among the many avatars of parodic activity in post-Soviet Cuba should not be glossed over or dismissed altogether. By grafting Mateo Palmer's text onto the background that I have just outlined, I will also discuss the importance of the site of intellectual production within the shifting, but still fearful, asymmetry between center and periphery.

If we were to synthesize the quite sizeable secondary bibliography inspired by *Ella escribía poscrítica* (Araújo, Baujín, Cámara, Campuzano, Díaz Mantilla, Eichenbronner, Garbatzky, González, Morejón, Pérez-Hernández, Puyol, Riccio, de Toro), the recurring keywords would coalesce around the transgressive hallmarks of postmodernity, with parody taking center stage along with language-games, intertextuality, stylistic hybridity, palimpsestic eclecticism (novel-testimony-essay-pseudo-autobiography), play with popular culture (graffiti), extreme self-reflexivity, and multiple de-centered subjectivities.[9] The fabric of *Ella escribía poscrítica* is woven from countless titles of canonical texts, both literary and theoretical, precise and altered quotes, overt or veiled references to well-known writers (Borges, Asturias, Cortázar, Piñera, Sarduy, Cabrera Infante, Martí, Ortiz, Macedonio Fernández, Huidobro, García Márquez, Calvino, Kafka, Mistral, Neruda, María Zambrano,

Laura Esquivel), critics (Jameson, Lyotard, Fanon, García Canclini), and fictional characters (Carpentier's Mackandal, 31, or Menegildo, 47; Lezama Lima's Oppiano Licario, 58, and Foción and Fronesis, 136–137), snippets of letters, song lyrics, lecture notes and interviews (both authentic and apocryphal, often undistinguishable), graffiti from Havana's G Street (21–24) followed by solemn Latin inscriptions enshrined on the walls of the University of Havana (80–81), neologisms, political innuendo, allusions to Cuban syncretic religions (Elleguá, Ochún, Changó, Yemayá, San Lázaro, *güijes*, *ñánigos*) and recurring references to practices and concepts explicitly linked by the narrator to the "postmodern" dimension of Cuban/pan-Caribbean culture, including *choteo* (14–15), transculturation, neobaroque, and carnival (91). When it comes to Latin American literary genealogy, Mateo Palmer singles out *testimonio* as an evanescent narrative mode whose postmodern afterlife lingers only in a parodic guise ("Postentrevista testimonialmente objetiva" [Testimonially objective post-interview], 182). By any standards, *Ella escribía poscrítica* is an unconventional book. As it happens, its kaleidoscopic confluence of aesthetic, cultural, and political discursive modes and references ends up turning it inside out in a gesture that, paradoxically, combines in equal measure *bona fide* vulnerability and defiance.

When gauged in relation to postmodern parody, as delineated by Hutcheon, the "trans-contextualizations" accumulated throughout *Ella escribía poscrítica* display an astonishing range of (self-)ironic distancing, "from scornful ridicule to reverential homage." While it seems that there remains no parodic path that has not been taken by Mateo Palmer, the "post" in the title specifically foregrounds the book's "undisciplined" (Pérez-Hernández) engagement with a particular "order of discourse," the one of academic criticism. Whereas the obscurity of jargon-filled critical idiom bears the brunt of Mateo Palmer's "postcritical" mockery, several Cuban writers (Carpentier, Lezama Lima, Piñera, Cabrera Infante, Sarduy) get more than a nod of recognition in a long chapter dedicated to "illustrious antecedents to postmodernity in Cuban literature" (90–121). Unsurprisingly, parody is also the pivot of Mateo Palmer's fine-grained analysis of Cabrera Infante's "The Death of Trotsky Narrated by Several Cuban Writers, Years Later or Before" (José Martí, Virgilio Piñera, Lydia Cabrera, Lino Novás Calvo, Alejo Carpentier, Nicolás Guillén, José Lezama Lima), an anthology-worthy parodic segment of the novel *Tres tristes tigres* (published in Barcelona in 1967, translated into English as *Three Trapped Tigers* in 1971). Unencumbered by the fact that—as far as I could determine—*Tres tristes tigres* has not been published in Cuba, Mateo Palmer joins a slew of scholars who have come to regard "The Death of Trotsky" as an all-time epitome of Cuban literary parody. However, what makes her approach most memorable is that it is not conceived in the semblance and image of "disciplined" academic criticism. Simultaneously foundational and deconstructive, it stands on its own, and it stands out.

Footnotes in *Ella escribía poscrítica*—a grand total of 128—deserve separate scrutiny. The Borgesian penchant for apocryphal references resonates, for example, in footnote 91 (140) citing a non-existent work by Mateo Palmer herself (*Cartas a Athos*) published by a non-existent press, Editorial Pon El Huevo, whose name is funny in and by itself [Lay an Egg] but turns into pure mockery once we realize that it is also a pun on Pinos Nuevos [New Pine Shoots], an official book series launched in 1994 with the explicit goal of promoting young writers (*los novísimos*) (Martín Sevillano, 80). Even though Mateo Palmer scatters sufficient clues for decoding the parodic register of footnote 91 (footnote 92 cites "Historia de la eternidad" by Borges, and Pinos Nuevos is mentioned throughout the book), overall the inter(con)textual labyrinth of *Ella escribía poscrítica*—which I have reproduced only partially and somewhat randomly—represents a major challenge for most readers. Without a map and a compass—Borgesian pun intended—this maze becomes increasingly difficult to navigate once we enter the domain of inside jokes and oblique anecdotes (Cuban "epitaphs", 40–41), or deeply codified allusions to the rituals, trials, and tribulations of Cuban *literati* (126–178, passim). As it happens, references to everyday reality do not always serve as signposts or offer a reprieve from the obscure, as in the instance when we stumble upon a seemingly random remark about "importing" tropical vegetables, such as yucca and yam, from Lithuania and Warsaw (29). The fact that it represents a snippet from a satirical verse that circulated in Cuba during the Special Period is, of course, of little relevance as long as the reader is able to decipher it in the intended register of poking fun at the absurdities of Cuba's entanglement with the Soviet-led Council for Mutual Economic Assistance. Inevitably, many such details will flow past the non-Cuban reader's eyes without being registered as factual, apocryphal, or parodic, or simply not being registered at all. In spite of my relative familiarity with the context, as I was reading and rereading *Ella escribía poscrítica* I remained leery of "short circuiting" parody and taking too much at face value. The 2005 Cuban reprint of the book by Letras Cubanas, as well as the 2010 Atom Press version I consulted for this chapter, surprised me with an appendix I had not seen before: a curious text allegedly penned by a certain Ínclita de Mamporro, clearly a fictitious professor from a non-existent university. While it was evident that Ínclita de Mamporro was one of Mateo Palmer's invented alter egos—along with Surligneur-2, Dulce Azucena, la Abanderada Roja, Intertextual, la Siemprenvela, Mitopoyética, Lafeministadesatada—I was unaware of the circumstances surrounding this particular imposture.[10]

Without the most helpful note from two "editors" (215), I would not have known that this text was first delivered by Mateo Palmer, alias Ínclita de Mamporro, at a public event in Havana in November 1996 to "commemorate" the one hundredth (sic!) anniversary of *Ella escribía poscrítica* and that the speech was subsequently published under the title "Ella no escribía poscrítitica: exorcizaba sus demonios" [She Was Not Writing Postcriticism, She Was Exorcising Her Own Demons] in *Unión*, the official journal of the UNEAC (National Union of Writers and Artists of Cuba). Actually, critic José Quiroga, who underscores the asynchronous experience of time in post-Soviet Cuba, could have used Mamporro's "futuristic" text as a perfect illustration for his brilliant argument. As for Mateo Palmer, in her meticulously staged performance as Ínclita de Mamporro, she turned self-parody into an irreverent act of defiance of Cuban cultural establishment. Mateo Palmer's playful choice to use as earrings (as if they were earrings) the two official medals she had been awarded for her contributions to Cuban education and culture (Pérez Hernández, *Indisciplinas*, 72; Araújo, 81) converted a stereotypically "feminine" sartorial signifier into a marker of political transgression. According to Hutcheon, self-parody "is not just the artist's way of disowning earlier mannerisms by externalization...It is a way of creating a form out of the questioning of the very act of aesthetic production" (10). In the end, Mateo Palmer's protean transformation into Ínclita Mamporro sent a strong message about what it means to be an artist and an intellectual in a country where cultural production is controlled—albeit not stifled— by an authoritarian regime. No laughing matter, indeed.

As often happens in Cuba, the political turned out to be an important touchstone for an apparently frivolous act. In a country of "extensive politicization" (Dopico Black, 133), whose Constitution identifies as the highest goal of its citizens "the construction of socialism and advancement toward a communist society" (Article 5), any serious intellectual engagement with foreign theories of postmodernity—which is at the core of *Ella escribía poscrítica*—could be construed as an act of dissidence.[11] In a retrospective article, "Postmodernismo y Criterios," Mateo Palmer recognized the extreme polarization in Cuban debates around postmodernity and its avatars: while postmodernism was perceived by many intellectuals as a potentially powerful tool for representing the otherwise silenced or distorted voices of the marginalized, it was flatly rejected by the most dogmatic sectors of the Cuban regime as the latest threat to the revolutionary project (9). As if on cue, in an essay published in 1999, Rafael Hernández—who could be considered a surrogate, if not a standard-bearer, of the cultural establishment (Grenier, "Temas")—brandishes a rhetoric that depicts postmodernism as the devil (re)incarnate of imperialist meddling in Cuba:

> From a political point of view, culture represents a system of resistance to forces that break down social cohesion. To borrow from the language of biology, we can say that such pathologies, both external and internal, grow more virulent in times like these. There are no more effective mechanisms for neutralizing the invasion of antigens of the (post)modern world, and for repairing dysfunctions in our own system, than those provided by the many facts of culture. In their response to foreign and hostile entities, cultural products act according to the principles of immunity, not as the kind of ideological condom whose ineffectiveness is well known. Culture can generate a more trustworthy system of antibodies and bodily repair. (51)

Hernández underscores both the militant ethos of the intellectuals and the fundamental role that genuinely Cuban culture is destined to play in resisting a foreign infiltration of the postmodern "antigens." Today, his tirade may read like an unintended pastiche of official rhetoric—a post-newspeak of the post-Soviet era—but, again, it should not be dismissed as innocuous or irrelevant. To the contrary, it helps us imagine what Mateo Palmer might have been up against when she undertook her "postcritical" experiments. I would argue that *Ella escribía poscrítica* is both a product of and a reflection upon Cuba's "postmodern condition" as an offspring of "rapid changes and nonlinear development" resulting in "pastiche and bricolage of disconnected modernizations within postmodernity" (Prizant, 82). Ultimately, these conditions "render it difficult to locate what is real in Cuba; the bizarre, the surreal, and the illogical frequently converge to frame reality" (Prizant, 82). Granted,

Hernández's discourse fits the "bizarre" and "surreal" categories much better than Mateo Palmer's book.

Paradoxically, state control might be contributing to the constant (re) activation of "parodic antibodies" (Bakhtin, *Notes Made*, 133) both in Cuban "practice of everyday life" (*choteo*), and in literary and artistic production. As many critics have observed, the double-voiced encoding associated with parody lends itself to challenging authoritarian power (Hariman; Howe; Hutcheon) and, in tandem with irony and satire, can be deployed as a powerful tool to circumvent government control. If these strategies were politically irrelevant, why, then, as Hutcheon wonders (78), would authoritarian regimes put so much effort into denigrating parody, or dismissing satire as trivial? There is little doubt that the cultural policy of the Cuban Revolution was mapped out by Fidel Castro on June 30, 1961, in his address to a gathering of intellectuals at the National Library in Havana. Commonly referred to as "Words to the Intellectuals", the speech proclaimed the "right" of the Revolution to safeguard its own existence by drawing the lines between what was allowable in artistic endeavors undertaken on the island ("within the Revolution") and what was unacceptable ("against the Revolution"). Artist, writer, and critic Coco Fusco remarks that as a "benchmark of Cuba's cultural policy regarding expressive freedoms" the binary within/ against the Revolution hinged on a paradox: on one hand, it sounded "as an absolute commandment" while, on the other, it was vague enough to accommodate even the most arbitrary and unpredictable shifts in government decisions ("Editorial. Cuba"). Ironically enough, since 1961 this approach has also enabled "the recurrence of periods of official relaxation in cultural policy, easing of censorship and encouragement—or at least acceptance—of experimentation and innovation" (Miller, 677).[12] *Ella escribía poscrítica* and the concomitant performance of Mateo Palmer impersonating Ínclita de Mamporro might have capitalized precisely on such relaxation of state control in the wake of the Special Period. As Mateo Palmer's book amply demonstrates, coloring outside the lines of the officially sanctioned revolutionary discourse is, inevitably, a liminal practice in a space that is more alternative than blatantly oppositional.

Throughout the years, "Within the Revolution, everything, against the Revolution, no rights at all" has been quoted, misquoted, misremembered, mistranslated, glossed, and glossed over or, at the very least, taken out of context (Randall). Along with Castro's other catchphrases, such as "Patria o muerte, venceremos" [Homeland or death,

we will triumph] or "Historia me absolverá" [History will absolve me],
"Words to the Intellectuals" has lent itself to relentless jokes, parodies, and spoofs. Inevitably, in the course of intergenerational repetitions the political edge of some of these gestures has become dulled.
However, the defamiliarizing power of parody may be more resistant
to being reabsorbed into the matrix of power (Butler) than our postmodern wisdom would allow us to admit. "Intelectuales sin palabras"
("Intellectuals without Words"), a short-lived installation by Cuban
artist Hamlet Lavastida (b. 2003) during the 2009 Havana Biennial, is
a case in point. As described by Fusco ("Editorial"; *Dangerous Moves*,
18–21), Lavastida's artwork consisted of a brief quote from Castro's
famous speech stenciled outside one of Havana's art galleries. The fact
that "Lavastida's stenciled words were removed shortly after they had
been installed" (Fusco, "Editorial") suggests, however, that in the eyes
of the regime this act was much more than just a "blank" parody that
had lost its bite.

In the course of more than two decades, *Ella escribía poscrítica* has
not lost much of its critical bite either. The enduring power of parody
in Mateo Palmer's now "classic" text may be attributed, in equal measure, to her ludic engagement with Western theories of postmodernity
and her intensely personal rendition of what it meant to be multi-tasking
as a woman, a writer, a mother, a teacher, a mentor, a cook, a nurse,
a mechanic, and an intellectual during the worst crisis in Cuba's modern history. According to José Quiroga, the splintered identities of the
writer/narrator/critic who struggles to stay afloat amidst the everyday
chaos of a shipwrecked utopia sends a powerful political message: "This
fragmentation can be understood by relating it to appeals for unity that
took place throughout the Special Period when 'resistance' as a mode
of action was insisted upon in all official discourse" (126). Faltering on
the brink of exhaustion when grappling with daily challenges, Mateo
Palmer goes in and out of a post-Borgesian library of Babel and brings
her readers down to earth. She reminds us that the main drama of the
Special Period unfolded in the domestic sphere, with women bearing the
brunt of material shortages and remaining at the forefront of the daily
struggle. The narrator's/protagonist's/writer's small-scale crises refract
the apocalyptic magnitude of the Special Period through a series of
fleeting vignettes: reporting the loss of her only pair of heels, concoct-
ing family meals out of insipid food rations, fixing her bike, or franti-
cally searching for such basic items as asthma medication (39). Mateo

Palmer's predicament becomes etched in our minds as a mock epic of sorts whereby her real struggle (*lucha*) stands in stark contrast to the disembodied myth of revolutionary quest, and its masculine pathos of sacrifice and heroism.

The complex interplay between the irreverent treatment of postmodernist theories and the fragmented chronicle of the topsy-turvy reality of the Special Period also serves as a reminder that profound inequalities continue to determine the production and diffusion of global academic knowledge. Mateo Palmer is acutely aware of the many degrees of separation between the geopolitical and historical contingency of *her* moment (the Special Period), and the theory and practice of academic scholarship in places where postmodernism had been galvanized by material excess. Cuba in 1995 may seem a surprising time and an inhospitable place from which to make a decisive critical intervention, but this is precisely what *Ella escribía poscrítica* has accomplished: in the crucible of the extreme material scarcity of the Special Period, Mateo Palmer forged a dialogue with a discourse whose theoretical matrix and critical practice had been molded in/by the United States and (western) Europe. Aesthetically and ideologically disobedient, to paraphrase Oroza, she carved out her *poscrítica* not as a peripheral mimicry of the "center" but, rather, as a highly personalized version of Cuban *canibaleo*. She demonstrated that self-representation in Cuba—and of a Cuban woman writer, in particular—does not have to be stymied or impoverished by material conditions. To be sure, her day-to-day experience with drastic scarcity reveals two facets of production of knowledge outside of privileged (imagined) communities: on one hand, the extreme frustration with the lack of material resources—tellingly illustrated by all the books and journals identified as indispensable for her research that are lost, stolen, checked out, or otherwise unavailable in the library (20–21); and, on the other, the astonishing creativity *inspired* by that very lack (*el arte de inventor y resolver*). Ultimately, Mateo Palmer's post-critical bricolage is a powerful reassertion of Audre Lorde's time-tested dictum that "the master's tools will never dismantle the master's house."

Notes

1. The extraordinary proliferation of taxonomies involving the prefix "post-" needs to be acknowledged, but also deemed too wide-ranging as to fall within the scope of this article. Beyond the most obvious appellations

(postmodern, postcolonial, post-socialist), we might consider post-memory, post-history, post-Cold War, post-politics, post-democratic, post-human, post-occidental, post-digital, and the already mentioned post-truth.

2. A magisterial reflection on the intricacies of Cuban "postmodern condition" is provided by Catherine Davies in "Surviving (on) the Soup of Signs." Davies's article is well-grounded in ample bibliography and rich in historical layering. Translations of major theorists of postmodernity began reaching Cuba in the late 1980s and continued throughout the Special Period: Fredric Jameson's "El posmodernismo o la lógica cultural del capitalismo tardío" appeared in Cuba's flagship journal *Casa de la Américas* in 1986, and, thanks to the indefatigable work of Desiderio Navarro, articles by Manfred Pfister, Hal Foster, Linda Hutcheon, Ihab Hassan, Susan Rubin Suleiman, and Erika Fisher-Lichte, among others, were published in Navarro's journal *Criterios* in the early 1990s.

3. Further differentiation between postmodernism, postmodernity, and postmodern can be found in Irvine.

4. In the context where there is little shame in plagiarizing and no shaming of plagiarism, illegal digital delivery of pirated materials in the form of "paquete semanal" ("weekly package") merits special attention. More than any other distinctly Cuban experience, it foregrounds a peculiar symbiosis between unofficial networks peddling copyrighted wares and the Cuban regime tolerating and enabling such practices: "In parallel to…structural constraints on internet access, various workarounds have emerged in Cuba. One well-documented phenomenon is USB sharing, which since the mid-2000s has become an efficient system for digital media circulation in Cuba. Over time this form of distribution has become standardized in a commercial format known as *el paquete* (the package). These compilations comprise one terabyte of diverse media content – television, movies, software, magazines and music – all updated on a weekly basis. The paquete typically includes: the latest episodes of TV shows direct from the United States, Spain, Mexico, Brazil, and Colombia; a selection of new documentaries; Cuban television shows; the latest music videos; and multiple TV programs from Miami…Because of its illegal nature, this infrastructure is hidden. Except for some cases of commercial trading of internet access, the Cuban authorities have tolerated the existence of these networks" (Rodríguez, 182–183). Beyond the weekly *paquete*, Tom Astley provides a detailed account of the use of USB as a powerful vehicle to disseminate all kinds of ideologically problematic and otherwise unavailable materials (foreign music videos, films, and books) while Vicente Morín Aguado refers to this practice as "the people's Internet." See also San Pedro, Balaisis (163), and Pertierra.

5. For a truly comprehensive overview of myriad facets of inventiveness in Cuba, I recommend *Beans and Roses: Everyday Economies and Morality in Contemporary Havana Cuba* by María Padrón Hernández.

6. While invention and innovation do not necessarily go hand-in-hand, it is important to note that Cuban "technological disobedience" is in good company as one of the many encarnations of "grassroots innovations" which, according to Angus Donald Campbell, include "do-it-yourself or DIY (United States), hacking (England), jugaad (India), 自主创新 or zizhu chuangxin (China), Trick 17 (Germany), gambiarra (Brazil), système D. (France), and jua kali (Kenya). Descriptions within South Africa include: in isiZulu, izenzele; in Sesotho, iketsetse; and in Setswana, itirele; all refer to doing it yourself and being self-sufficient" (32). See also Lastovicka and Bettencourt; and Jencks and Silver. In reference to Latin American art history, Dezeuze recalls the theory and practice of Brazilian artist Hélio Oiticica, who in 1967 coined the motto "on adversity we thrive" ("da adversidade vivemos"). Nicholas Balaisis, in turn, furnishes a useful synthesis of Oroza's theory (154–155).

7. Some trends in post-Soviet Cuban literary production and, in particular, the so-called dirty realism championed by Pedro Juan Gutiérrez, can be seen as a mutation of the "porno tropic tradition" studied by McClintock in the context of Anglophone and Francophone literatures and, particularly, travel writing.

8. Studies of parody in Cuban literature tend to focus on individual authors rather than on broader overviews, with bibliographies on Arenas, Piñera, Cabrera Infante, Sarduy, and Padura being particularly prolific. See, for example, Lisenby, Rowlandson, Ruiz Barrionuevo, Bartolotto, Lange, and Manzari.

9. Mateo Palmer's work has been recognized most recently through such prestigious awards as the residency in the International Writing Program at the University of Iowa (2015) and the 2016 National Prize for Literature in Cuba. For an overview of Mateo Palmer's intellectual and literary trajectory, see José Antonio Baujín's *laudatio* delivered at the National Prize for Literature ceremony on February 12, 2017 ("Un graffiti MAGGIE").

10. Pérez-Hernández' playful interview with Mateo Palmer ("Del regreso de un libro"), conducted in conjunction with the launch of the revised and expanded version of *Ella escribía poscrítica* and published by the journal *Temas*, provides a wealth of informative details that shed light on some of the most opaque aspects of the book.

11. The entire Article 5 reads as follows: "The Communist Party of Cuba, Martian and of Marxist-Leninist, the organized vanguard of the Cuban nation, is the superior leading force of the society and the State,

organizing and guiding the common efforts aimed at the highest goals of the construction of socialism and advancement toward the communist society." Furthermore, the 2002 amendment to Article 3 pronounced "social revolutionary political system" as "irrevocable."

12. Regardless of the to-and-fro in cultural policies, any kind of critical or parodic treatment of Fidel or Raúl Castro is considered taboo and unequivocally "against the Revolution." See Fusco, *Performance and Politics in Cuba*, for specific examples from visual and performance arts. For additional bibliography on Cuban cultural policies, studies by Kumaraswami and Grenier are particularly thorough and balanced.

WORKS CITED

Araújo, Nara. "Repensando desde el feminismo los estudios latinoamericanos." *Lectora* 5–6 (1999–2000): 55–65. Print.

Astley, Tom. "The People's Mixtape: Peer-to-Peer File Sharing Without the Internet in Contemporary Cuba." In *Networked Music Cultures*. Edited by Raphaël Nowak and Andrew Whelan. London: Palgrave Macmillan, 2016. 13–30. Print.

Bakhtin, Mikhail. "From Notes Made in 1970–71." In *Speech Genres and Other Late Essays*. Edited by Caryl Emerson and Michael Holquist and translated by Vern W. McGee. Austin: Texas University Press, 1986. 132–158. Print.

———. *The Dialogic Imagination: Four Essays*. Edited by Michael Holquist and translated by Caryl Emerson and Michael Holquist. Austin: Texas University Press, 1981. Print.

Balaisis, Nicholas. *Cuban Film Media, Late Socialism, and the Public Sphere: Imperfect Aesthetics*. New York: Palgrave, 2016. Print.

Bartolotto, María Celina. "Fake for Its Own Sake: A Staged Performance of Choteo in Sarduy's *De donde son los cantantes*." *Chasqui* 38.1 (2009): 16–28. Print.

Baujín, José Antonio. "Un grafiti MAGGIE. Discurso de elogio de Margarita Mateo en la entrega del Premio Nacional de Literatura 2016." *Revolución y Cultura* (April–June 2017): 13–15. http://www.ryc.cult.cu/wp-content/uploads/2017/04/2-2017a.pdf. Web.

———. "Una recreación posmoderna del topos del ensayismo." *Revista Universidad de La Habana* 247 (1997): 216–217. Print.

Baym, Geoffrey, and Jeffrey P. Jones. "News Parody in Global Perspective: Politics, Power, and Resistance." *Popular Communication* 10.1–2 (2012): 2–13. Print.

Benítez-Rojo, Antonio. *The Repeating Island: The Caribbean and the Postmodern Perspective*. Translated by James Maraniss. Durham: Duke University Press, 1992. Print.

Beverley, John. "The Im/Possibility of Politics: Subalternity, Modernity, Hegemony." *The Latin American Subaltern Studies Reader.* Edited by Ileana Rodríguez. Durham: Duke University Press, 2001: 47–63. Print.

Butler, Judith. "From Interiority to Gender Performatives." *Camp: Queer Aesthetics and the Performing Subject.* Edited by Fabio Cleto. Ann Arbor: University of Michigan Press, 1999. 361–368. Print.

Cabrera, Jenny Cruz, María Regina Cano Orúe, and Dmitri Prieto Samsónov. "(Post)-Soviet Diaspora in Cuba." *International Journal of Cuban Studies* 8.2 (2016): 263–295. Print.

Cabrera Infante, Guillermo. *Three Trapped Tigers.* Translated by Donald Gardner and Suzanne Jill Levine in Collaboration with the Author. New York: Marlowe & Company, 1971. Print.

Cámara, Madeline, and David L. Frye. *Cuban Women Writers: Imagining a Matria.* New York: Palgrave Macmillan, 2008. Print.

Camnitzer, Luis. "La corrupción en el arte/el arte de la corrupción" (1995). *Universes in Universe* (March 2012). http://u-in-u.com/es/magazine/articles/2012/corrupcion-arte/. Web.

Campbell, Angus Donald. "Lay Designers: Grassroots Innovation for Appropriate Change." *Design Issues* 33.1 (2017): 30–47. http://www.angusdonaldcampbell.com/wp-content/uploads/2016/11/006_DESI_a_00424_Campbell_WEB_vB.pdf. Web.

Campuzano, Luisa. *Cuban Women Writers at the End of the 90s: A Thematic/Bibliographic Map.* http://masteres.ugr.es/gemma/pages/actividades/actividades-granada/actividades-2012-2013/luisa-campuzano-3cubanwomenwritersattheendofthe90s/!. Web.

Cano, Lidia, and Xiomar García. *El postmodernismo: Esa fachada de vidrio.* La Habana: Ciencias Sociales, 1994. Print.

Casamayor-Cisneros, Odette. *Utopía distopía e ingravidez: reconfiguraciones cosmológicas en la narrativa postsoviética cubana.* Madrid/Frankfurt: Iberoamericana/Vervuert, 2012. Print.

———. "Floating in the Void: Ethical Weightlessness in Post-Soviet Cuba Narrative." *Bulletin of Latin American Research* 31 (2012): 38–57. Print.

Castro Ruz, Fidel. *Speech to Intellectuals.* June 30, 1961. http://lanic.utexas.edu/project/castro/db/1961/19610630.html. Web.

Chatman, Seymour. "Parody and Style." *Poetics Today* 22.1 (2001): 25–39. Print.

Coombe, Rosemary J. *The Cultural Life of Intellectual Properties: Authorship, Appropriation, and the Law.* Durham: Duke University Press, 1998. Print.

Cuba's Constitution of 1976 with Amendments Through 2002. https://www.constituteproject.org/constitution/Cuba_2002.pdf?lang=en. Web.

Davies, Catherine. "Surviving (on) the Soup of Signs: Postmodernism, Politics and Culture in Cuba." *Latin American Perspectives* 27.4 (2000): 103–121. Print.

De la Campa, Román. *Cuba on My Mind: Journeys to a Severed Nation.* London: Verso, 2002. Print.

De la Nuez, Iván. "El espejo cubano de la posmodernidad. Más acá del bien y del mal." *Plural* 238 (1991): 21–32. Print.

De Mamporro, Ínclita. "Ella no escribía poscrítica: exorcizaba sus demonios." *Unión* 9.26 (1997): 91–92. Print.

Dentith, Simon. *Parody.* London: Routledge, 2000. Print.

Dezeuze, Anna. *Almost Nothing: Observations on Precarious Practices in Contemporary Art.* Manchester: Manchester University Press, 2017. Print.

Díaz Mantilla, Daniel "Escribir en crisis. Margarita Mateo entre el ensayo y la ficción." *Temas* 81 (2015). http://temas.cult.cu/articulo_academico/escribir-en-crisis-margarita-mateo-entre-el-ensayo-y-la-ficcion/. Web.

Dopico, Ana Maria, "Picturing Havana: History, Vision, and the Scramble for Cuba." *Nepantla: Views from the South* 3.3 (2002): 451–493. Print.

Dopico Black, Georgina. "The Limits of Expression: Intellectual Freedom in Postrevolutionary Cuba." *Cuban Studies* 19 (1989): 107–144. Print.

Duvall, John N. "Troping History: Modernist Residue in Fredric Jameson's Pastiche and Linda Hutcheon's Parody." *Style* 33.3 (1999): 372–390. Print.

Eichenbronner, Ana. "Autorreferencialidad y metaficción en narradores cubanos del siglo XXI." IV Coloquio Internacional Literatura y Vida. Rosario, Junio 2016. http://www.celarg.org/int/arch_coloquios/eichenbronner.pdf. Web.

Ferrari, Guillermina de. *Community and Culture in Post-Soviet Cuba.* New York/London: Routledge, 2015. Print.

Fornet, Jorge. "Escritores y mercado editorial en Iberoamérica." *Revista Malabia* 49 (2007). http://www.revistamalabia.com/index.php/archivo/36-numero-49/45-escritores-y-mercado-editorial-en-iberoamerica.html. Web.

Fusco, Coco. "Editorial. Cuba: The Fading of the Subcontinental Dream." *E-flux Journal* 68 (2015). http://worker01.e-flux.com/pdf/article_9004585.pdf. Web.

———. *Dangerous Moves: Performance and Politics in Cuba.* London: Tate Publishing, 2015. Print.

Garbatzky, Irina. "Teorías del archivo, formas de la huida. Sobre *Teoría del alma china* de Carlos A. Aguilera." *Acta Literaria* 53 (2016): 77–93. Print.

Garrido Castellano, Carlos. "On Truth and Opacity: Symbolic Translation and Legibility in Contemporary Text-Based Cuban Art." *Revista Mitologías* 12 (2015): 223–236. Print.

Genette, Gérard. *Palimpsests: Literature in the Second Degree.* Translated by Channa Newman and Claude Doubinsky. Nebraska University Press, 1997. Print.

González, María Virginia. "Estrategias para construir una tradición: (re)lecturas en la obra de Margarita Mateo Palmer." In *Literaturas caribeñas: Debates, reescrituras, tradiciones*. Edited by Guadalupe Silva and María Fernanda Pampín. Buenos Aires: Universidad de Buenos Aires Facultad de Filosofía y Letras, 2015. 47–72. Print.

———. *La construcción ensayística del Caribe en la obra de Margarita Mateo Palmer*. http://2012.cil.filo.uba.ar/ponencia/la-construcci%C3%B3n-ensay%C3%ADstica-del-caribe-en-la-obra-de-margarita-mateo-palmer. Web.

———. "La transgresión del ensayo: *Ella escribía poscrítica* de Margarita Mateo Palmer." Edited by Graciela Salto. *Memorias del silencio. Literaturas en el Caribe y Centroamérica*. Buenos Aires: Corregidor, 2010. 216–219. Print.

Greenblatt, Stephen. "Resonance and Wonder." *Bulletin of the American Academy of Arts and Sciences* 43.4 (1990): 11–34. Print.

Grenier, Yvon. "Temas and Anathemas: Depoliticization and 'Newspeak' in Cuba's Social Sciences and Humanities." *Revista Mexicana de Análisis Político y Administración Pública* 5.2 (2016): 155–182. Print.

———. "Cultural Policy, Participation and the Gatekeeper State in Cuba." *Cuba in Transition* 24 (2014): 456–473. Print.

Hariman, Robert. "Political Parody and Public Culture." *Quarterly Journal of Speech* 94.3 (2008). 247–272. Print.

Hernández Busto, Enrique. "Signos de la isla." *Plural* (July 1992): 25–28. Print.

Hernández, Rafael. *Looking at Cuba: Essays on Culture and Civil Society*. Translated by Dick Cluster. Gainesville: University of Florida Press, 2003. Translation of Hernández, *Otra guerra*. La Habana: Editorial de Ciencias Sociales, 1999. Print.

Hernández-Reguant, Ariana. *Cuba in the Special Period: Culture and Ideology in the 1990s*. New York: Palgrave Macmillan, 2009. Print.

———. "Copyrighting Che: Art and Authorship Under Cuban Late Socialism." *Public Culture* 16.1 (2004). 1–29. Print.

Hernández Salván, Marta. *Mínima Cuba: Heretical Poetics and Power in Post-Soviet Cuba*. Albany: SUNY Press, 2015. Print.

Howe, Linda S. *Transgression and Conformity: Cuban Writers and Artists After the Revolution*. Madison: University of Wisconsin Press, 2004. Print.

Huggan, Graham. *The Postcolonial Exotic: Marketing the Margins*. London and New York: Routledge, 2001. Print.

Hutcheon, Linda. *A Theory of Parody: The Teachings of 20th-Century Art Forms*. London: Routledge, 1985. Print.

Ichikawa, Emilio. "Disloque ideológico de la Postmodernidad (Una mirada desde La Habana)." *Apuntes postmodernos* 8.1–2 (2000): 47–58. Print.

Irvine, Martin. 'The Postmodern.' 'Postmodernism.' 'Postmodernity.' Approaches to Po-Mo. http://faculty.georgetown.edu/irvinem/theory/pomo.html. Web.

Jameson, Fredric. "Postmodernism, or the Cultural Logic of Late Capitalism." *New Left Review* I 146 (1984): 53–92. Print.

Jencks, Charles, and Nathan Silver. *Adhocism: The Case for Improvisation.* Boston: MIT Press, 2013. Print.

Johnson, Peter. "Can You Quote Donald Duck?: Intellectual Property in Cyberculture." *Yale Journal of Law & the Humanities* 13.2 (2001). http://digitalcommons.law.yale.edu/yjlh/vol13/iss2/4/. Web.

Knapp, Trischa G. *The Daily Show 9 Rhetoric: Arguments, Issues, and Strategies.* Lanham, MD: Lexington Books, 2011. Print.

Kumaraswami, Par. *The Social Life of Literature in Revolutionary Cuba: Narrative, Identity, and Well-Being.* New York: Palgrave Macmillan, 2016. Print.

Lange, Charlotte. *Modos de parodia: Guillermo Cabrera Infante, Reinaldo Arenas, Jorge Ibargüengoitia y José Agustín,* 22. 2008. Bern: Peter Lang. Print.

Lastovicka, John, and Lance Bettencourt. "Lifestyle of the Tight and Frugal: Theory and Measurement." *Journal of Consumer Research* 26 (1999): 85–100. Print.

Lévi-Strauss, Claude. *The Savage Mind.* Chicago: University of Chicago Press, 1966. Print.

Lightbody, Sarah. "Ordo Amoris Cabinet 'The Eternal Object: Notes on a Film'." *Theoretical Beach.* http://www.diangohernandez.com/the-eternal-object-notes-on-a-film-by-sarah-lightbody/. Web.

Lisenby, David. "Frustrated Mulatta Aspirations: Reiterations of 'Cecilia Valdés' in Post-Soviet Cuba." *Afro-Hispanic Review* 31.1 (2012): 87–104. Print.

Lorde, Audre. *The Master's Tools Will Never Dismantle the Master's House.* https://collectiveliberation.org/wp-content/uploads/2013/01/Lorde_The_Masters_Tools.pdf. Web.

Loss, Jacqueline. *Dreaming in Russian: The Cuban Soviet Imaginary.* Austin: University of Texas Press, 2014. Print.

———. "Despojos de lo soviético en Cuba: la estética del adiós." *Otro Lunes. Revista Hispanoamericana de Cultura* 8 (2009). http://www.otrolunes.com/html/este-lunes/este-lunes-n08-a11-p01-2009.html. Web.

Loss, Jacqueline, and Manuel Prieto, Eds. *Caviar with Rum: Cuba-USSR and the Post-Soviet Experience.* New York: Palgrave Macmillan, 2012. Print.

Lyotard, Jean F. *The Postmodern Condition: A Report on Knowledge.* Minneapolis: University of Minnesota Press, 1984. Print.

Manzari, H. J. "A Postmodern 'Play' on a Nineteenth Century Cuban Classic: Reinaldo Arenas' *La Loma del Ángel.*" *Decimonónica* 3.2 (2006): 45–58. Print.

Mañach, Jorge. *Indagación del choteo.* Barcelona: Linkgua, 2007. Print.

Marcus, George E. "The Debate Over Parody in Copyright Law: An Experiment in Cultural Critique." *Yale Journal of Law & the Humanities* 1.2 (1989): 295–316. http://digitalcommons.law.yale.edu/yjlh/vol1/iss2/3. Web.

Martín Sevillano, Ana Belén. *Sociedad civil y arte en Cuba: Cuento y artes plásticas en el cambio de siglo (1980–2000)*. Madrid: Editorial Verbum, 2008. Print.

Mateo Palmer, Margarita. *Ella escribía poscrítica*. Atom Press, 2010. Print.

———. "Postmodernismo y criterios: prólogo a una antología y para un aniversario." *El posmoderno, el postmodernismo y su crítica en Criterios*. http://www.criterios.es/pdf/mateopost.pdf. Web.

McClintock, Anne. *Imperial Leather: Race, Gender and Sexuality in the Colonial Contest*. London: Routledge, 1995. Print.

Mendand, Louis. "Parodies Lost. The Art of Making Fun." *The New Yorker*, September 20, 2010. http://www.newyorker.com/magazine/2010/09/20/parodies-lost. Web.

Miller, Nicola. "A Revolutionary Modernity: The Cultural Policy of the Cuban Revolution." *Journal of Latin American Studies* 40 (2008): 675–696. http://journals.cambridge.org/abstract_S0022216X08004719. Web.

Morejón, Idalia. "Ella escribía poscrítica: de los márgenes al centro de la polémica." *Unión* (1997): 87–90. Print.

Morín Aguado, Vicente. "The Strange Case of Cuba's Gilbert Man." *Havana Times*. February 14, 2015. http://www.havanatimes.org/?p=109346. Web.

Mosquera, Gerardo. "Juan Francisco Elso: Sacralisation and the 'Other' Postmodernity in New Cuban Art." *Third Text* 41 (1997–98): 75–84. Print.

Muguiro Altuna, Carlos (Ed.). *Las formas de la estalgia (cubana)*. Special Issue *Kamchatka: Revista de análisis cultural* 5 (2015). Print.

Müller, Beate. *Parody: Dimensions and Perspectives*. Amsterdam: Rodopi, 1997. Print.

Nelson, Anne. *Cuba's Parallel Worlds: Digital Media Crosses the Divide*. Washington, DC: Center for International Media Assistance, 2016. Print.

Oroza, Ernesto. "Technological Disobedience: From Revolution to Revolico. com." *Technological Disobedience*. http://www.technologicaldisobedience. com/. Web.

Oroza, Ernesto and Pénélope Bozzi. *Objets Réinventés: La Création Populaire à Cuba*, Paris: Ed. Alternatives, 2002. Print.

Oxford Dictionaries. *Word of the Year 2016*. https://www.oxforddictionaries. com/press/news/2016/12/11/WOTY-16. Web.

Padrón Hernández, María. *Beans and Roses: Everyday Economies and Morality in Contemporary Havana, Cuba*. Ph.D. Dissertation in Social Anthropology, School of Global Studies University of Gothenburg, 2012. https://gupea. ub.gu.se/bitstream/2077/29082/4/gupea_2077_29082_4.pdf. Web.

PBS. "The Bizarre, Brilliant and Useful inventions of Cuban DIY Engineers." http://www.pbs.org/newshour/updates/bizarre-brilliant-useful-inventions-cuban-diy-engineers. Web.

Pérez-Hernández, Reinier. *Indisciplinas críticas: la estrategia poscrítica en Margarita Mateo Palmer y Julio Ramos*. Leiden: Almenara, 2014. Print.

———. "Del regreso de un libro." *Temas* 53 (2008): 189–195. Print.

Pertierra, Anna Cristina. "Private Pleasures: Watching Videos in Post-Soviet Cuba." *International Journal of Cultural Studies* 12.2 (2009): 113–130. Print.

Price, Rachel. *Planet/Cuba: Art, Culture, and the Future of the Island*. London: Verso 2015. Print.

Prieto, Abel. *El humor de Misha: La crisis del "socialismo real" en el chiste político*. Buenos Aires: Colihue, 1997. Print.

Prizant, Yael. *Cuba Inside Out: Revolution and Contemporary Theatre*. Carbondale: Southern Illinois University Press, 2014. Print.

Puñales-Alpízar, Damaris. *Escrito en cirílico: el ideal soviético en la cultura cubana posnoventa*. Santiago: Cuarto Propio, 2013. Print.

Puyol, Johanna. "Entrevista con Margarita Mateo. Rompiendo moldes." *La Jiribilla* 343 (2007). http://www.lajiribilla.co.cu/2007/n343_12/343_15.html. Web.

Quiroga, José. *Cuban Palimpsests*. Minneapolis: University of Minnesota Press, 2005. Print.

Randall, Margaret. *Exporting Revolution: Cuba's Global Solidarity*. Durham: Duke University Press, 2017. Print.

Ravelo Cabrera, Paul. *El debate de lo moderno-postmoderno*. La Habana: Pinos Nuevos, 1996. Print.

Riccio, Alessandra. "Maggie Mateo despilfarra su patrimonio. Pensar y escribir en el período especial." *Inti: Revista de Literatura Hispánica* 1.59 (2004): 113–122. Print.

Rodríguez, Fidel A. "Videos to the Left: Circumvention Practices and Audiovisual Ecologies." *Geoblocking and Global Video Culture*. Edited by Ramón Lobato and James Meese. Amsterdam: Institute of Network Cultures, 2016. 178–188. Print.

Rojas, Rafael. "The Archive's Ashes." Translated by Ariana Hernández-Reguant and Susannah Rodríguez Drissi. *Cuba Counterpoints. Public Scholarship about a Changing Cuba*. https://cubacounterpoints.com/archives/3816. Web.

Rose, Margaret A. *Parody: Ancient, Modern, and Post-modern*. Cambridge: Cambridge University Press, 1993. Print.

———. "Post-modern Pastiche." *British Journal of Aesthetics* 31.1 (1991): 26–38. Print.

———. *Parody/Meta-Fiction: An Analysis of Parody as a Critical Mirror to the Writing and Reception of Fiction*. London: Croom Helm, 1979. Print.

Rowlandson, William. "Cabrera Infante and Parody: Tracking Hemingway in *Tres Tristes Tigres*." *The Modern Language Review* 98.3 (2003): 620–633. Print.

Ruiz Barrionuevo, Carmen. "Parodia y espejeo de la escritura en *Tres tristes tigres*: 'la muerte de Trotsky referida por varios escritores cubanos, años después—o antes'." *América: Cahiers du CRICCAL* 20 (1998): 191–198. http://www.persee.fr/doc/ameri_0982-9237_1998_num_20_1_1349f. Web.

Said, Edward. *Orientalism*. New York: Vintage Books, 2003. Print.

Sánchez Aguilera, Osmar. *Otros pensamientos en La Habana*. La Habana, Letras Cubanas, 1994. Print.

San Pedro, Emilio. "Cuban Internet Delivered Weekly by Hand." http://www.bbc.com/news/technology-33816655. Web.

Santana, Andrés I. *Nosotros, los más infieles: Narraciones críticas sobre el arte cubano (1993–2005)*. Murcia: CENDEAC, Centro de Documentación y Estudios Avanzados de Arte Contemporáneo, 2007. Print.

Schur, Richard L. *Parodies of Ownership: Hip-hop Aesthetics and Intellectual Property Law*. Ann Arbor: University of Michigan Press, 2009. Print.

Segre, Erica. "'El convertible no convertible': Reconsidering Refuse and Disjecta Aesthetics in Contemporary Cuban Art." *Latin American Popular Culture: Politics, Media, Affect* (2013): 109–138. Print.

Shklovsky, Viktor. "Art as Technique." *Russian Formalist Criticism*. Edited by Lee T. Lemon and Marion J. Reis. Lincoln: University of Nebraska Press, 1965. 3–24. Print.

Sklodowska, Elzbieta. *Invento luego resisto: El Período Especial como experiencia y metáfora (1990–2015)*. Santiago de Chile: Cuarto Propio, 2016. Print.

———. *La parodia en la nueva novela hispanoamericana (1960–1985)*. Amsterdam and Philadelphia: John Benjamins Publishing, 1991. Print.

Smith, Marlin H. "Note: The Limits of Copyright: Property, Parody, and the Public Domain." *Duke Law Journal* 42 (1993): 1233–1272. Print.

Snyder, Emily. "'The Fist of Lázaro Is the First of His Generation': Lázaro Saavedra and New Cuban Art as Dissidence." *Cuban Studies* (2015): 193–202.

Tanuma, Sachiko. "Post-Utopian Irony: Cuban Narratives During the 'Special Period' Decade." *Political and Legal Anthropology Review* 30.1 (2007): 46–66. Print.

Toro, Alfonso de. "Margarita Mateo: Posicionalidades y estrategias de hibridación." http://home.uni-leipzig.de/detoro/wp-content/uploads/2014/03/2006_MagaritaMateo.pdf. Web.

———. "Meta-autobiografía/autobiografía transversal posmoderna o la imposibilidad de la historia en primera persona: Alain Robbe-Grillet, Sere Doubrovsky, Assia Djjebar, Abdelkebir y Margarita Mateo." *Estudios Públicos* 107 (2007): 214–308. https://dialnet.unirioja.es/servlet/articulo?codigo=2381186. Web.

Venegas, Cristina. *Digital Dilemmas: The State, the Individual, and Digital Media in Cuba*. New Brunswick, NJ: Rutgers University Press, 2010. Print.

Waugh, Patricia. "Literary Evolution: The Place of Parody." In *Metafiction: The Theory and Practice of Self-Conscious Fiction*. Edited by Patricia Waugh. London: Routledge, 1984. 63–86. Print.

Weiss, Rachel. *To and From Utopia in the New Cuban Art*. Minneapolis: University of Minnesota Press, 2011. Print.

Yoss. "Lo que dejaron los rusos." *Temas* 37–38 (2004): 138–144. Print.

Zeitlin, Marilyn A. *Contemporary Art from Cuba: Irony and Survival on the Utopian Island*. Arizona State University Press, 1998. Print.

Zurbano, Roberto. *Los estados nacientes: Literatura cubana y postmodernidad*. La Habana: Editorial Pinos Nuevos, 1995. Print.

CHAPTER 9

Elective Affinities: The Spectacle of Melodrama and Sensationalism in *Cinco esquinas* by Mario Vargas Llosa

Jorge Carlos Guerrero

Mario Vargas Llosa's novel about the political uses of the press during Alberto Fujimori's regime is a playful parody of the aesthetics and politics of yellow journalism. Based on the premise that the aesthetics of melodrama are intrinsic to sensationalism, I argue that the novel ironically imitates the excesses of journalism through the melodramatization of its narrative form. A pervasive irony renders visible the textual use of melodrama's hyperbole and exaggeration in the parody of discourses, genres, and texts, which establishes a vision of the perils of democratic culture under the spectacle of yellow journalism. *Cinco esquinas'* double-encoding serves to warn that, behind the outcome of the novel's melodramatic plot—that is, the end of the regime and guerrilla warfare, as well as the triumph of justice with the incarceration of the major culprits—Peru's democracy is threatened by the degradation of public discourse.

J. C. Guerrero (✉)
Department of Modern Languages and Literatures, University of Ottawa,
Ottawa, ON, Canada
e-mail: jguerrer@uottawa.ca

© The Author(s) 2018   195
H. C. Weldt-Basson (ed.), *Postmodern Parody in Latin
American Literature*, Literatures of the Americas,
https://doi.org/10.1007/978-3-319-90430-6_9

Cinco esquinas [*Five Points*] (2015) revolves around the manipulation of yellow journalism, and the way it affects the lives of individuals living in the last few months of Fujimori's rule (1990–2000). The two initial chapters outline the novel's two storylines: the erotic versus the criminal and the political. In the first storyline, Rolando Garro, the unscrupulous editor of the weekly tabloid *Destapes*, triggers a long chain of events, ultimately leading to the end of the authoritarian regime, when he blackmails Enrique Cárdenas, one of Peru's wealthiest entrepreneurs. The editor uses photographs of an orgy, in which Enrique Cárdenas participated years earlier, to request funding in order to expand the tabloid's coverage and reach. When he refuses to collaborate, *Destapes* publishes the pictures. The editor, whose sensationalist publication has been secretly at the service of the Doctor (Vladimiro Montesinos, Fujimori's head of intelligence), is killed for not having obtained authorization for the blackmail of such a powerful figure in Peru's economic upper-class. At this point, Retaquita (Julieta Leguizamón), Garro's closest collaborator and disciple at the weekly, accuses Enrique Cárdenas of the murder. He is arrested but later released on bail. The scapegoat for the crime is Juan Peineta, a destitute and senile old man, a former popular reciter of *criollo* music and poetry whose career had been ruined by Garro's tabloid. As tensions rise, the true wheels of power are revealed: Retaquita is brought before the Doctor. He offers her a generous salary if she is willing to become the new editor of *Destapes*. In turn, she must blindly follow his orders and publish stories on political opponents. Retaquita takes the job but, as she learns of Montesinos's hand in the death of her mentor, she undertakes the role of private detective, managing to gather evidence of her boss's machinations, and turns against him when she publishes a special issue of *Destapes* denouncing his crime. The second storyline involves Enrique Cárdenas and his wife, Marisa. They both share a close friendship with Luciano Casabellas, a respected attorney who is married to Chabela, Marisa's best friend. Terrorism, rampant political violence, nightly curfews, Garro's blackmail, the public humiliation due to the exposure of the photos, the brief incarceration of Enrique, the negotiations conducted by Luciano and members of the economic elite with the Doctor to free him: these matters strengthen the relationship between the four characters to the point that their heterosexual lives are radically transformed. Sexual desire brings them closer together into an expanding erotic relationship, first involving Marisa and Chabela, then Enrique, and lastly Luciano.

The novel's concluding installment serves as a coda to the events depicted earlier: Set three years after the regime's demise, during the government of Alejandro Toledo (2001–2006), the two couples reflect about their recent experiences and the current state of Peru.

Cinco esquinas' reworking of a plurality of codes, genres, and texts, including the author's *La tía Julia y el escribidor* [*Aunt Julia and The Scriptwriter*], the detective-type novel, the erotic novel, *criollo* music, and yellow journalism is, to adopt Linda Hutcheon's definition, "a form of repetition with ironic critical distance, marking difference rather than similarity" (*A Theory of Parody*, xii). My argument is that critical distance from the intertexts is realized through the playful exacerbation of the melodramatic mode. Peter Brooks, in *The Melodramatic Imagination. Balzac, Henry James, Melodrama, and the Mode of Excess*, defines the "essence of melodrama" as "a dramaturgy of hyperbole, excess, excitement, and 'acting out'" (viii). He further argues that "melodrama...generally operates in the mode of romance, though with its own specific structures and characters" (30). The novel's encoding of intertexts in the mode of romance serves to criticize what it identifies as the discursive properties of yellow journalism: first and foremost amongst them, its aesthetics of melodrama. Irony makes visible the extensive parody by flaunting the novel's recourse to melodramatic devices in a manner that seeks to mirror the use of melodrama in yellow journalism. The ostentatious textual display "provides a framing that," in Hutcheon's perspective of the trope, "makes signals, such as, quotation marks, understatement and echoic mention into markers of irony" (*Irony's Edge*, 153). I propose that the flaunted melodramatic devices act as triggers by having "a 'meta-ironic' function, one that sets up a series of expectations that frame the utterance as potentially ironic" (154). Consequently, the novel's display of a repository of melodramatic excess is interpreted as a textual strategy directed at eliciting a double-reading of the playful imitation of codes and texts. For the analysis of the novel's recourse to melodrama, I will mainly rely on Brooks' theorization of the mode.[1] Moreover, I will delimit the scope of the analysis to *criollo* music, journalism, and *La tía Julia y el escribidor*.[2]

Carlos Fuentes has called melodrama the "central fact of private life in Latin America," and the sole context in which "Latin Americans recognize each other ecumenically" (qtd. in Podalsky, 57). Brooks asserts that melodrama is modernity's pre-eminent imaginative mode and, as such, it is a crucial mode of expression in modern literature (3). Vargas Llosa has long expressed a fascination for it, and stated the conviction that literature truly engages readers when it explores melodrama. In *The Perpetual Orgy, Flaubert and Madame Bovary*, Vargas Llosa asserts that "[r]eality is only melodramatic, there is only bad taste in life: the exclusion of everything else creates a sense of unreality" (19). He associates melodrama with his "basic realist fixation: the melodramatic element moves me because melodrama is closer to the real than drama, as tragicomedy is closer to the real than either pure comedy or pure tragedy" (19). The appeal of the mode is evident in his works, and perhaps most notably in *La tía Julia y el escribidor*, a novel about melodrama and soap operas.

The author has also written extensively about journalism, and he has denounced the political uses of it during the Fujimori regime. In *Notes on the Death of Culture: Essays on Spectacle and Society*, he propounds that the barrier separating serious journalism from yellow journalism has become progressively blurred and that this tendency, which he sees as the product of a civilizational shift characterized by cultural decline and the ascendancy of entertainment as the supreme value, is a menace for democracy (45).[3] One explanation for its supremacy is perhaps captured in the assertive statements about melodrama's pre-eminence, which can be extended to yellow journalism, for both share commonalities. In effect, there is a well-established correlation between sensationalist representation and melodrama. Ben Singer maintains that the melodramatic mode should be viewed as a "cluster concept" that encompasses a plurality of fictional and non-fictional texts (44) and Shelley Streeby holds that "the sensational and sentimental…exist on a continuum" (15). Studies of the sensationalist press in Latin America coincide in underlining the same continuities. Guillermo Sunkel argues that sensationalism applies the aesthetics of melodrama to the treatment of stories (83). Similarly, according to Marcel Velázquez, in Peru the sensationalist press "reivindica el imperio de las pasiones, el lenguaje oral, las jergas, los refranes, el cuerpo como un espacio de poder, una cultura plebeya donde lo oral y lo visual son más importantes que los razonamientos escritos, y donde abunda la parodia y la ridiculización de algunas figuras asociadas con el poder político" (187) [vindicates inflamed passions, colloquial language, sayings, slang, the power of the body as an expressive social phenomenon, popular culture conceived as the primacy of oral and visual elements, and the abundant parody and mocking of political figures]. The appeal of melodrama for Vargas Llosa (melodrama as a reflection of life, a mode that casts back pathos and parody) partly explains the public fascination with yellow journalism, as well. Both melodrama and sensationalism "work by provoking affect and emotional responses in readers" (Streeby, 15) and are important mediators of modern subjectivities (Anker, 22). The extensive use of the sensationalist press during the Fujimori regime is a patent example of melodrama's productivity as a mode in public discourse.[4]

Cinco esquinas ostentatiously displays the recourse to melodrama in the very titles of its chapters. The paratext, the transitional and transactional zone, as Gérard Genette defines it, stresses its function as a "privileged place of pragmatics and textual strategy," and indicates the hyperbolic use of melodrama (2). Headings, such as "Una visita inesperada" [An Unexpected Visit], "El empresario y el abogado" [The Businessman and the Lawyer], "La cueva de los chismes" [The Cave of Gossip], "Un negocio singular" [A Strange Affair], "La agonía de Quique" [Quique's Agony], "El escándalo" [The Scandal], "La Retaquita tiene miedo" [Retaquita's Fears], "Extrañas operaciones en torno a Juan Peineta" [Strange Maneuvers around Juan Peineta], "La noche más larga del ingeniero Cárdenas" [Engineer Cárdenas's Longest Night], "El latifundista y la chinita" [The Landowner and the Chinese Girl], and "Desarreglos y arreglos conyugales" [Matrimonial Agreements and Disagreements] theatrically clarify the informational content of the action. The combination of the selected binary oppositions, adjectives, nouns, diminutives, and superlatives, serves to emphasize the enigmatic and dangerous, the emotional, the erotic, and the sentimental, and to organize characters in fixed categories. These paratextual elements are markers of irony, for they clearly imply the flaunted amplification of the aesthetics and structures of melodrama, especially in a novel about Peru's recent past. *Cinco esquinas* is thus playful and critical, parodic and political, suggesting the doubleness of postmodernism. In Hutcheon's understanding, postmodern works subvert dominant ideologies from within because there is no stable standpoint of truth or reality outside of the received ideologies from which one might launch a critique of them (*Politics*, 90–95). Nevertheless, as I will discuss, *Cinco esquinas* articulates a critique that emanates from a firm, albeit playfully constructed perspective about cultural decline as embodied in the ascendancy of sensationalism.

The organization of the novel, with most chapters centering on either the popular or the upper-class characters, points, from the beginning, to the "scene of dramatic confrontation and peripety," which "takes us to the core of melodrama's premises and design" (Brooks, 25). The two initial chapters construct a scene that is doubly dramatic: The sudden and unexpected sexual encounter between the two wives, Chabela and Marisa, triggers the erotic plot, and it is a major turning point in the lives of both couples. Rolando Garro's visit to Enrique Cárdenas with the intent of blackmail transforms the lives of all characters in the novel, and ultimately leads to the demise of the Fujimori regime.

The meeting of Enrique Cárdenas and Rolando Garro is a highly tense situation in which the dichotomies of melodrama are in full evidence. One of the most striking features of melodrama is the extent to which characters tend "to say, directly and explicitly, their moral judgments of the world" and how they "launch into a vocabulary of psychological and moral abstractions to characterize themselves and others" (Brooks, 36). In this case, the interaction of cultural, moral, and social opposites, of virtue and corruption, leads to the grandiose phraseology of both characters: Rolando Garro's discourse, introduced in direct style, centers on the ethics of journalism; it provokes in Enrique Cárdenas a long sequence of damning thoughts, represented in free indirect style. The aristocratic magnate directs his business interests in mining from the twenty-first floor of a skyscraper overlooking Lima. Rolando Garro only magnifies his influence by commenting that it must give him a feeling of tremendous power to have Lima "a sus pies" (22) [at his feet]. In the eyes of Enrique Cárdenas, the journalist is the most abject of characters, an animal figure crawling on the ground. The entrepreneur sees in him a creature with a mousy smile, rodent eyes, squeaky high-pitched voice, small and shifting eyes, and an emaciated body (23). Such a lowly being smells horribly and can only dress in a ridiculous fashion: tight corduroy purple pants and yellow shoes with thick platforms that make him look taller (24). To him, the editor of *Destapes* is the embodiment of "*huachafería*" [ugliness and bad taste] (24). This word also means ridiculously pretentious, a qualification corroborated by Garro's opening speech about the ethics of his profession, all the while presenting Cárdenas with a folder containing the pictures of the orgy with which he intends to blackmail him. Anticipating a possible question about how he came to have the pictures, he categorically states that he is professionally forbidden from revealing sources (25). In sum, the scene organizes the polarization and the hyperdramatization of forces in conflict, and posits a world of decisive moral clarity.

Initially, the characters reside and operate in disparate sectors of Peruvian society, but criminality, terrorism, and the actions and measures of the Fujimori regime render porous these otherwise compartmentalized parts of Peru, and their interaction triggers the plots. The fundamental bipolar contrast and clash, which is a defining structural property of melodrama, involves the elite and the popular classes. The characters belonging to the economic and professional elite of the country exhibit aristocratic habits and qualities. Enrique Cárdenas and Luciano Casabellas have their offices in the upscale San Isidro neighborhood of Lima. Luciano, a lawyer in a highly prestigious firm, is associated with British aristocratic sophistication. According to his wife, he is "el hombre más conservador y puritano del mundo" (40) [the most conservative and Puritan man in the world]; everything in his office, books, paintings and furniture, is "vagamente británic[o]" (43) [vaguely British]. Both couples reside in the wealthiest neighborhoods, and are attended to by butlers, housemaids, and chauffeurs. Enrique and Marisa have the Golf Course Apartment and, echoing Garro's comment about Enrique's power, the narrator underscores that they have the city "a sus pies" [at their feet]. In effect, from the balcony of their penthouse, they often sit observing the sea of lights of Lima (18). Paintings by artists such as Wildredo Lam and Fernando de Szyslo hang on the walls. Similarly, Chabela and Luciano live in affluence. They have a mansion with a large garden, where there is a swimming pool and two Great Danes running around the trees (19). They are members of a global elite with experience studying and working abroad, where they continue to have business and professional interests. They often spend weekends in their secondary residence in a posh area of Miami and travel there in business class (33). Enrique and Marisa have an apartment in one of the buildings of Brickell Avenue overlooking the sea and Key Biscayne. On the walls of the their living room hang works by Lam, Soto, Morales, and, in the bedroom, there are paintings by Szyszlo, Gerardo Chávez, and Fernando Botero, and two of Victor Vasarely's prints (35). In sum, they are in the "alto mundo" [world of the rich and famous], as the special issue of *Destapes* dedicated to Enrique melodramatically puts it (127).

In contrast, the inhabitants of Cinco esquinas, the heart of the Barrios Altos neighbourhood, live in dire poverty, and their lives generally reflect the decay of the area, which is in ruins. The novel establishes a parallel between these ruins and the deterioration of characters such as a Juan

Peineta. The title of the chapters centered on the character are emphatic in this regard. Chapter 4, the first to introduce Juan Peineta, is entitled "Una ruina de la farándula" [The Vestiges of the Entertainment World]; in the character's own thoughts, the present years are "[l]os de mi decadencia" (64) [my phase of decadence]. The reciter is by vocation of melodramatic temperament. Juan Peineta's repertoire includes selected poems by José Santos Chocano, Amado Nervo, Gustavo Adolfo Bécquer, Juan de Dios Peza, Juana de Ibarbourou, Gabriela Mistral, and, especially, the *criollo* songs of Felipe Pinglo.[5] In his old age, he is still passionate about reciting. The multiple references to the music of Felipe Pinglo, a composer, popular poet, and singer, point to *criollo* music as an intertext. Major events in the novel, including the finding of the body of the crime, take place at the feet of Felipe Pinglo's statue, erected at the heart of Cinco esquinas because it was in this area that the poet had composed his most famous songs.[6] Juan Peineta is very old, progressively forgetful, and suffering from dementia. He walks the streets trying to reminisce about the past of the neighborhood, and his own artistic and sentimental trajectory. He knows that Juan Peineta is his artistic name, but he is unable to recall his real name. However, the name of his idol Felipe Pinglo is always in his mind. He is uncharacteristically heedful when it comes to the artist, the object of an "admiración sin límites" [boundless admiration] inherited from his father (67). He made a career of reciting poems and especially the lyrics of the maestro's songs, which were always the highlight of his shows.

Juan Peineta has a special memory of one of the musician's most famous songs, entitled "El Plebeyo," which literally means "plebeian" or "commoner". The melodramatic song tells the story of the plebeian Luis Enrique who despairs due to the "infamante ley" [infamous law] that forbids a commoner from "amar a una aristócrata" [loving an aristocrat]. The popular song is not transcribed in the novel, but constantly present in the otherwise fading memory of Juan Peineta. His warm recollections of the song express both connections to his past and also his penchant for melodrama in popular art. His father was present in the Alfonso XIII Theater when the artist Alcides Carreño performed Pinglo's most famous song "El Plebeyo" for the first time (68). And, when Juan Peineta got married to his wife Anastasia, they deposited the bride's bouquet at the foot of the bard's statue. The parodic inversion of "El Plebeyo" in *Cinco esquinas* becomes evident when considering that Enrique, the plebeian in the song, is the aristocratic protagonist of the novel, and Retaquita, the plebeian character, becomes, as will be discussed further below, the object of his unrequited love.

This ironic inversion of popular melodrama hints at the novel's larger reference to the melodramatic model of Pedro Camacho's script in *La tía Julia y el escribidor*. In it, the protagonist, Varguitas, often visits the scriptwriter's office and takes great interest in his hand-drawn map, which is inscribed with strange symbols and initials labeling each district of the city. He realizes that Camacho "había aislado en círculos rojos los barrios disímiles de Miraflores y San Isidro, de la Victoria y del Callao... Había clasificado los barrios según su importancia social. Pero lo curioso era el tipo de calificativos, la naturaleza de la nomenclatura" (30) [he had singled out altogether the dissimilar districts of Miraflores and San Isidro, La Victoria and El Callao...He had classified the districts of Lima according to their social status. But the curious thing was the type of descriptive adjectives he had used, the nature of his nomenclature].[7] When asked, the scriptwriter defends what he qualifies as his artistic classification for he explains: "No me interesa toda la gente que compone cada barrio, sino la más llamativa, la que da a cada sitio su perfume y su color...En mis obras siempre hay aristócratas o plebe...La mesocracia no me inspira y tampoco a mi público" (31) [It's not all the people who live in each district, but only the flashiest, the most immediately noticeable, those who give each section of the city its particular flavor and color...In my works there are always blue bloods or the hoi polloi...The bourgeoisie doesn't inspire me or interest me—or my public, either]. Camacho's artistic classification is reworked in *Cinco esquinas*, a novel that playfully abides by the same melodramatic techniques. Its characters are also classified as aristocrats and plebeians, and live in their respective spaces embodying local color and flavor.

Cinco esquinas also alludes to Pedro Camacho's art of storytelling and his enabling rituals or performances. In a visit to the tiny lodgings of the scriptwriter, Varguitas and Julia discover in awe that he wears costumes while writing his scripts. Camacho's explanation to the inquiring couple is the following: "¿Por qué no voy a tener derecho, para consubstanciarme con personajes de mi propiedad, a parecerme a ellos?...¿Qué mejor manera de hacer arte realista que identificándose materialmente con la realidad?" (77) [And why shouldn't I have the right to become one with characters of my own creation, to resemble them? What better way is there of creating realistic art than by materially identifying with reality?]. The total identification with the characters and their reality entails a blurring of the narrative voice. All the melodramatic stories in the even-numbered chapters of *La tía Julia y el escribidor* involve an omniscient narrator, and the consubstantiation is achieved through the internalization of melodramatic speech within the narrator. Although the figure behind the costume is never revealed, the author of the stories, inspired by Camacho's scripts, is Varguitas himself, for they are clearly stylistic exercises or pastiches of the sort that the aspiring author is continuously writing in the odd-numbered chapters.[8] A similar effort at concealment is present in *Cinco esquinas*, where the third-person omniscient narrator intermixes narration and directly and indirectly quoted speech, with relatively identifiable markers which render very accessible the identification of speakers. Vargas Llosa has commented on his efforts to reach what he calls "invisibilidad formal" [formal invisibility] and to avoid that "el lenguaje destruyera la relación del lector con la historia" [language destroy the relationship between the reader and the story] (Rodríguez Marcos, "Vargas Llosa"). In this respect, the novel does not have the "visibly inventing narrator" which, according to Patricia Waugh, characterizes many postmodernist works (22). The discreetness of the third-person narrator suggests the consubstantiation proclaimed by Pedro Camacho. One of the consequences of the adoption of such a narrative perspective is that ironic intent must be inferred from the narrator's discourse, and from a plurality of textual clues. As in Varguita's pastiches, which reveal the narrator's worldview, the narrator of *Cinco esquinas* has the same proclivity to make judgments, notably about yellow journalism. Nevertheless, the expression of the narrator's position is always articulated in an exaggerated and hyperbolic manner, and ideological positioning is thus deflated through the playful parody of melodramatic discourse. Consequently, *Cinco esquinas* adopts Camacho's notion of narrative consubstantiation, but the narrator's use of melodramatic speech to vehicle ideas implies ironic distance. This does not mean that, in postmodern fashion, the ideological position is deconstructed but, rather, that the novel ironically reflects on the narrator's discourse, and, in this manner, underscores the possible provisionality of the ideas espoused.

In a novel that flaunts melodrama, the etymology of the word—*melos* for music and *drama* for deed, action, and play—accentuates the textual importance of the character Juan Peineta. The novel playfully combines its parts melodramatically, *melos* and *drama*, declamation, action, and dialogue. Juan sees himself as an artist and poet. His discourse is a long lamentation, for he made the tragic mistake of betraying art (71).

Unlike the scriptwriter Pedro Camacho, Juan Peineta's all-consuming vocation is declamation; however, they share the same devotion for their art, are abused by the entertainment industry, have passionately loved their partners, and end up suffering varying degrees of madness. The perils of Pedro Camacho's dramatic confusion—when his stories lose coherence, and his characters and the plots of one story begin appearing in another—echo Juan Peineta's experience. The reciter begins mixing up poems and *criollo* songs in a spiral that ends with him being unable to distinguish art from food. Interned in a psychiatric hospital, he wonders if poetry is eaten with ice cream, and when the nurse jokingly answers that it is, rather, consumed with rice, Juan Peineta orders "ketchup, más bien" (262) [ketchup, instead].

Juan Peineta's artistic and personal trajectory was sealed by the entertainment industry. He was a successful artist who recited before loving audiences in stadiums, social clubs, and *peñas criollas*, the traditional venues dedicated to *criollo* music. He had also recited in radio programs, and managed to have his own weekly program, called "Hora de poesía" (70) [Poetry Hour]. However, it all changed when he was offered to work for a program in *América Televisión*; the most successful vaudeville and comedy team of Peruvian television had lost one of its members, and the television mogul Celonio Ferrero happened to fancy Juan Peineta for the part. Although the proposal deeply wounded his pride as an artist, he accepted because it would allow the couple to live better, and also get his wife Anastasia the medical treatment that she desperately needed for her terminal illness (72). In the present, the widower sees his television stunt as a tragic mistake, for it was a fatal act of disloyalty towards his vocation as an artist and poet. His role in the show had been to recite poems only to be suddenly shut up with slaps that would make the public crack up laughing (106). These parallels between Juan Peineta and Pedro Camacho, and their peril at the hands of the entertainment industry, are significant for, as I will discuss below, this reworking can be read as an ironic commentary on the narrative form of *Cinco esquinas*.

The stirring of base desires is the primal dramatic form of melodrama (Booth, 38). *Cinco esquinas* ironically accentuates the journalist's commerce with base desires. In this respect, the first scene in the editorial office reveals a merciless Rolando Garro. He is unhappy because Ceferino, the publication's photographer, has failed to obtain truly harmful pictures of the actress whom they have nicknamed The One-Eyed Woman. He explains that the objective is to discredit and sink the actress so that she is dismissed from the show. Many of the victims are selected randomly, and their good name can be easily reinstated if they pay, unless the editor has taken offense at their reactions to the tabloid's criticism, in which case he is relentless. In this instance, the actress had regretted the existence of shameful publications such as *Destapes* (54). Retaquita has been charged with writing the damning article and Rolando Garro anticipates that it will be "genial y letal" (56) [great and lethal]. He is always satisfied with the professional work of his top journalist because she competently unearths the dark side of people. In his view, she embodies his notion of journalism, "capaz de matar a su madre por una primicia, sobre todo si era sucia y escabrosa" (56) [capable of killing her mother for a story, especially if it was something dirty and lurid]. She became a journalist thanks to him, and he takes pride in the disciple who has always proven a "devoción perruna" (56) [canine devotion] to him. Rolando Garro enjoys the power that he has over his victims and draws satisfaction from knowing how much they despise him since he sees in it a form of "reconocimiento" (55) [recognition].

The need for some form of acknowledgment is shared by all characters who inhabit Cinco esquinas. In stark contrast with the multiple family ties of upper-class roles, the lower-class characters are orphans. Rolando Garro is alone in the world. He does not even know his birth name because his parents abandoned him at a hospice. His adoptive parents initially named him Rolando Torres. However, since he fled his foster home at an early age, he has little information about the past and prefers not to think about his mysterious origins. He is a troubled man who takes multiple pills in order to avoid days of madness and depression, and because, on the authority of his psychiatrist, he runs the risk of "volverse loco de verdad o de quedarse tieso" (57) [going crazy or dying]. His health problems or "maldito carácter" [damned character] never allowed him to form a stable relationship, and he fears ending up as a beggar in the streets, from which he had risen when he discovered his vocation for "la chismografía periodística" (58) [journalistic gossip].

His disciple, Retaquita, in Rolando Garro's eyes, has an innate ability to make people expose "sus vergüenzas al aire" (55) [their intimate secrets]. As with all main characters whose perspectives are privileged in chapters exclusively focused on them, the initial scene outlines her personality. She is riding a bus to work and, whenever necessary, brandishes a giant needle that hung from her belt in order to fend off men who might try to fondle and harass her. As menacing as her giant needle is the grotesque discourse with which she imprecates her abusers: "La próxima vez que te arrimes te clavo esto en esa pichula inmunda que debes tener...Estás prevenido, concha tu madre" (87) [Next time that you come near me I will pin it into your filthy prick...You are forewarned, motherfucker]. She is also alone in the world. She spent her early years walking the streets of Cinco esquinas with her father, selling *emolientes*, a traditional drink made of various medicinal plants, herbs, and seeds. In spite of living almost in destitution, her father ensured that she finish school. Retaquita's passion for yellow journalism is such that she keeps a meticulously classified collection of tabloids for study at home. Her notion of the profession is tied to her traumatic past and thirst for vengeance; she feels that her job allows her to take revenge on a hostile world (92). The publications that she admires, and where she learned the tools of the trade, are those that she routinely saw in kiosks as a child. The tabloids attracted numerous people who, unable to pay, would just observe the pictures of naked women and read the big blazing red letters denouncing the most foul secrets "que destruían las credenciales de las gentes aparentemente dignas y prestigiosas del país" (93) [capable of destroying the reputation of the most apparently decent and prestigious people in the country]. Rolando Garro made it possible for her to enter the profession as a card-holding journalist. Retaquita is now completely devoted to her mentor. She idealizes, in hyperbolic terms, "el periodista más afamado del país" [the most celebrated journalist in the country], and the man she secretly loves (94).

The most telling parodic section of the novel centers on yellow journalism. Unlike all other sections, chapter 21, entitled "Edición extraordinaria de *Destapes*" [Special Issue of *Destapes*], presents a collection of the tabloid's parts, ostensibly put together by Retaquita. The issue is about the investigation into Rolando Garro's death with several parts reworking discursive and visual properties of yellow journalism, ranging from its rhetoric to typographic representation (letter font and size, lower and upper cases, typeface). The elements selected to reproduce the tabloid's aesthetic and rhetorical structure in narrative form put forward a textual decoding of the sensationalist press that is comically reductive. The special number of *Destapes* has five major parts: the editorial, three interviews, and the transcription of the Doctor's secret recordings. The headline is "Destape Político-Criminal" [Uncovering Politics and Criminality], and the subtitles of the sections are "Lo sabemos pero lo hacemos" [We Know the Risks, but Still Do It],

"Un forastero pervertido, un millonario emboscado y la orgía de Chosica" [A Perverted Foreigner, A Tricked Millionaire and the Chosica Orgy], "El asesinato de un periodista y la amenazada libertad de expresión en el Perú" [The Murder of a Journalist and Free Expression under Threat in Peru], and "Las grabaciones secretas" [The Secret Recordings]. All the self-explanatory titles are further expanded in paragraphs typeset in italics; these invariably develop a narrative of the journalists' heroic undertakings to uncover the truth. Of special note is the reproduction of the earlier edition of *Destapes* about the orgy and the compromising pictures of Enrique Cárdenas, considered necessary background information to the current story. Additionally, the editor apologizes for having wrongly denounced the magnate to the police. The first inference to be drawn is that the tabloid dramatizes the role of the journalists as much as it dramatizes the story. Second, this self-referentiality is articulated in a melodramatic mode. The tabloid opposes the role of the conscious, courageous and righteous journalists against criminals who infringe the law and pose an existential threat to the press and the nation. The special issue's rhetoric thus appeals to a grandiloquent discourse of heroic qualities and moral abstractions. Third, the introduction of the story of nudity and sex blurs the barriers between the private and public spheres. Enrique Cárdenas is the object of an editorial apology, and therefore publicly vindicated, while, at the same time, readers are reminded of the recent scandal involving nudity and sex. In sum, the section is a comically reductive parody of tabloid journalism. Its reading of sensationalist discourse underscores, first and foremost, its aesthetics of melodrama, its proclivity to parody and ridicule, its disregard for the demarcations of the private and public spheres, its fabrication and manipulation of facts, and its self-referencing as self-promotion. Moreover, the critical parody of sensationalism also suggests the use of similar devices and techniques in a novel that interweaves eroticism and the recent history of authoritarian politics and terrorism in Peru. The text thus ironically suggests that the novel's narrative form is infused with the same stuff of yellow journalism.

In this way, ironic markers make visible what I call the playful melodramatization of narrative form. The most notable example of textual irony is in the mystery surrounding Rolando Garro's name. The character is puzzled by his adoptive parents' decision to change his last name from Torres, their name, to Garro (57). Roland Georges Garros was a hero and martyr of World War I, and, in Retaquita's mind and

Destapes' epic narrative, Rolando Garro is indeed a hero, despite his shortcomings. However, the textual discussion of onomastics ironically undermines this view. In the same playful spirit, early on, the text anticipated this moment of hero-making through one of Rolando Garro's jocular remarks. He tells Retaquita that they will probably be killed, but they should take comfort in knowing that statues will be erected in their memory as "mártires del periodismo" (173) [martyrs of journalism]. This is, indeed, what Retaquita is presently doing in honor of her secret love. The death of her mentor and only family has left her all alone (173). She has developed the theory that Rolando Garro's extortion was done in the service of the tabloid, for he wanted it to be Peru's leading publication, and also a publication independent from government meddling, not "el desaguadero del régimen" (276) [the regime's drain]. She undertakes the secret investigation of the Doctor in order to realize her mentor's alleged mission. Consequently, Retaquita's commitment is, to a great extent, about retribution, and, as indicated earlier, about exorcising her trauma and social resentment. She, as all the main characters in the novel, utters at one point the word "vengeance," a key emotion that moves melodramatic action.

Chapter 20, significantly entitled "Remolino" [Whirlpool], for it alludes to Retaquita's use of the word "desaguadero" [drain] to describe *Destapes'* role, introduces all the narrative perspectives and temporal frames of the novel; the telescoping of dialogues functions as a *mise en abyme*, and, as such, serves to render textual intention more overtly (Hutcheon, *Narcissistic Narrative*, 55). The interweaving of paragraphs about gossip and scandal, politics and sex, together with the gory details of torture, further reflects the playful mirroring of yellow journalism. For instance, an exchange between Retaquita and Ceferino in the editorial office re-enacts the initial scene in which her mentor scolded the photographer Ceferino; Retaquita reveals the same professional zeal and even the language of her predecessor. The Doctor has assigned her the task of tarnishing the reputation of a member of the opposition, senator Arrieta Salomón, and she reprimands Ceferino because his pictures are not good enough to "hundir[lo] en el ridículo" (259) [demean and ridicule him]. In a meeting with the Doctor, Retaquita discusses the published article; her new boss rejoices in the fabricated story, for the senator will have to focus all of his energies on convincing everyone that he "no es un violador de sirvientas ni un maricón al que se lo tira su chofer" (265) [is neither a rapist of maids nor a queer who sleeps with his chauffeur]. In another interwoven scene, Retaquita meets with Ceferino at a restaurant to plot the upcoming special issue of the tabloid dedicated to the Doctor. The meeting of the journalists at the restaurant is framed by images of sexual intercourse. In this manner, Enrique's sexual initiation with Chabela and Marisa precedes and follows a conversation about journalism and politics.

Significantly, to these scenes are added those of Juan Peineta's torture and reclusion. When working for *América Televisión* in the program Los Tres Chistosos, Juan Peineta had caught the attention of Rolando Garro, who soon began to criticize his work in *Última Hora*, a tabloid where he worked before his founding of *Destapes*. Instead of heeding the advice of colleagues who recommended that he bribe the journalist, he wrote a letter to the editor. As a consequence, the journalist's defamation campaign grew until the channel dismissed him. His termination occurred at the time his wife Anastasia needed the medical treatment for her brain tumor. She soon died and Juan Peineta, who was not able to work as a reciter or comedian ever again, made it his mission to take revenge. His notion of retribution involved writing letters to newspapers and numerous authorities over the years. In the process, he acquired a reputation for being a madman and Rolando Garro's archenemy (113). In the detailed torture session conducted by the Doctor's henchmen and supervised by a judge, a confused Juan Peineta has trouble remembering the journalist, and repeatedly begs them to stop. They promise that, if he signs a fabricated confession, the judge will send him to a psychiatric hospital, where his life will improve; instead of living in dire poverty, there will be food and medical attention. Subsequent scenes focus on the artist's descent into madness in the hospital. In this manner, the chapter's interweaving of such disparate scenes ranging from politics and sex to the gory details of torture, the plotting of heroes and tormentors, scenes of innocence and villainy, mirrors the special issue of *Destapes*. It is a parody of the sensationalist appetite for base desires and the instigation of emotional responses in readers. The chapter, entitled "Whirlpool," thus reflects the notion of *Detapes* as the "drain" of the regime.

The scene of torture also confirms Juan Peineta as the most melodramatic of characters, because he is the unredeemed victim of the two dark forces at work in the novel: the sensationalist press and the politics of the regime. Melodrama is "an expressionistic form" about the articulation of the characters' "moral and emotional states and conditions, their intentions and motives"; yet melodrama also "has recourse to non-verbal means of expressing its meanings...particularly in climatic moments and in extreme situations" (Brooks, 56). This recourse to silence, or "text of muteness," is "central to the representation of its most important meanings" (62). The silencing of Juan Peineta, his torture and descent into madness, as well as his disappearance as a speaking subject in the novel, mobilize emotions that cannot be articulated in verbal registers, and concomitantly stress his textual importance. Juan Peineta has always regretted his tragic mistake in the most melodramatic fashion: "de puro angurriento le clavaste una puñalada al arte" (84) [sheer avarice led you to stab art in the back]. Once his career as a comedian was over, he could not be a reciter again because he had diminished his vocation in the eyes of his audience. I suggest that Juan Peineta's tragic mistake, his betrayal of art, can be read as a textual commentary about *Cinco esquinas'* extensive engagement with the melodramatic mode. Moreover, it is possible to see in Juan Peineta an autobiographical allusion; the character incessantly criticizes the yellow press and warns citizens about its excesses, an intellectual position reminiscent of Mario Vargas Llosa's view of the irrelevance of intellectuals in public life today.[9] Also, considering that Juan Peineta is the textual equivalent of Pedro Camacho, the scriptwriter whose work is only known to the reader thanks to Varguita's pastiches, the notion of an autobiographical reference is reinforced. Therefore, Juan Peineta's error functions as an ironic and even comical commentary on the author and the novel's aesthetic choices—namely, its melodramatically compromised narrative form.[10]

The novel's pervasive irony is patent in the last chapter, entitled "¿Happy End?," for it contrasts the optimistic perspective of the upperclass characters with evident textual markers that stress contradiction and skepticism. Three years have elapsed since the fall of the regime, and their exchanges, interwoven with reminiscences, reveal their present circumstances and their evaluation of the recent past. They are all happy because they have survived the personal and national ordeal; they have also strengthened their relationship as couples and as friends, so much so that the novel concludes with the consolidation of the *ménage à quatre*. The country is better off, although there are still some pockets of guerrilla activity; the Doctor and Fujimori, as well as the major guerrilla leaders, Abimael Guzmán of the Shining Path and Víctor Polay of the Túpac Amaru Revolutionary Group, are in jail. Besides, in their view the current president, the *"cholo"* [half-breed] Toledo, is doing things well for the country (312).

The last chapter places greater attention on Enrique, the character whose peripety structures the novel. He is reading a book when Marisa interrupts him with a comment about his recent ordeal. Enrique begs her not to bring it up ever again: "No hablemos nunca más de esa maldita historia" (307) [Let's not talk ever again about that damned past]. She replies that her husband is the most contradictory of individuals because, although he refuses to discuss the past with her, he watches "el programa tan ridículo de esa mujerzuela" (307) [that slut's ridiculous program]. Surprisingly, he has become an ardent follower of Retaquita's new sensationalist television program. He is constantly reminded of the past when he watches *La hora de la Retaquita* [Retaquita's Hour]. His opinion of the journalist has radically evolved. He tells Marisa that Retaquita was "clave para la caída de la dictadura" [key to the demise of the dictatorship], and that her valiant exploits merit her current success with the most popular program on television (308). When Marisa leaves the room, Enrique acknowledges to himself his attraction towards the journalist; he sees something "fascinante" [fascinating] in her (309). He admires her extraordinary and even exemplary trajectory; the story of "una muchacha del montón" [an average girl] who brought down the "todopoderoso Doctor" (318) [almighty Doctor]. Retaquita has not brought down the regime alone, as Enrique's superlative statement suggests. *Destapes* narrated the epic exploits of the journalist, and Enrique was perhaps influenced by it, or is now by her nightly television program. The fact remains that the language that he uses to recount her trajectory is highly melodramatic and reminiscent of the message and rhetoric of *Destapes.*

At the same time, in a previous chapter, the novel has ironically articulated Retaquita as a character firmly on the side of virtue. In the structure of Manichean conflicts that defines melodrama, "[v]irtue is almost inevitably represented by a young heroine" (Brooks, 32). One of the most notable textual strategies to organize the confrontation of forces is through the contrast between dark and light. Retaquita's meeting with the Doctor in his secret headquarters is a clear instance of the trope of light penetrating darkness; it is what Shelley Streeby, writing in the context of Mexican sensational journalism, has called a "rhetoric of exposure, of bringing hidden horrors into the light of day," a trope with clear links to sensational literature (132). In the middle of the night, the Doctor's men take her, head covered, to his secret headquarters, a place ironically underplayed as "refugio secreto" (228) [secret refuge].

The Doctor is immediately impressed with Retaquita, who intimately fears meeting her mentor's fate. He praises her audacity. In order to protect herself, Retaquita has denounced Enrique Cárdenas to the police, and given multiple interviews warning that if anything were to happen to her, it would be the entrepreneur's doing. Her complaint and newly acquired public visibility have thus guaranteed her safety. Surprisingly, the meeting of the tiny and frail-looking girl with the embodiment of the regime's masculine power, which is suggested in the connotation of *"hombre fuerte"* [strong man/strongman], leads to the affirmation of her virile powers.[11] The Doctor's spontaneous reaction is to contrast her small physical size with her "huevos tan grandes. Unos ovarios tan grandes, quiero decir, perdona" (232) [such big balls. Or rather such big ovaries, I mean, sorry]. The comment evokes an earlier allusion to her masculinity, when she was introduced riding a bus and brandishing a giant needle (87). Thus, through the references to male genitalia, the text grotesquely enacts melodrama's standard ritual of the confrontation of antagonists, of virtue and villainy, and the expulsion of one of them (Brooks, 17). The Doctor's admiring attitude anticipates that Retaquita is now the active force and motor of plot, the *"hombre fuerte"* [strong man/strongman] has met his match.

Conversely, the novel has contrasted Retaquita's with Enrique's trips to the core of darkness. The character's longest night, as the chapter dedicated to his brief incarceration is entitled, refers to his sexual abuse by a fellow inmate in jail. He finds himself in a dark room crowded with men. When an inmate tries to touch him, he moves away frightened. He soon feels safe next to a big and strong man, who grabs him by the waist. The *"hombre fuerte"* [strong man] seems to be "uno de los capos" [one of the leaders] and Enrique offers to pay for his protection. The inmate explains that he is lucky because he is also the strongman: "Aquí, yo soy autoridad" (219) [Here, I represent authority]. However, he soon requests sexual favors and the text details, at some length, Enrique's submission. He cries all night, acknowledging his cowardice and confusedly begging forgiveness. The abuser's titles, first *"hombre fuerte"* [strong man] and then "capo" [leader] have a double referent, for the scene is intended to function as the mirror image of Retaquita's interaction with the Doctor. Both characters meet the *"hombre fuerte"* [strong man/strongman], but Enrique's encounter is allegorical in nature, and serves to comment on the social sectors behind the regime. Fujimori's government initially had the support of economic circles sympathetic to the president's liberal economic reformism and heavy-handedness with terrorism. Enrique's incarceration and his ordeal at the hands of the strongman are the novel's strong condemnation of his class, which was willing to forfeit its liberty for a putative national good, only to find itself becoming complicit in its own oppression.

The encounter with the Doctor ironically stresses the binary opposition between Enrique and Retaquita. Enrique flirts with the idea of meeting her: "de saber cómo hablaba cuando no estaba representando en la pantalla el papel de hurgadora de intimidades" (309) [of knowing how she spoke when she was away from the cameras divulging the intimate lives of people]. The character's fantasy of getting to know Retaquita must be discarded if he is to fulfill his role in the story of the melodramatic song "Plebeyo." The novel has inverted the roles of the story and, as previously mentioned, Enrique is the aristocratic character who falls in love with the plebeian Retaquita. The song's third stanza sums up the lover's fate: "Así en duelo mortal / Abolengo y pasión, / En silenciosa lucha / Condenarnos suelen / A grande dolor; / Al ver que un querer / Porque plebeyo es / Delinque si pretende / La enguantada mano / De fina mujer" [In fatal duel / Lineage and passion, / In a silent struggle / Often condemn us / To great suffering; / When witnessing the love / Of a commoner / Commit a crime for courting the gloved hand / Of a refined woman]. The lover is condemned to secretly love because lineage and passion are insurmountable barriers. Enrique likewise can only flirt with the idea. According to the law of unrequited love, he must resign himself to watching Retaquita every evening.

The parallel story of "El latifundista y la chinita" [The Landowner and the Chinese Girl] comically corroborates this reading. This section, chapter 20, functions almost as a chapter-length parenthesis. In the middle of a conversation between the two couples, Luciano decides to reveal a deeply held family secret. The story involves a similar inversion of the song "El Plebeyo." It is about the love story of his *criollo* grandfather and his Chinese grandmother. Conservative Don Casimiro, the owner of very large landed estates and employer of numerous peasants who lived in his properties, married the daughter of the village's butcher. Luciano is therefore partly Chinese, but had never spoken of his background because "fue siempre un tabú" (189) [it was always taboo]. A relationship between individuals of such extreme ethnic and social backgrounds in Peru of the late nineteenth and early twentieth century was unthinkable. In Luciano's view, his grandfather was authoritarian and racist, as all the members of his class. In fact, he never learned his grandmother's name because she was forced to change it to Laura, and her family was sent away to avoid any shameful reference to her Chinese background. Luciano still does not know much more about her, but feels better after the confession because the shameful family secret "[le] quemaba las entrañas" (195) [was burning inside him]. The melodramatic story of star-crossed lovers who represent different classes and ethnicities is a variation of the "Plebeyo" song, and the tale shares the melodramatic undertones of Latin America's foundational fictions. More significantly, it suggests that the characters are still bound by the values of the past to the extent that it has taken until the present for Luciano to reveal the shameful genealogy to family and friends. It also playfully underscores the pervasiveness of melodrama.

This recurrent emphasis on contradiction stresses the aesthetics and politics of the novel. Enrique's contradiction, his refusal to discuss the past, but his fascination with Retaquita's brand of journalism, reflects the novel's own recourse to the melodramatic mode to tackle Peru's recent history. Enrique, as *Cinco esquinas*, opts for the appeal of the melodramatic imagination in approaching the past. Contradiction also refers to the novel's conclusion. The optimistic outlook of the characters is expressive of melodrama's need for moral certainty, for the prevalence of justice, and, at least in Enrique's view, for virtue finally recognized with Retaquita's redemption. However, the text indicates that view as willful. After all, Peru's newly recovered democracy seems to be in the hands of the sensationalist press. The barriers between the private and the public realms have been abolished, and characters such as Enrique, who were victims of yellow journalism's disregard for such demarcations, now are enthralled by it. Furthermore, his notion of the past is informed by Retaquita's narrative to the point that he seems to have also assimilated her melodramatic language. In this manner, the novel ironically concludes, conveying a skeptical perspective of culture and politics. The evaluation of Peru's democratic culture is thus questioned.

In conclusion, *Cinco esquinas'* recourse to the melodramatic mode puts parody to sharp political effect by bringing attention to the influential commerce of base desires in journalism during the Fujimori regime. Parody fulfills the following functions: it establishes a correlation between melodrama and sensationalism, and indicates the use and abuse of the mode in sensationalist discourse. Furthermore, the novel playfully mirrors yellow journalism's appropriation of melodrama through its own melodramatization of narrative form. The pervasive irony serves to undercut the discourse of yellow journalism, and to reflect on the aesthetics and politics of the novel.

In this regard, the novel emphasizes that melodrama should belong to the realm of fictional discourse, not journalism. It is a perspective that Vargas Llosa has held for a long time. Literature, in his view, is a compensatory fantasy, and any incursions of fantasy outside the circumscribed artistic domain are dangerous.[12] The novel's criticism of yellow journalism is grounded in the same reasoning, and Retaquita's influence over Enrique is a cautionary tale in this regard. Notwithstanding this perspective, which contradicts the major postmodern tenet that one cannot step outside that which one contests, the novel is profoundly playful about this contradiction for the following reasons. First, it embraces and rejects melodrama, and, in this manner, as Hutcheon puts it, "may indeed be complicitous with the values it inscribes as well as subverts, but the subversion is still there" (*Politics*, 106). Second, it reflects ironically on its ideological position through the character of Juan Peineta, who both alludes to the author's ideas and the novel's narrative form. Lastly, the emphasis on contradiction and skepticism in the last chapter can be taken as a metatextual commentary on the novel's aporias. In this regard, irony serves not to deconstruct the novel's ideology, but at least to underscore its possible provisionality as opposed to its definitive affirmation.

Rolando Garro, Juan Peineta, Retaquita, and Enrique are subjects bereft and without guidance. They embody pathos, melodrama's dominant affect. The popular characters are alone in the world, all orphaned by diverse circumstances, and often without recourse to the primary marker of social identity—that is, their names. In this disenchanted situation, melodramatic characters tend to seek escape from, rather than face, the alienating effects of their situation. In the case of Rolando Garro and Retaquita, the quest to escape takes the form of yellow journalism, which is a compensatory vocation that helps them regulate their traumas and resentments. As for Enrique, who has been shaken by the ordeal, he ironically derives guidance from Retaquita's televised discourse. The character who is left completely bereft, without compensatory recourse, is Juan Peineta. Silenced and reduced to insanity, locked up in the psychiatric hospital, he can only continue to long for a lost plenitude and presence, and thus represents melodrama's "longing for a fullness of being of an earlier, still sacred universe" (Brooks, 5). The fate of Juan Peineta, as an image of Pedro Camacho, of Varguitas, and therefore of the author, suggests irony about the novel's longing for a world as it should be, a world where there is place for programs such as "Poetry Hour," Juan Peineta's former show, as opposed to "Retaquita's Hour."[13]

Cinco esquinas condemns the economic elite for its support of the regime, and Enrique's incarceration and his ordeal at the hands of the strongman allegorically portrays its political submission. Parody is also the means of exposing this elite's mentality, as the thoughts and speeches reveal their conservative and even racist perspectives, as exemplified in their conversation about Luciano's secret genealogy, and their conde-scending assessment of the "half-breed" president, when they comment that the "*cholo*" is managing things well (312). In this context, both the parody of *criollo* music and the plotting of Enrique in the melodramatic story reminiscent of foundational fictions establish an ironic correlation between literary form and the elite's system of values, which underscores their backwards conservatism despite their membership in a postmodern global elite, and their erotic adventures. The parody of their speech and the "Plebeyo" song serve to empty their discourse of any sense of truth and affective import.

The novel's playful engagement with the melodramatic mode also suggests broader ideological implications. Melodrama, as Brooks and others have pointed out, exists to articulate the moral crisis brought on by the disenchantment of the modern world, and its overwhelm-ing presence in diverse media in the contemporary world might also be a response to the need brought about by the current crisis in values decried by *Cinco esquinas*. However, while it addresses an epistemolog-ical crisis, "[m]elodrama cannot figure the birth of a new society—the role of comedy—but only the old society reformed" (Brooks, 12). On this subject, the final chapter serves as a necessary coda, a supplement to the events of the past three years. The upper-class characters end with an optimistic outlook about Peru, but textual markers point, rather, to skepticism, insinuating that the melodramatic closure is not the novel's conclusion. The textual recourse to irony and parody deflate, through self-reflexivity, the exaggeration of melodrama. Thus, the conventional outcomes of melodrama are framed in a manner that stress the need for greater critical scrutiny of the contradictions of the present historical moment.

Notes

1. Melodrama, in Brooks' reading, is a vital and nuanced aesthetic response to the experience of a post-Enlightenment crisis in values. He argues that classic melodrama confronts the crisis brought about by the French Revolution. This major event overturned the legitimacy of the sacred world and its earthly delegates (the aristocracy, the Church, and the state), and placed the individual at the nucleus of cultural, political, and social life. Melodrama's answer to this experience of uncertainty is the positing of a world of decisive moral clarity. This mode's "polarization and hyperdramatization of forces in conflict represent a need to locate and make evident, legible, and operative those large choices of ways of being which we hold to be of overwhelming importance even though we cannot derive them from any transcendental system of belief" (viii).
2. All translations are mine, unless otherwise noted.
3. In his native Peru, yellow journalism has an extended readership. In Lima, where *Cinco esquinas* is set, "la franja de consumidores de la prensa sensasionalista bordea el 60% de los lectores de la prensa escrita; por ello, con más de un millón y medio de lectores diarios es la industria cultural más extendida en el rubro de las publicaciones periódicas" (Velázquez, 182) [the readers of the sensationalist press amount to 60% of the total readers of written publications; they represent about a million and a half people, and thus contribute to making the sensationalist press the most important cultural industry in terms of daily publications].
4. Rubén Gamarra Garay provides a detailed account of the network involving publishing figures and the government authorities. In the 1990s, there were several publications founded with the objective of favoring the regime. The newspapers *El Chino, La Chuchi, Conclusión, El Tío, El Men y La Yuca*, in addition to the tabloids *La Repúdica* and *Repudio*, were all created during the municipal and presidential campaigns of 1995, 1998, and 2000, and used to attack and bring discredit to members of the opposition, and, to a lesser extent, to independent journalists who reported negatively on the government. The publications were widely popular amongst voters (273–274).
5. Felipe Pinglo Alva (1899–1936) was an influential and prolific poet and songwriter, who is also known as the father of Peruvian *criollo* music. In 2016, the Peruvian government declared his works part of the National Cultural Heritage.
6. The location is also the site of the Barrios Altos massacre, which took place on November 3, 1991. Fifteen people, including an eight-year-old child, were killed, and four more injured, by assailants who were later determined to be members of Grupo Colina, a death squad made up

of members of the Peruvian Armed Forces, and acting in concert with the head of intelligence, Montesinos. The murder of innocent partygoers became a symbol of human rights abuses during the Fujimori regime, and was cited as one of the reason's for the request of extradition from Chile, where the former president had been residing since 2005, by the Peruvian government in 2007 (Burt, 384).

7. The translations of *La tía Julia y el escribidor* are taken from the pages of Vargas Llosa, *Aunt Julia and the Scriptwriter, 1977*. Translated by Helen Lane. Farrar, Straus & Giroux, 1982. 49–50.

8. As Carlos Alonso points out, "although the subject matter is unequivocally Camacho's radio serials, the text obviously does not reproduce the actual scripts over which the Bolivian feverishly labors, since they are not written in the dialogic format characteristic of that genre. They are, rather, condensed prose renditions of the actual radio broadcasts. The resulting question regarding the provenance of these chapters can only be resolved textually by proposing that the even-numbered chapters...the "Camacho" installments of the novel, are the work of the aspiring writer Varguitas, who has produced them as exercises for mastering the craft of storytelling" (50).

9. In his *Notes on the Death of Culture*, Vargas Llosa regrets that "intellectuals have disappeared from public debates, at least the debates that matter. It is true that some still sign manifestos, send letters to newspapers and become involved in polemics, but none of this has any serious repercussion in the running of society where economic, institutional and even cultural matters are decided by the political and administrative classes, and by the so-called powers that be, where intellectuals are conspicuous by their absences" (38).

10. In his book on Flaubert, Vargas Llosa refers critically to two irreconcilable strands in modern literature. On the one hand, literature for popular consumption exhibits "most abject conformism in the face of the established order" (233); and, on the other, a form of "experimental literature that is so esoteric that it is accessible to a small educated class" (234). However, more recently, in *Notes on the Death of Culture*, he seems to suggest that the contemporary demand for accessible books is such that writers are hard pressed to accommodate this requirement: "For the culture in which we live does not favor, but rather discourages, the indefatigable efforts that produce works that require of the readers an intellectual concentration almost as great as that of their writers. Today's readers require easy books that entertain them and this demand creates a pressure that becomes a powerful incentive to writers" (26). Nevertheless, he also explains that "[i]f literature is just about entertainment...then literary fictions cannot compete with those supplied by our screens, be they

big or small. Illusions forged by words demand the active participation of readers, an imaginative effort, and, with respect to modern literature, complex feats of memory, association and creation, something that film and television images do not require of their viewers" (214).

11. The novel has qualified the Doctor in these terms early on when, in a conversation between Enrique and Luciano, the latter reminds him that, after much consultation with other lawyers and economic leaders—in essence, the country's elite—the Doctor is really "[e]l hombre fuerte de este gobierno" (81) [the government's strongman].

12. Vargas Llosa has repeatedly advocated his notion of the compensatory function of literature in the following manner: "Los hombres no están contentos con su suerte y casi todos...quisieran una vida distinta de la que llevan. Para aplacar—tramposamente—ese apetito nacieron las ficciones. Ellas se escriben y se leen para que los seres humanos tengan las vidas que no se resignan a no tener. En el embrión de toda novela hay una inconformidad y un deseo inalcanzado" (*Contra viento*, 2 and 419) [Human beings are not happy with their fate and almost all of them...would like to have to lead another different life. To appease this appetite deceitfully, fictions were born. They are written and read to provide human beings with the lives they are unresigned to not having. At the core of every novel there is nonconformity and unfulfilled desire].

13. In *Notes on the Death of Culture*, Vargas Llosa has portrayed, although not in ironic tone, a Western civilization bereft of guidance that turns "fleeting entertainment into the supreme aspiration of human existence as well as the right to view with cynicism and disdain everything that is boring or worrying, and remind us that life is not just entertainment but also drama, pain, mystery and frustration" (50).

WORKS CITED

Alonso, Carlos J. "*La tía Julia y el escribidor*: The Writing Subject's Fantasy of Empowerment." *PMLA* 106.1 (1991): 46–59. Print.

Anker, Elisabeth. *Orgies of Feeling: Melodrama and the Politics of Freedom.* Durham, NC: Duke University Press, 2014. Print.

Booth, Michael. *English Melodrama.* London: Herbert Jenkins, 1965. Print.

Brooks, Peter. *The Melodramatic Imagination. Balzac, Henry James, Melodrama, and the Mode of Excess*, 1976. New Haven, CT: Yale University Press, 1995. Print.

Burt, Jo-Marie. "Guilty as Charged: The Trial of Former Peruvian President Alberto Fujimori for Human Rights Violations." *International Journal of Transitional Justice Journal* 3.3 (2009): 384–405. Print.

Gamarra Garay, Rubén. *La prensa chicha de Montesinos.* Lima: AFA Editores, 2001. Print.

Genette, Gerard. *Paratexts: Thresholds of Interpretation. 1987.* Cambridge: Cambridge University Press, 1997. Print.

Hutcheon, Linda. *Narcissistic Narrative. The Metafictional Paradox.* Waterloo: Wilfrid Laurier University Press, 1980. Print.

———. *A Theory of Parody: The Teachings of Twentieth-Century Art Forms.* New York: Methuen, 1985. Print.

———. *Irony's Edge: The Theory and Politics of Irony.* London: Routledge, 1995. Print.

———. *The Politics of Postmodernism.* 1989. London: Routledge, 2002. Print.

Podalsky, Laura. "Disjointed Frames: Melodrama, Nationalism, and Representation in 1940s Mexico." *Studies in Latin American Popular Culture* 12 (1993): 57–73. Print.

Rodríguez Marcos, Javier. "Vargas Llosa: La pornografía es erotismo mal escrito." *Babelia* March 4, 2016. http://cultura.elpais.com/cultura/2016/03/02/babelia/1456923139_366965.html. Web.

Singer, Ben. *Melodrama and Modernity: Early Sensational Cinema and Its Contexts.* New York: Columbia University Press, 2001. Print.

Streeby, Shelley. *Radical Sensations: World Movements, Violence, and Visual Culture.* Durham: Duke University Press, 2012. Print.

Sunkel, Guillermo. *La prensa sensacionalista y los sectores populares.* Bogotá: Grupo Editorial Norma, 2002. Print.

Vargas Llosa, Mario. *La tía Julia y el escribidor.* Editorial Seix Barral, 1977. Print.

———. *Aunt Julia and the Scriptwriter, 1977.* Translated by Helen Lane. Farrar, Straus and Giroux, 1982. Print.

———. *The Perpetual Orgy. Flaubert and Madame Bovary.* 1975. Translated by Helen Lane. Farrar, Straus and Giroux, 1986. Print

———. *Contra viento y marea*, Vol. 2. Seix Barral, 1986. Print.

———. *Notes on the Death of Culture: Essays on Spectacle and Society.* 2012. Translated by John King. Farrar, Straus and Giroux, 2015. Print.

———. *Cinco esquinas.* Penguin Random House Grupo Editorial, 2015. Print.

Velásquez, Marcel. "El mal/estar en la cultura chichi: la prensa sensacionalista." In *Industrias Culturales. Máquina de deseos en el mundo contemporáneo.* Edited by Santiago López Maguiña, Gonzalo Portocarrero, Rocío Silva Santisteban, Juan Carlos Ubilluz, and Víctor Vich. Red para el Desarrollo de las Ciencias Sociales en el Perú, 2007. 181–198. Print.

Waugh, Patricia. *Metafiction: The Theory and Practice of Self-Conscious Fiction.* 1984. London: Routledge, 2002. Print.

CHAPTER 10

Postmodern Transpositions of the Latin American *novela de la tierra*: *Maldito amor* by Rosario Ferré and *La otra selva* by Boris Salazar

Helene Carol Weldt-Basson

The Latin American *novela de la tierra* refers to regionalist novels written in the 1920s through the 1940s that emphasized the effects of nature on man and the strong connection between the two. The *novela de la tierra* is considered a foundational text in the development of Latin American fiction, and therefore, it is no surprise that contemporary novelists have entered into dialogue with these novels through parody. In the prologue to the novella *Maldito amor* (1985) [*Sweet Diamond Dust*], Rosario Ferré states that "Puerto Rico también produjo su novela de la tierra, *La llamarada*, de Enrique Laguerre (1935) donde la nacionalidad se perfila alrededor del infierno del Cañaveral" (10) [Puerto Rico also produced its own novel of the land, *La llamarada* by Enrique Laguerre where

H. C. Weldt-Basson (✉)
University of North Dakota, Grand Forks, ND, USA
e-mail: helene.weldtbasson@und.edu

© The Author(s) 2018
H. C. Weldt-Basson (ed.), *Postmodern Parody in Latin American Literature*, Literatures of the Americas,
https://doi.org/10.1007/978-3-319-90430-6_10

nationality is outlined by the surrounding hell of the sugar cane industry (my translation)].[1] She later adds that *Maldito amor*:

> Intenta, de alguna manera, parodiar esa visión de la historia y de la vida señorial de la hacienda, arrebatarle al mito su poder de conferir autoridad e identidad, ya que la tierra (y la sociedad que generó entre nosotros) constituyó siempre en nuestro caso una realidad conflictiva e insuficiente. . . . El regreso a la romántica vida de la tierra . . . que proponen . . . *Solar Montoya* y *Cauce sin río* de Laguerre . . . constituyó desde sus comienzos una actitud reaccionaria, insostenible en el mundo moderno. (10)
>
> Attempts, in some way, to parody this vision of history and of the lordly life of the hacienda, to rob the myth of its power to confer authority and identity, since la land (and the society that it generated among us) always constituted a conflictive and insufficient reality in our case. The return to the romantic life of the land . . . that *Solar Montoya* and *Cauce sin río* propose . . . constituted from the beginning a reactionary attitude that is unsustainable in the moderrn world.

It seems clear from Ferré's words that *Maldito amor* is a parody of Laguerre's *La llamarada* that seeks to undermine the ideological tenets upon which Laguerre's novel is based. As we shall see, Ferré not only deconstructs the previous novel in terms of its economic and class ideology, but also from a feminist standpoint.

It is this focus on fiction as ideological discourse that leads to the combination of an analysis of Ferré's parody in *Maldito amor* with that of another postmodern transposition, that of the Colombian writer Boris Salazar, who incorporates *La vorágine*, Colombia's most famous *novela de la tierra*, into his novel *La otra selva* (1991) [*The Other Jungle*]. *La otra selva* has been studied as a parody of José Eustasio Rivera's exposé of the rubber industry by Natalia Crespo in her book *Parodias al canon: Reescrituras en la literatura hispánica contemporánea*. Crespo views *La otra selva* as a "feminist" (understood loosely) reworking of *La vorágine* in the sense that, in Salazar's novel, the protagonist, who is the writer Rivera, reworks his novel to include two chapters written from the perspective of Alicia, the female character who has no direct voice in the original version of *La vorágine*. Crespo states that *La otra selva*, "rescata el machismo de su predecesora literaria y hace de ello un motivo de reflexión" (293) [rescues *machismo* from its literary predecessor and makes it a cause for reflection]. Although on the surface Salazar's novel appears to be a parody of *La vorágine* that "criticizes" the original novel for not giving a voice to its female characters, an analysis of the ideological workings of *La otra selva* will illustrate that (1) the supposed "voice" given to Alicia ultimately reflects dominant male ideology and is not a true female viewpoint; and (2) Salazar's intention, more than a parody of *La vorágine*, is to imitate the detective novel using as its basis the biography of José Eustasio Rivera written by Eduardo Neale-Silva titled *Horizonte Humano: Vida de José Eustasio Rivera*. The real hero of *La otra selva* is not Rivera or Alicia, but the nameless detective who narrates a good portion of the novel.

Before entering into an analysis of these two pairs of texts, it is necessary to define what is meant by "parody" and "ideology" in this study. Parody has been variably defined by such critics as Gérard Genette, Margaret Rose, and Linda Hutcheon. It is not my intention to review the multiple definitions of parody provided by different authors, but simply to explain how I use the term here. Noé Jitrik is one of the few Latin Americanists who attempt to theorize parody specifically in terms of Latin America. In his article "Rehabilitación de la parodia" in the collection *La parodia en la literatura latinoamericana* edited by Roberto Ferro, Jitrik stresses the desirability of employing a model of parody for Latin American literature that has not been developed by other countries and on the basis of other literatures. Jitrik defines parody as an imitative act that intends to "llegar a otra parte" [to arrive elsewhere]. According to Jitrik:

> La "parodia" se define en la pura diferencia de las identidades textuales o como producto de una interacción. En el primer caso, se trata de un efecto canónico, el "desfiguramiento burlón". Para la segunda acepción, el efecto sería la modificación de la lectura pero no solo del texto base, sino de las dos instancias: el cambio en la lectura del texto A, lleva a ver el texto B de otro modo". (15)
>
> Parody is defined as the pure difference in textual identities or as a product of an interaction. In the first case, it is a question of a canonical effect, the "mocking disfigurement." In the second sense, the effect would be the modification of the reading but not only of the base text, but of both instances: the change in the reading of text A, makes one see text B in a different light.

Although Jitrik shuns foreign definitions, his discussion of parody is not dissimilar from Genette's in *Palimpsests*, where he states that "the most rigorous form of parody, or minimal parody, consists...of taking up a familiar text literally and giving it new meaning" (16). Genette further refines this definition by indicating that this transformation of one text by another can have different functions, so that when the function is playful, the text is a parody; if it is satirical, it should be termed a travesty; and if it is serious or polemical, instead of parody, the term "transposition" should be used. Another Spanish language critic, Juan Carlos Pueo, is at odds with this aspect of Genette's definition of parody. According to Pueo, at least in the case of postmodern parody, hypertext (the parodying text) and hypotext (the parodied text) can never be separated, and, in addition to recognizing the presence of the hypotext within the hypertext, there must exist, on the paradigmatic level, an ironic distance between the two, or one cannot speak of parody *per se*:

> La labor del receptor no depende sólo del reconocimiento del modelo . . . sino de su necesidad de establecer qué tipo de relación mantienen los textos en juego para ofrecer un nuevo texto.. . . Es el receptor quien debe constatar que entre el sentido que estas referencias producen en el hipotexto convocado y el sentido con que aparecen en el hipertexto hay una relación no de analogía . . . sino de contraste irónico. (108)
>
> The task of the receiver does not only depend on recognition of the model . . . but on his necessity of establishing what type of relationship the texts in play maintain in order to offer a new text . . . It is the receiver who should establish that between the meaning these references produce in the convoked hypotext and the meaning with which they appear in the hypertext there is a relationship not of analogy . . .but of ironic contrast.

In this sense, Pueo is more specific than Jitrik because, although both critics emphasize the condition that a hypertext must operate some sort of change on its hypotext that confers new meaning, for Pueo, this relationship must be ironic, in order for parody to exist. It is this definition that I shall adopt for the purpose of this study, which is to show the distinct ideological relationships that the novels *Maldito amor* and *La otra selva* bear with regard to the *novela de la tierra*.

The term "ideology" is significantly more complicated to define. According to Göran Therborn in *The Ideology of Power*, ideology refers to:

> That aspect of the human condition under which human beings live their lives as conscious actors in a world that makes sense to them to varying degrees. Ideology is the medium through which this consciousness and meaningfulness operate . . . Thus, the conception of ideology employed

here deliberately includes the everyday notions and "experience" and elaborate intellectual doctrines, both the "consciousness" of social actors and the institutionalized thought-systems and discourses of a given society. (1)

Therborn explains that human subjectivity is "being in the world." "Being" is both existential and historical, while "in the world" is inclusive (being a member of a meaningful world) and positional (having a particular place in that world). Thus, there are four forms of human subjectivity:

1. inclusive-existential, which refers to ideological discourse that ascribes meaning to the world, such as mythologies, religion and moral discourse;
2. inclusive-historical ideologies that refer to humans as members of historical worlds and are fundamentally ideologies of inclusion and exclusion in social groups, such as tribes, states, nations, and churches;
3. positional-existential ideologies that refer to one's relationship to the Other in the existential world, such as gender distinctions; and
4. positional-historical ideologies that refer to positionality in social worlds, such as occupations, positions of political power, and membership in different classes. These four categories often overlap (Therborn, 22–24).

Therborn further stipulates that to "conceive of a text or utterance as ideology, is to focus on the way it operates in the formation and transformation of human subjectivity" (1). Thus, it is my intention to illustrate that, while *Maldito amor* is an ideological parody of *La llamarada* from both a feminist, social, and postcolonial standpoint, *La otra selva* is a playful parody of the hard-boiled detective novel, whose ultimate ideological underpinnings reinforce dominant male ideology.

It is surprising that, to date, no one has examined the relationship between *Maldito amor* and *La llamarada*, given that Ferré was explicit about this connection in the prologue to her novel. Socorro Velázquez Lara, in her dissertation titled *La parodia como poder subversivo feminista en la narrativa de Rosario Ferré*, is the only critic who examines *Maldito amor* as a parody of the *novela de la tierra*. Velázquez Lara identifies specific traits common to this genre and then illustrates how Ferré employs them in her parody, without any specific reference to Laguerre's novel.

By ignoring Ferré's predecessor, Velázquez Lara's study fails to capture the ideological thrust of Ferré's novel and only touches the surface of Ferré's parody of the genre. Her analysis of the "parody" is reduced to the observation that Ferré imitates the telling of a story of various generations of a family; ironically parodies her own family tree; echoes the force of nature in the description of hurricanes, rains, and fires; shares the *novela de la tierra's* repudiation of racial prejudice; portrays Gloria as a personification of barbarism; and, ultimately, expresses solidarity with the writers of the *novela de la tierra* (178–200). Given that Ferré has already stated in the introduction to *Maldito amor* that she seeks to deconstruct the myths upon which the *novela de la tierra* was written, Velázquez Lara presents an unfortunate misinterpretation of Ferré's parody.

Similarly, in "Rosario Ferré en el espejo", Marie Murphy sees *Maldito amor* as a parody of the romance plot, without any reference to *La llamarada* or the *novela de la tierra* (regionalist) genre (140). Although her observations are not erroneous, Ferré's parody is a clear textual transposition of *La llamarada*, and much more specific than these other critics indicate. In order to comprehend the transformation that Ferré operates on Laguerre's novel, it is necessary to provide a brief synopsis and critical overview of his work.

The protagonist of *La llamarada*, who is also the novel's first-person narrator, is Juan Antonio Borrás. Borrás is the son of a coffee plantation owner, who, after graduating from college, obtains a position as the manager of a sugarcane plantation. Borrás is anxious to achieve economic success, but during his employment at the *Central*, he becomes aware of abuses of the workers and their desperate plight. Much of the novel presents the struggle in Borrás's consciousness between recognizing the injustices of the condition of the plantation workers, most of whom are black, and his need to suppress this recognition to pursue his own economic and class interests. Although at the novel's end Borrás abandons the sugarcane industry, his return to manage his family's coffee plantation upon his father's death, and his submersion in his identification with the beautiful mountain terrain that brings him peace, mark an affirmation of acceptance of the status quo and his bourgeois values.

Two excellent essays examine the ideological implications of Laguerre's *La llamarada*. Rogelio Escudero Valentín in "El desarrollo de un conflicto insospechado en *La llamarada*, novel del Cañaveral puertorriqueño" deconstructs the ideology of social class behind the novel's proposition of the patriarchal structure of the hacienda system as a valid alternative to capitalist exploitation, while Lola Aponte Ramos exposes the racism implicit in the protagonist's contradictory attitudes toward black people in "Enrique Laguerre y la memoriosa construcción del blanquito en *La llamarada*." According to Escudero Valentín, despite the novel's condemnation of imperialism, it presents "una defensa explícita del modo de producción patriarcal existente en las montañas de nuestro país antes de 1898" (123) [an explicit defense of the patriarchal mode of production that existed in the mountains of our country before 1898], presenting the "vida patriarcal como depositario de la puertorriquenidad" (126) [patriarchal life as the depository of Puerto Ricanness]. Escudero Valentín astutely notes that Borrás is caught between the socialism of Don Polo and a nature that is connected to the patriarchal way of life, bastion of the good old days (129) and illustrates how the novel presents a progressive fusion of Borrás with nature that prefigures his eventual rejection of Don Polo's socialist ideology and return to the mountain to live happily ever after (132).

In a similar vein, Aponte Ramos focuses on the racial ideology behind *La llamarada*. Although Borrás acknowledges some black ancestry, attends the *bomba* (a black dance party), and recognizes the achievements of many of his schoolmates of mixed race, the novel is characterized by racial contradictions and a general process of what she calls "dárselas de blanquito", which refers to the assumption of upper-class values, on the "insistencia en un orden de mundo occidental, asumido como natural" (896) [the insistence upon the occidental world order, assumed as natural]. According to Aponte Ramos, the novel's ending reaffirms European (white) class values:

> La relación saber/tenencia de la tierra/linaje europeo adquiere su mayor relevancia cuando, al finalizar la novela, Borrás hereda un cafetal en la montaña, allí, bajo la constitución del poder heredero de linaje claro . . . Tenemos pues que la herencia confirmadora de linajes y legitimadora de saberes, es decisiva en la constitución de los universos relatados pues mientras la tenencia de la industria de azúcar se da gracias a la apropiación por manejos turbios . . . el mundo de la tenencia de la tierra heredada se describe a partir de las fiestas de acabe y el paisaje de belleza llena de paz. Coincide la tenencia legitimadora con el matrimonio de Borrás y la francesa, esto es la integración de su yo con el linaje europeo que reclama. Importante será subrayar que la vida de obrero que recoge el café ni siquiera es aludida. (897)

The relationship knowledge/possession of the land/European lineage acquires its greatest relevance when, at the end of the novel, Borrás inherits a coffee plantation in the mountain, there, under the constitution of hereditary power of clear lineage . . . The confirmatory inheritance of lineages and legitimizing of knowledge, is decisive in the constitution of related universes since while the possession of the sugarcane industry was achieved thanks to its appropriation by turbid means, the world of possession of inherited land is described parting from the celebrations of the end of the harvest and a beautiful landscape filled with peace. The legitimizing possession coincides with Borrás's marriage to the French woman, that is, to the integration of his "I" with the European lineage. It is important to underscore that there is no allusion to the life of the coffee plantation worker who gathers the coffee.

Escudero Valentín and Aponte Ramos offer detailed analyses of how *La llamarada* conforms to traditional patriarchal ideology and the notion of supremacy of European lineage. I will now illustrate how Ferré transposes *La llamarada* to express the opposite ideology (feminist/socialist/postcolonial) through an imitation of certain elements from the previous novel in *Maldito amor*.

The first, and perhaps most important, change that *Maldito amor* operates on *La llamarada* involves narrative perspective. *La llamarada* is told from the viewpoint of a single first-person narrator, the protagonist Juan Antonio Borrás. Everything the reader is told in the novel is filtered through Borrás's perspective. None of the female characters (Sarah, Delmira, Pepiña) is given a direct voice. In contrast, *Maldito amor* is narrated by several different narrators that include Hermengildo, Titina, Arístides, Laura, and Gloria. Their accounts of events often conflict, and thus Ferré renders a postmodern version of the *novela de la tierra* that implicitly questions the value of Borrás's narration as an isolated viewpoint (and thus the ideology he espouses within it). By including female narrators, Ferré takes the first step toward offering a "feminist" standpoint on the story.

La llamarada recounts the rivalry between two patriarchal haciendas, prior to their absorption by the U.S. run *Central* for which Borrás works. These two haciendas are Santa Rosa (which used to be owned by the Alzamora family) and Palmares (which was previously owned by the de Moreau family). *Maldito amor* parodies this relationship through the rivalry depicted between the *Central Justicia* and the *Central Ejemplo*. The *Central Justicia* is the sugarcane factory owned by Ubaldino De La Valle, while the *Central Ejemplo* is the North-American-owned factory that has progressively taken over the local sugarcane industry in Puerto Rico. Ferré transposes the rivalry between local sugarcane factories into a rivalry between the local and the imperialistic enterprises. Although the reader may initially be fooled into believing that this is a fight between good (*Central Justicia*) and evil (*Central Ejemplo*) through Hermengildo Martínez's idealized narration of Ubaldino as national hero, as the novel progresses, it becomes clear that the *Central Justicia* is just as abusive to its workers as the *Central Ejemplo*. Consequently, the name "Central Justicia" is ironic and is employed in *Maldito amor* as a tool to debunk the patriarchal ideology (the return to the "just" patriarchal hacienda system) proposed in Laguerre's novel.

Two of the female narrators in *Maldito amor* fuse gendered and racialized perspectives. Titina is a black ex-slave and Gloria is a mulatto. Through these two narrators, women and black people are given a voice that they did not have in *La llamarada*. Furthermore, since black workers comprised the workforce in the sugarcane industry, their appropriation of elements from *La llamarada* in their narration also reflects the social viewpoint of the worker class.

The character Titina is a reworking of two distinct characters that appear in *La llamarada*: Pablo Roldán and José Dolores. Siño Pablo is a very old white worker who operates the iron gate to the Santa Rosa estate. In *La llamarada* we are told that "junto al portón una casita, cercada de pedazos de madera techada en cinc viejo: el hogar de Siño Pablo" (32) [next to the gate a small house, enclosed by wood, roofed with old zinc: Mr. Pablo's home]. This house is echoed in the house whose ownership has been promised to Titina by Ubaldino in *Maldito amor*: "Sí, Señor, hace cinco años que el Niño Ubaldino nos prometió que nos iba a regalar la casita de tablones y techo de zinc en que hemos vivido siempre" (26) [Yes, Sir, it's been five years since Niño Ubaldino promised us that he was going to give us the house made of wood with a zinc roof in which we have always lived]. Later on, a black house-servant named José Dolores is presented as "un hombre de más de cien años que por lo ágil y avispado que es, no da manifiestas señales de ancianidad. Cuando se quita el amplio sombrero de cogollos muestra su pelo ensortijado y níveo que hace contraste con el rostro negro de líneas severas" (39) [a man of more than one hundred years old who because of his agility and quick-wittedness, does not show manifest signs of old age].

Titina reminds the reader of José Dolores because Hermengildo refers to her as "la criada sempiterna de esa familia" (35) [the everlasting maid of that family] (*Sweet Diamond Dust*, 24), implying she is very old. In *La llamarada*, the house with the zinc roof is of no particular significance, other than it is a servant's residence. However, in *Maldito amor* it becomes important as a sign of the abuses of the patriarchal system. The house ends up burning in the fire Gloria sets, but as she tells Titina: "De todas maneras, Arístides y sus hermanas jamás hubiesen permitido que Néstor y tú heredasen la casita que Don Ubaldino les había legado" (85) [don't you see none of it matters any more, that Arístides and his sisters would never have let you keep the bungalow Niño Ubaldino had left to you in his will] (*Sweet Diamond Dust*, 85). Titina is thus treated as if she were still a slave, and not as a faithful worker who deserves remuneration from the De La Valle family.

A second element that is a mere mention in *La llamarada* but is picked up and developed in *Maldito amor* is the reference to Juan Campos Morel's romantic musical composition titled "Maldito amor." In Laguerre's novel, there is the following reference: "un peón picaba yerba silbando una vieja danza de Morel" [a laborer chipped at the herbs whistling an old dance by Morel]. Not only does this music provide the title for Ferré's novel, but the song is incorporated into her text in two passages that illustrate *Maldito amor*'s parodic intentions. As Malva E. Filer points out in her article "Polifonía y contrapunto: La crónica histórica en *Maldito amor* y *The House on the Lagoon*", the novel parodies the song through Gloria's voice. The first time the song appears in the novel, it is quoted accurately through Elvira De La Valle's voice. She sings the song when she is falling in love with Don Julio Font: "Ya tu amor/es un pájaro sin voz/ya tu amor/se perdió en mi corazón/no sé por qué/me marchita tu pasión/y por qué no ardió" (20) [Your love is now a songless bird/Your love, my dear, is lost in my heart/I don't know why your passion wilts me/And why it never flamed!] (*Sweet Diamond Dust*, 9). At the end of the novel, when Gloria decides to burn down the entire hacienda and *Central Justicia* in an apocalyptic attempt to finally put an end to the abuses perpetrated by the family, she sings a parodic version of the song: "ya tu amor/es un pájaro con voz/ya tu amor/anidó en mi corazón/ya sé por qué me consume esta pasión y por qué ardió" (85) [Your love is a bird which has found its voice/Your love has finally nested in my heart/Now I know why it burns/When I remember you] (*Sweet Diamond Dust*, 85).

Ferré recontextualizes the song so that it no longer refers just to a love affair *per se* but, rather, to the context of the burning of the *Central Justicia* and justice for the workers who now are a bird "which has found its voice" through Gloria's actions. Filer states that the modified song sung by Gloria is the "expresión de una coinciencia adquirida, de autoafirmación y rebeldía por parte de este personaje [y] sirve de epitafio al mundo representado por Ubaldino" (320) [expression of an acquired consciousness, of self-affirmation and rebellion on the part of this character (and) serves as an epitaph to the world represented by Ubaldino]. Moreover, by destroying the testament, the document by which normally the hereditary power of lineage is confirmed, Gloria subverts the action whereby Juan Borrás inherits his father's patriarchal coffee plantation.[2] Obviously, the excessive romanticism of the song is also critiqued, not only through its parody, but also through the outcome of Elvira's love affair with Julio Font. Although they marry, he is an abusive husband who silences and beats her.

Perhaps the most significant parody of elements from *La llamarada* is achieved through the re-contextualization of the fire motif. The "blazing fire" appears not only in the novel's title, but throughout the novel in two forms. Borrás constantly speaks of the "llamarada de odio" [the blazing fire of hate] between the workers and the management of the *Central*. Moreover, in the novel, the worker Segundo Marte sets fire to the sugarcane fields on several occasions, as a method to force management into meeting the demands of the striking workers. Although the workers' complaints are justified, Segundo Marte is converted into an "evil" figure when he attempts to murder Juan Borrás. As a result, he is shot, his death is made acceptable, and the crisis of the workers is pushed into the novel's background and once again ignored. In contrast, the blazing fire that occurs in *Maldito amor* is not accomplished by a striking worker, but by the mulatto Gloria Camprubí. Although she stood to inherit the entire *Central Justicia* through Laura's final testament, Gloria burns both the testament and the hacienda, thus not only preventing it from falling into the hands of the imperialistic *Central Ejemplo*, but also apocalyptically terminating the reign of the De La Valle family and the patriarchal structure that is praised in *La llamarada*. Gloria thus simultaneously represents women, black people, and the workers, whose plight is to some degree united in *Maldito amor*. Gloria's actions and version of events contradicts the idealistic portrayal of the hacienda system and the De La Valle family in Hermengildo's discourse. Hermengildo's narrative can be thought of as another version of *La llamarada* that is debunked by the female narrative voices (Titina, Gloria, Laura) in Ferré's text.

In addition, it is worthwhile noting that the name De La Valle is also an intertextual reference to Laguerre's novel. In *La llamarada*, the character Delmira Alzamora is the illegitimate daughter of Ramiro Del Valle, who eventually marries into the De Moreau family, accentuating the rivalry between the Alzamora and De Moreau families.

The episode in which a worker's hand is cut off is an element in both *La llamarada* and *Maldito amor*. In *La llamarada*, the worker's hand is severed during the sugarcane harvest, and it is eventually amputated when gangrene sets in because of inadequate medical care. The criticism here is aimed at the medical care system, rather than at the *Central* (127). However, in *Maldito amor*, the worker's hand is cut off by machinery that is not properly operated by the older worker in charge of it. Doña Elvira demands that her husband, Julio Font, the owner of the sugar mill, pay a monthly stipend to the injured worker since the hacienda is at fault, something he refuses to do. Once again, the element is reworked to show the abuses of the paternalistic hacienda system, and a woman is made the voice of justice and equality for the workers (24).

Finally, the character Gloria, much like Titina, appears to be a fusion of two characters from *La llamarada*: Sarah and Delmira. At the beginning of Laguerre's novel, Juan Borrás reminisces about his school days and romance with a poor girl named Sarah: "Y luego vino el amor a señalarme otros rumbos....Centro de este hervor de anhelos era Sarah, muchachita sentimental, que conocí en uno de esos suburbios de gente pobre que conserva cierto orgullo" (23) [And then love came to signal other paths to me...The center of these boiling desires was Sarah, a sentimental girl whom I met in one of those slums of poor people who have some pride]. Arístides' description of his relationship with Gloria when he was a student is quite similar: "A mi auténtico interés por los estudios se añadió mi dicha de conocer por aquellos años a Gloria Camprubí, una mulata hermosa...Había nacido en un barrio de Guamaní y era pobre" (50) [I was a good student and I knew it; and then one day my happiness was complete when I met Gloria Camprubí at the university, one of those mulatto beauties who are used to stopping traffic] (*Sweet Diamond Dust*, 40–41). However, there is also a connection between Delmira Alzamora and Gloria, since Delmira is a mulatto woman who is desperately in love with Juan Borrás. Gloria is also a mulatto, but reverses the relationship portrayed in *La llamarada*, because it is Arístides who is madly in love with her. Just as Borrás spurns Delmira to marry Pepiña, Gloria spurns Arístides to marry his brother Nicolás. While Delmira is portrayed as weak and sterile, Gloria is a strong, passionate woman who gives birth to Nicolasito. Through Gloria, Ferré contests the traditional portrayal of women as a commodity for reproduction that the reader encounters in *La llamarada*. According to Zaira Rivera Casellas, the "tragic mulatto woman" (*la mulata trágica*) is a common trope in Puerto Rican literature and most often she is portrayed as a voiceless figure (104). Aponte Ramos notes that *La llamarada*'s Delmira is just such a figure: "la mujer muere víctima de la pasión insatisfecha: *el locus* de la mulata trágica se cumple" (902) [the woman dies a victim of unsatisfied passion; the locus of the tragic mulatto woman is fulfilled]. However, *Maldito amor*'s Gloria parodically reappropriates this figure, converting Gloria into a woman of both voice and action who survives and triumphs at the end of the novel.

In summary, Ferré's novel, as a polemical or ironic parody of Laguerre's *La llamarada*, deconstructs two types of ideological discourses present in the novel. First, the novel questions what Therborn terms the "positional-historical" ideology proposed in *La llamarada*: the return to the patriarchal hacienda system as justice for the workers. The discourse that purports the idyllic union of man and nature on the coffee plantation naturalizes the bourgeois class ideology behind this economic model. Ferré exposes the workings and misconceptions of this ideology in her transformation of Laguerre's work. Similarly, Ferré uses her parody as a means to subvert the positional-existential ideology regarding race that is propagated throughout *La llamarada*. Borrás' rejection of the mulatto Delmira, his marriage to the European Pepiña, and his inheritance of the coffee plantation through his lineage are acts that naturalize the racial subtext of black people as inferior, despite statements in praise of black heritage made in the novel. Through black and mulatto characters (Titina and Gloria), Ferré debunks notions of racial inferiority and gives a voice to the previously marginalized, a characteristic of postcolonial fiction.

As already noted, at first glance, Boris Salazar's novel *La otra selva* also appears to parody *La vorágine* in ways that give voice to women. However, a deeper look into this novel from a feminist standpoint suggests both that the novel naturalizes stereotypes about women, and that the actual focus of the novel is displaced from the female characters to the detective/narrator whose actions parody those of the hard-boiled detective novel. There is a complicated set of interrelations between the detective plot, *La vorágine*, and the biography of José Eustasio Rivera written by Eduardo Neale-Silva that I attempt to elucidate below.

First, it is necessary to show how Salazar appropriates and transposes elements from the biographical work by Neale-Silva titled *Horizonte Humano* (1960), starting with the novel's title. In chapter 18, Neale-Silva states that upon arrival in New York (where Rivera travelled to have his novel translated and made into a movie), "se halló ante *una selva de edificios*" (418) [he found himself before *a jungle* of buildings] (my emphasis). This is likely where Salazar got the idea of portraying New York as the "other jungle". Rivera's adventures in New York thus parody those of his protagonist Arturo Cova in the Colombian jungles.

Second, this parallel between Rivera and his novel's protagonist is suggested by Neale-Silva, who highlights the autobiographical content of *La vorágine* in his biography of Rivera: "Hay en la figura del héroe elementos de la idiosincracia de Rivera y aun detalles autobiográficos pero no de identidad" (301) [There are in the hero's figure elements of Rivera's idiosyncrasies, and even autobiographical details, but no identity]. Salazar's novel emphasizes numerous parallels between Rivera and Cova, putting into play the suggestions made in the Neale-Silva biography. For example, the fleeting sexual encounter that Rivera has with the woman in the hotel parallels Cova's many romantic involvements (with Alicia, Clara, and Zoraida) in *La vorágine*. His inability to commit to Clara Weingest when she falls in love with him is similar to Cova's inability to commit to Alicia, and the character Rivera underscores this connection by stating:

> La hermosa suave . . . pronunciaba unas palabras que hubieran cabido en los labios de Arturo o de Alicia. Huir, partir, lanzarse hacia lo desconocido en la esperanza de que allá habrá una mejor oportunidad para el amor. Él conocía los resultados de esos viajes. Él sabía que la muerte era la única compañía posible . . . Temía que él y ella repitieran la historia que había llevado a Arturo y Alicia hacia su desconocido final. (144)
>
> [The soft beauty . . . pronounced words that could have come from the lips of Arturo or Alicia. Flee, leave, launch oneself toward the unknown in the hope that there there will be a better opportunity for love. He knew the results of those trips. He knew that death was the only possible companion. . . He feared that he and she would repeat the story that had led Arturo and Alicia to their unknown ending.]

Moreover, Claire explicitly questions what relationship there might be between Cova and Rivera (73) in one passage, while the narrator indicates in another the physical similarity between the two: "Cuando me mostró la foto de Arturo Cova que acompañaba la primera edición de *La vorágine*, me di cuenta de que entre Cova y el poeta había más de una afinidad" [When he showed me the picture of Arturo Cova that accompanied the first edition of *La vorágine*, I realized that there was more than a simple affinity between Cova and the poet].

La otra selva appropriates numerous other details from *Horizonte Humano*, including the advertisement placed in the newspaper to exchange Spanish lessons for English lessons and the response by Claire Weingest, as well as the café where the Colombians in New York gather, the flight of the Colombian aviator Benjamín Méndez, the idea of Rivera's prodigious memory, and the rumor that there were nefarious plans to steal his unpublished manuscript, *Mancha de aceite* (referred to as *Mancha negra* in Salazar's novel). Salazar's portrayal of Weingest in the novel is strikingly similar to Neale-Silva's description: "Optó por una otoñal 'miss' que ya sabía bastante castellano y que además de ser inteligente, tenía el atractivo de disponer de automóvil propio" (422) [He opted for a 'miss' in her autumn, since she knew a good deal of Spanish and, in addition to being intelligent, she had the attraction of owning her own automobile]. Rivera's prodigious memory becomes a key factor in the novel's detective fiction structure because this is what determines the need for the "bad guys" led by Lesmes to murder Rivera in order to eliminate any traces of his manuscript. Neale-Silva tells the following anecdote:

> Pronto observó el crítico que Rivera parecía estar citando partes de su novela como si la tuviera delante de los ojos.
> —Es que me sé el libro de memoria.
> —¡No puede ser! ¡No lo creo!
> Y de palabra en palabra se llegó a un convenio: el poeta habría de demostrar ante varios testigos que en realidad tenía tan prodigiosa memoria. (389)
> Soon the critic observed that Rivera seemed to be citing parts if his novel as if he had it before him.
> —"It's that I know the book by heart."
> —"It cannot be! I don't believe it!"
> And from word to word they arrived at an agreement: the poet was to demonstrate before various witnesses that in reality he had such a prodigious memory.

Salazar appropriates this detail through Lesmes' decision to kill Rivera as the only method by which he can possibly eradicate his novel *La mancha negra* because, if they destroy the manuscript, Rivera will still be able to retain what he wrote in his mind because "Si alguien quería poseer los escritos del poeta tenía que acabar con su memoria prodigiosa (155) [If someone wanted to possess the poet's writings they had to do away with his prodigious memory].

Furthermore, Salazar seizes on the rumors quoted in Neale-Silva's text that suggest that Rivera was poisoned, instead of dying a natural death: "Muy variadas y peregrinas son las versiones que ha dado el vulgo de cómo murió Rivera. Los más alarmistas han llegado a sostener que fue envenenado" (445) [Very varied and weird are the versions that the masses have given of how Rivera died. The most alarmist have sustained that he was poisoned]. Indeed, this is how Salazar portrays Rivera's death at the Polyclinic Hospital in New York, when experts conjecture that he actually died of viral encephalitis or bronchial pneumonia with a cerebral abscess (Neale-Silva, 480). In any case, Salazar appropriates the details of the Neale-Silva biography to convert Rivera's life into a piece of detective fiction through constant reference to the paradigms of this fictional genre. Before discussing the implications of this second level of parody in *La otra selva*, I will trace the pertinent elements that construct the transposition from biography to detective novel.

According to John Scaggs in *Crime Fiction*, the hard-boiled detective novel consists of the following elements: a detective who is heroic; a common man, yet a man of honor; he must have a client whom he mistrusts, the action must take place in an urban setting, and there is the presence of a *femme fatale* (Scaggs, 55–59). Scagg adds:

> There is little analysis of clues and associated analytic deduction. Rather, the hard-boiled detective's investigations, involving direct questioning and movement from place to place, parallel the sort of tracking down of a quarry that is characteristic of the frontier romance and the Western. . . the private eye is . . . an alienated individual who exists outside or beyond the socio-economic order of family, friends, work, and home. . . . He drinks and smokes a lot . . . a single, masculine lifestyle. (59)

The parallels with Salazar's novel are clear: his detective, the unnamed narrator, proves himself to be a heroic when he turns on his mistrusted client, Lesmes (to whom we will shortly return), and attempts to save Rivera's life. The novel takes place in New York, an urban environment, and the detective's friend María, who poses as the sexy actress Lupe Vélez, passes for the traditional *femme fatale*. There are constant references made by the narrator to drinking Jack Daniels (smoking and drinking too much), and to his status as a loner. He wanders through New York City, following Rivera's footsteps. To this, we should add, at the same time that the narrator is a detective, he is also a Colombian journalist and writer.

The interesting question that this second level of imitation raises is how do the detective-novel elements affect the overall meaning and effect of *La otra selva*? This question brings us back to issues of ideology construction and the worldview naturalized in the novel.

In *Anatomy of Murder: Mystery, Detective and Crime Fiction*, Carl D. Malmgreen examines the ideology behind detective fiction. According to Malmgreen, detective fiction features:

> A heroic protagonist and divides its interest between the heroic detective and the squalid world he or she inhabits. That world may defeat the detective, but in the process he earns the reader's respect, admiration, and concern. Detective fiction is thus conservative (and even nostalgic) in a "modern" way, celebrating an ethos of the Individual. The "mean streets" of detective fiction re-create a frontier setting in which independence, self-reliance, professionalism, personal integrity and a private code of ethics are valorized; the operatives of detective fiction are "lone rangers" re-situated in the urban frontiers of the twentieth-century. (192)

According to John Scaggs, Philip Marlowe (the detective who is possibly the model for Salazar's narrator) is "an idealized figure, a questing knight of romance transplanted into the mean streets of the mid-twentieth century. Like the questing knight, Marlowe's is a quest to restore justice and order motivated by his own personal code of honor" (62).

Thus, the "hero" of Salazar's novel is not the alleged protagonist, José Eustasio Rivera, nor is it the character from *La vorágine*, Alicia, to whom Salazar grants a voice in his novel. Rather, it is the unnamed narrator who is the detective that ultimately seeks justice in the novel. It is the narrator who attempts to rescue Rivera from the enemies who are trying to kill him, although he is ultimately unsuccessful in this endeavor. The focus on the male detective as hero has important implications for understanding both the purpose of Salazar's "parody" and the ideological underpinnings of *La otra selva*.

If we now return to Jitrik's definition of parody offered at the beginning of this study, we will recall that, in order for parody to be parody, one text must imitate another in order to "arrive elsewhere" and to make the reader read the imitated text "in a different light." Moreover, in Pueo's definition, parody necessitates an ironic appropriation of a former text. Ferré's *Maldito amor* was an excellent example of parody in these senses, because, as we saw, it obliges the reader to re-read the *novela de la tierra La llamarada* very differently than it was intended. Ferré ironically exposes the abuses and ideological underpinnings of the patriarchal hacienda system that is praised and seen nostalgically in *La llamarada*.

However, when we apply Jitrik's and Pueo's definitions of parody to *La otra selva*, and ask ourselves how does the novel lead us to re-read *La vorágine* in a different light, it is my belief that the novel falls short of what parody should be in these critics' terms. Although Natalia Crespo discusses *La otra selva* as a parody of *La vorágine*, by "rescuing it from *el machismo*" of the original novel, it is difficult to argue that *La otra selva* results in a differential or ironic reading on two counts. First, I would argue that *machismo* is already evident and not in any way ideologically disguised or defended in *La vorágine*. Second, although *La otra selva* purports to contest *machismo* by giving the character Alicia a voice, any "feminist/anti-machista" message behind this (which would afford a differential reading) is controverted in three ways:

1. Alicia's own voice repeats many stereotypes of women and does not constitute an enlightened female perspective;
2. other male–female relationships portrayed in the novel (such as the one between Claire Weingest and Rivera) repeat the same dynamics that exist between Alicia and Arturo Cova in *La vorágine*, which counteracts any attempts to "update" or ironically re-read the regionalist novel through parody; and
3. as alluded to in my discussion of detective fiction, by making the narrator/detective into the hero (instead of perhaps a female character), Salazar distracts attention from any possible feminist or female-centered parody of *La vorágine*.

An examination of these three elements will illustrate that, although *La otra selva* intertextually plays with elements from *La vorágine*, there is ultimately no reworking of the text that leads us to re-read *La vorágine* in a new or ironic light.

Let us begin by examining the "voice" created for Alicia in *La otra selva*. The protagonist, Rivera—who is, of course, male—feels that one of his greatest achievements before his death is reworking *La vorágine* to include Alicia's voice in two chapters.

"Voice" is a somewhat complicated narrative term that has been variably used. James Phelan defines narrative voice as "the fusion of style, tone, and values" (46) and "voice exists in the space between style and character" (47). Bakhtin's writings imply that "voice" is inextricably linked to the notion of an opinion or worldview (184). Thus, the mere "acoustic fact" (Martínez-Bonati, 1–3) of discourse is not sufficient to create a "voice." In this sense, the granting of words to Alicia may give her an "acoustic" voice in the novel, but what is the worldview ascribed to Alicia behind these words, and is this what Bakhtin would term a "double-voiced discourse" behind which we can also hear the "words" of a narrator/author? And, if so, is this the narrator/author the Rivera protagonist who creates Alicia or Salazar himself? Does this entity agree or disagree with Alicia? As one can see, the question of "voice" is no simple matter.

In *Redreaming America*, Debra Castillo points out that, in *La otra selva*, "Alicia's clear-eyed understanding of her role as a token object serves as this novel's most straightforward acknowledgment of the mechanisms of control in the masculinist text. By a sleight of hand, suggests Alicia...even when women speak in their own voices...they do so as characters created by others and for other purposes" (122). I would argue that *La otra selva*, rather than problematizing these mechanisms of control, puts them into play in ways that subvert the idea of female agency. If we examine the two chapters of the novel in which Alicia speaks, it is very clear that the discourse betrays patriarchal ideology behind its stance. Michelle Barrett defines four mechanisms through which patriarchal ideology has traditionally inscribed women in literary works: stereotypes, compensation, collusion, and recuperation (Barrett, 109–111). Stereotyping refers to the portrayal of women according to a fixed, traditional model. Compensation "elevates the moral value of femininity"; collusion emphasizes "women's consent to their own subordination" and recuperation is the process through which men challenge attempts to controvert the historically dominant meaning of gender (Greene and Kahn, 21–19). In chapter 16 of *La otra selva*, the first of the two that give "voice" to Alicia, the character refers to herself as "una mujer que no tiene las palabras ni la inteligencia para contar lo que nos ha ocurrido en esta selva que todo lo puede" [a woman who doesn't have the words nor the intelligence to recount what has happened to us in this jungle that is all powerful]. I would argue that this is an excellent example of what Barrett terms "stereotyping" by having a female character portray herself as incapable and unintelligent. Second, Alicia's discourse in this chapter implies a form of compensation (elevation of femininity) by appealing to her role as mother of Arturo's child as a reason for his love and attention, as an aspect of female biology that makes women superior. On page 109, she states that Arturo was happier to have defeated his rival than to be with her, "Alicia, la madre de su hijo" [Alicia, the mother of his child] and then again, on page 110, that he seeks the signs "que merezco ser la madre de su hijo" [that I deserve to be the mother of his child]. These statements implying a superiority associated with motherhood ultimately suggest female compensation. Similarly, in chapter 23, Alicia seems to view herself as a sexual object, stating "Acaso mi vientre flojo recuerda el de la muchacha que podía mirarse en el espejo sin temor?" (155) [Perhaps my flabby stomach recalls that of the girl who could look in the mirror without fear?]. Moreover, both chapters focus almost exclusively on Alicia's relationship with Arturo Cova, which to some degree reinforces the stereotype of women existing for and through men. Very little of Alicia's discourse is dedicated to fear of death in the jungle, concern for the fate of her child, and other possible topics. Thus, the discourse becomes more male-centered than female-centered, although Alicia does on occasion bring female issues to the fore, such as Arturo's alleged idealization of her,[3] or her role as token object in the battle between men (Arturo and Barrera).

The second aspect of the novel that undermines the agency of women, and thus counteracts any voice given to Alicia, is the portrayal of the relationship between Claire and José Eustasio Rivera. If Salazar's intention were to criticize the *machismo* inherent in *La vorágine*, why does he replicate forms of *machismo* in Rivera's relationships with women in the novel? In chapter 21, Rivera underscores the parallels between himself and his character Arturo Cova, with regard to his reaction when Claire suggested they travel together to Africa. Rivera thinks:

> Las palabras le molestaron porque le hicieron recordar la suerte de alguien que él conocía muy de cerca y porque le demostraron que en últimas, todo marchaba hacia el mismo destino. . . . No era a ella a quien temía, sino a la fuerza femenina que siempre había tratado de imponerle un destino. (145)

> The words bothered him because they made him remember the fate
> of someone that he knew very well and because they demonstrated, in the
> final instance, that everything was marching toward the same destiny . . . .
> It wasn't she whom he feared, but rather the feminine force that had always
> tried to impose a destiny upon him.

Rivera, like Cova, is presented as a womanizer (he has a fleeting sexual encounter with the woman in the hotel and later is on the brink of propositioning María, the Lupe Vélez double), afraid of any stable relationship, and subscribing here to the myth of the devouring female or terrible mother. However, it is not so much Rivera's reaction as Claire's that defines the novel's stereotyping of female characters. In chapter 20, the regretful Claire, shocked at Rivera's withdrawal from their encounters subsequent to her proposal of the African trip, thinks to herself:

> Estabas preparada para aceptarlo todo, para saber de sus varias amantes, de su esposa esperándolo en Colombia, de sus hijos . . .. para todo menos para el silencio . . . Habrías preferido un infierno de celos y descubrimientos fatales a este silencio unánime y feroz que te atacaba desde el momento mismo en que él llamó para decirte que no podría volver a las clases de inglés porque tendría que ponerse a trabajar seriamente en su novela. A pesar de tu falta de malicia entendiste que el problema no era el tiempo que él pudiera dedicarte, sino su subida decisión de no verte más . . . de devolverte a tu mundo de soledad y vacío. (139)
>
> You were prepared to accept everything, to find out about his various lovers, his wife waiting for him in Colombia, his children . . . You were prepared for everything except silence . . . You would have preferred a hell of jealousy and fatal discoveries to this unanimous and ferocious silence that attacked you from the very moment in which he called to tell you that he would not be able to return to English classes because he would have to begin to seriously work on his novel. Despite your lack of suspicion, you understood that the problem was not the time that he could dedicate to you, but rather the sudden decision to not see you anymore . . . to return you to your world of solitude and emptiness.

When Claire is first presented in the novel, she is portrayed as an allegedly independent woman, who recognized the mediocrity of her relationship with her first boyfriend and preferred to thus remain single. However, in chapter 20, this vision of Claire Weingest is undermined by that of Claire as a desperate old maid who is willing to put up with any indignity with regard to her love for Rivera: lovers, wives, and children. Once again, the ideological stereotype of a woman whose life will be "emptiness and solitude" without a man, is found behind the novel's discourse. Furthermore, the portrayal of Claire as sympathizing with Rivera for his reaction is another good example of compensation. Claire is so emotionally superior, so empathetic, so "maternal" (in the character Rivera's own words) that she feels close to Rivera when she realizes that he is acting out of fear: "Debiste reconocer, sin embargo, que al saber de su temor lo sentiste más cercano, más próximo a tus miedos y a tus reacciones" (139) [You should recognize, however, that upon learning of his fear you felt he was closer to you, closer to your fears and reactions].

Rather than inverting the relationship between the romantic pairs (Claire/Rivera vs. Alicia/Arturo) in a way that would highlight a female-centered parody, Salazar simply imitates the same relationship that already exists in *La vorágine*. This has the effect of undermining the feminine voice that *La otra selva* is allegedly attempting to create through granting narrative voice to Alicia.

The final aspect of the novel that is somewhat incongruent with the alleged parodic aims of *La otra selva* is the conversion of Rivera's biography (and, subsumed in it, the allusions to *La vorágine*) into a piece of hard-boiled detective fiction. The element that ties these two aspects of the novel together is the character Lesmes. Salazar has selected the least memorable character from *La vorágine* (so much so that he makes the connection to the previous novel explicit on page 152 in order to ensure his recognition to the reader) and converted him into the villain of *La otra selva*. It is Lesmes who hires the narrator/detective initially to steal Rivera's manuscript, *La mancha negra*, which reveals details about the corruption of Colombian governmental officials with regard to petroleum deals with the United States. In *La vorágine*, the character "Petardo Lesmes" is a Colombian swindler who appears on two pages of the novel. Cova mocks him, alluding to his embezzlement of funds, and other similar activities (125–126). Theoretically, Lesmes is a "parody" of Petardo Lesmes, but only in the sense of pure imitation, since the character is not taken in a different direction or commented upon in any significant way through his appropriation (other than his possible insignificance within the original novel). His purpose is largely to physically connect the detective fiction parody to the *novela de la tierra* parody, but again, without signaling to the reader how to read the former text in a new light. On the other hand, the narrator's suspicion toward Lesmes, his eventual refusal to comply with his client's aims, and final attempts to rescue Rivera from Lesmes' murder attempts, all the while submerging himself in whorehouses and other lowly settings characteristic of urban detective fiction, serve to enhance the reader's heroic vision of the narrator/detective. None of this seems to have anything to do with Alicia, Claire, or the vision of women which Crespo has underscored as the purpose of the novelistic parody of *La vorágine*. This lack of connection is precisely my point. This juxtaposition functions as a distraction from any message that Salazar might have originally intended. Ultimately, the novel reads more as an imitation of hard-boiled detective fiction than as a parody of *La vorágine*, which is relegated to a mere intertextual allusion.

According to Dennis Porter in *The Pursuit of Crime*, detective fiction is characterized by a fixed ideological constant and numerous ideological variables. The ideological constant of detective fiction is the celebration of "traditional heroic virtues and...an ideology of hero worship" (126), as others have commented. However, within this ideological frame, there are many ideological variables, including who the hero is (male or female, young or old, and so forth). Nonetheless, Porter specifies that the genre is "potentially anathema to such ideological adversaries of heroic male action such as...social collectivists and radical feminists, whose purpose is to forge a new sensibility and new forms of human association" (126). In other words, Salazar could have somewhat altered the ideological thrust of detective fiction by adopting a female heroine, but remains within the tradition of the male hero, thus detracting from the alleged new "focus" on women.

I have chosen to connect two very different transpositions of the *novela de la tierra*, precisely to illustrate how Ferré's novel, *Maldito amor*, is a true parody, as defined by Jitrik and Pueo, while *La otra selva* is not. *Maldito amor* forces the reader to "re-read" *La llamarada* by Enrique Laguerre and subverts its ideology through a reworking of key novelistic elements taken from the former work. In contrast, *La otra selva*, while in itself an interesting read, fails as an attempt to rework the fundamental ideology of *la novela de la tierra*, or oblige us to read *La vorágine* in a new light. At best, it is a ludic imitation of detective fiction that perhaps aligns itself with *La vorágine* by creating a Colombian "national myth" of identity related to the fight against imperialism.[4]

Although *Maldito amor* and *La otra selva* are both postmodern texts that share many postmodern characteristics,[5] these two imitations of the *novela de la tierra* ultimately have little in common in terms of their aims. Both novels share metacritical examination on some level. Salazar's novel employs the narrator/detective's simultaneous role as writer to reflect on the novel's writing process, exposing its lack of truth value with comments such as "la literatura se puede burlar la precisión histórica" (29) [Literature can mock historical precision]. Ferré's multiple, contradictory narrators also constitute a metacritical examination of the truth-claims of her own parody, since the reader is never sure of what actually happened in many instances (who killed Nicolás? Who is Nicolasito's father?). According to Pueo, this type of metacriticism is inherent in all postmodern parody:

> La ironía de la parodia reside precisamente en este valor heurístico que pone en cuestión continuamente el valor de los textos parodiados y por extensión, el valor de cualquier texto. La parodia supone una conciencia de la fragilidad de los textos . . . para dar su perspectiva irónica no se limita . . . al hipotexto . . . sino [se dirige] hacia su propia constitución textual. (89)
>
> The irony of parody resides precisely in this heuristic value that continually questions the value of the parodied texts and by extension, the value of any text. Parody supposes a consciousness of the fragility of texts . . . In order to give its ironic perspective it does not limit itself to the hypotext but rather [directs itself] toward its own textual constitution.

Despite such similarities, the essential differences between these two works that superficially appear to share the same goals by imitating the *novela de la tierra* lie in the dialogue (or lack thereof) that the hypertexts succeed or fail in establishing with their respective hypotexts.

NOTES

1. Most of the translations of citations from *Maldito amor* have been taken from the English translation by Ferré herself (*Sweet Diamond Dust*), unless otherwise noted, as in this instance (where the original content was omitted from the prologue in English). All translations of other texts in this chapter are mine.
2. Although Gloria is allegedly named as the recipient in Laura's will, she indicates that, had the testament survived, there is no way the "legitimate" heirs (Arístides and his sisters, the blood relatives) would have allowed Gloria to receive the hacienda and *Central Justicia*. Thus, the destruction of the testament also becomes an apocalyptic act that symbolically destroys the patriarchal tradition of inheritance through lineage.

3. Although critics such as Crespo and Castillo insist that *La vorágine* idealizes women, Carlos Daniel Ortiz points out that, although the protagonist Arturo Cova desires an ideal love, from the onset of the novel "ha empezado a rechazar esa *mentira romántica* que resulta insuficiente para comprender el mundo, dado que hay en él una postura consciente con respecto a la falsedad de su objeto deseado" (n.p.) [(he) has begun to reject this romantic lie that is insufficient for understanding the world, given that there is within him a conscious position with respect to the falsity of his desired object]. Moreover, Ortiz insists that Alicia is in no way idealized in the novel, but instead "es presentada como una joven de ciudad de buena familia, inteligente. Ella se presenta rebelde con actitud sumamente práctica, con un proceder libre y autónomo, y con clara conciencia de la desventaja que tiene ser mujer para la sociedad de principios de siglo XX" (n.p.) [(Alicia) is presented as a young person from the city from a good family, intelligent. She is presented as rebellious, with a very practical attitude, with a free and autonomous behavior, and clear consciousness of the disadvantage of being a woman in the society of the early twentieth century].

4. Porter suggests that detective fiction from different countries creates different national myths. Although Salazar lives in New York City and, according to Castillo (111), his perspective is fully North American, *La otra selva*, written in Spanish and focused on a Colombian writer, can still be thought to contain "Colombian myths" of national identity.

5. Both novels also exhibit postmodern genre blending: Ferré mixes the romance novel and sub-genre of realist fiction, while Salazar blends biography and detective fiction. Ralph Cohen discusses this practice in "Do Postmodern Genres Exist?" 11–27.

Works Cited

Aponte Ramos, Lola. "Enrique Laguerre y la memoriosa construcción del blanquito en *La llamarada*." *Revista Iberoamericana* 69.205 (2003): 895–908. Print.

Bakhtin, Mikhail. *Problems of Dostoevsky's Poetics*. Edited and translated by Caryl Emerson. Minneapolis: University of Minnesota Press, 1984. Print.

Barrett, Michelle. *Women's Oppression Today: Problems in Marxist Feminist Analysis*. London: Verso, 1980. Print.

Castillo, Debra A. *Redreaming America: Toward a Bilingual American Culture*. Albany: State University of New York Press, 2005. Print.

Cohen, Ralph. "Do Postmodern Genres Exist?" In *Postmodern Genres*. Edited by Marjorie Perloff. Norman: University of Oklahoma Press, 1988. 11–27. Print.

248   H. C. WELDT-BASSON

82137Crespo, Natalia. *Parodias al canon: Reescrituras en la literatura hispánica contemporánea (1975–2000)*. Buenos Aires: Ediciones Corregidor, 2012. Print.

Escudero Valentín, Rogelio. "El desarrollo de un conflicto insospechado en *La llamarada*, novela del cañaveral puertorriqueño." *Revista de Estudios Hispánicos* 8 (1981): 123–146. Print.

Ferré, Rosario. *Sweet Diamond Dust and Other Stories*. Translated by Rosario Ferré. New York: Plume, 1988.

———. *Maldito amor y otros cuentos*. New York: Vintage Español, 1998. Print.

Filer, Malva E. "Polifonía y contrapunto: La crónica histórica en *Maldito amor* y *The House on the Lagoon*." *Revista Hispánica Moderna* 49.2 (1996): 318–328. Print.

Genette, Gérard. *Palimpsests: Literature in the Second Degree*. Translated by Channa Newman and Claude Doubinsky. Lincoln: University of Nebraska Press, 1997.

Greene, Gayle and Coppelia Kahn. "Feminist Scholarship and the Social Construction of Women." In *Making a Difference: Feminist Literary Criticism*. Edited by Gayle Greene and Coppelia Kahn. London: Methuen, 1985. 1–36. Print.

Jitrik, Noé. "Rehabilitación de la parodia." In *La parodia en la literatura latinoamericana*. Edited by Roberto Ferro. Buenos Aires: Instituto de Literatura Hispanoamericana, 1993. 13–32. Print.

Laguerre, Enrique A. *La llamarada*. 33rd ed. Baltimore: Editorial Cultural, 1996. Print.

Malmgreen, Carl D. *Anatomy of Murder: Mystery, Detective and Crime Fiction*. Bowling Green, OH: Bowling Green State University Popular Press, 2001. Print.

Martínez-Bonati, Félix. "El sistema del discurso y la evolución de las formas narrativas." *Dispositio* 5–6.15–16 (1980–1981): 1–18. Print.

Murphy, Mary. "Rosario Ferré en el espejo: Defiance and Inversions." *Hispanic Review* 65.2 (1997): 145–157.

Neale-Silva, Eduardo. *Horizonte humano: Vida de José Eustasio Rivera*. Mexico, D.F.: Fondo de Cultura Económica, 1960. Print.

Ortiz, Carlos Daniel. "La idealización de la mujer en *La vorágine*." *Espéculo* 36 (2007), n.p. Web.

Phelan, James. *Narrative as Rhetoric: Technique, Audiences, Ethics, Ideology*. Columbus: Ohio State University Press, 1996. Print.

Porter, Dennis. *The Pursuit of Crime*. New Haven: Yale University Press, 1981. Print.

Pueo, Juan Carlos. *Los reflejos en juego (Una teoría de la parodia)*. Valencia: Tirant Lo Blanch, 2002. Print.

Rivera, José Eustasio. *La vorágine*. Mexico, D.F.: Editorial Porrúa, 1978. Print.

Salazar, Boris. *La otra selva*. Bogotá: Tercer Mundo Editores, 1991. Print.

Scaggs, John. *Crime Fiction. The New Critical Idiom*. London: Routledge, 2005. Print.

Therborn, Göran. *The Ideology of Power and the Power of Ideology*. London: Verso, 1980. Print.

Velázquez Lara, Socorro. "La parodia como poder subversivo feminista en la narrativa de Rosario Ferré." Diss. Ann Arbor: University of Michigan, 1996. Print.

INDEX

© The Editor(s) (if applicable) and The Author(s) 2018   251
H. C. Weldt-Basson (ed.), *Postmodern Parody in Latin
American Literature*, Literatures of the Americas,
https://doi.org/10.1007/978-3-319-90430-6

Printed by Printforce, the Netherlands